Praise for
The Global Achievement Gap

"*The Global Achievement Gap* is thoughtful and inspirational. It describes how, in these changing times, schools too must change if the U.S. is to remain a strong economic and intellectual leader in the world, and it offers creative solutions and examples of success. This book will capture your head, your heart, and, I hope, your future actions. This is a *very* important book for anyone who cares about preparing young people for success in a rapidly changing global society. Every school board member, administrator, teacher, and parent in the nation should read this book."
—ANNE L. BRYANT, EXECUTIVE DIRECTOR, NATIONAL SCHOOL BOARDS ASSOCIATION

"*The Global Achievement Gap* is a 'must' read for all policymakers as Congress continues its debate on how best to reform the No Child Left Behind law with a measure of flexibility, and where the thin line between 'performing' and 'failing' must be more about competing in this global world than simply about passing a standardized test. It's time to stop harping on what's wrong with our schools and instead provide them with the tools—as author Tony Wagner eloquently lays out— that they need to produce competitive, connective, technologically proficient, hopeful young men and women ready to take on the challenges of a global economy and succeed."
—U.S. SENATOR DANIEL K. INOUYE

"Tony Wagner takes us deep inside the black box of school curriculum in a way few authors have done. What do we mean by rigor? By 21st century skills? Wagner shows us concretely what thinking skills really are, how current approaches to 'raising standards' cannot get us there, and what will. Everyone concerned with American education should read this book."
—LINDA DARLING-HAMMOND,
CHARLES E. DUCOMMUN PROFESSOR OF EDUCATION, STANFORD UNIVERSITY

"Tony Wagner has managed to penetrate the jargon and over-simplified responses to the pervasive underachievement that exists among our students. He has charted an important new direction and given us a way to get there. This book deserves to be powerfully influential."
—MEL LEVINE, AUTHOR OF *A MIND AT A TIME*

"Tony Wagner argues persuasively that old ways of teaching are completely unsuited to new ways of working. *The Global Achievement Gap* should be grabbed by business leaders to guide a much-needed conversation with educators."
—ROSABETH MOSS KANTER, HARVARD BUSINESS SCHOOL PROFESSOR
AND AUTHOR OF *AMERICA THE PRINCIPLED* AND *CONFIDENCE*

"In *Change Leadership*, Tony Wagner challenged my assumptions about the new skills instructional leaders must acquire to improve the quality of teaching and learning in classrooms. In his latest book, he continues to challenge my assumptions about the survival skills our students must acquire if they are to be prepared for creating solutions and resolving issues in the global society of the 21st century. This book is a 'must read' for the change agents in public education. Wagner presents a compelling case for rapid and urgent change in the present American education system."
—BETTY BURKS, DEPUTY SUPERINTENDENT,
SAN ANTONIO INDEPENDENT SCHOOL DISTRICT

"*The Global Achievement Gap* is a lucid—and scary—book. It chronicles how policies that intend to improve our schools are actually shutting down their abilities to help students learn how to think. Parents, teachers, administrators and policymakers urgently need to understand what Wagner is telling us."

—CLAYTON CHRISTENSEN, PROFESSOR, HARVARD BUSINESS SCHOOL,
AND AUTHOR OF *DISRUPTING CLASS*

"In *The Global Achievement Gap*, Tony Wagner offers a thoughtful analysis of where we are in American public education (behind the times), and what we need to do to adapt to the future that is upon us. Drawing upon years of accumulated wisdom as a teacher, principal, trainer, and well-traveled observer of schools, Wagner builds a persuasive case for change in the way we approach schooling, grounded in the question: what does it mean to be an educated person in the 21st century?"

—DR. RICHARD C. ATKINSON, PRESIDENT EMERITUS, UNIVERSITY OF CALIFORNIA

"School as we know it all too often does not engage students, teachers or leaders in the learning process and as a result we have a generation of students learning to 'do school' rather than learning the skills they really need to succeed. Tony Wagner makes a strong case for rethinking our entire approach to education and his argument is persuasive."

—LARRY STUPSKI, CHAIRMAN, STUPSKI FOUNDATION

"This insightful book calls for a much needed dialogue between educators, business leaders and policymakers on the future of American education. By using many real-life examples, the book is a very readable starting point for that discussion."

—CHARLES FADEL, GLOBAL LEAD FOR EDUCATION, CISCO

"Kudos to Tony Wagner. . . . Many people have been cursing the darkness of our education system, but by breaking down the many dilemmas that students, teachers, and parents face as well as examining different approaches that have been successful, Wagner lights a candle for those who want to help but don't know where to start. Whether we can transition through these exciting and perilous times will depend upon the culture we leave our young people. Tony Wagner has provided a map."

—JOHN ABELE, FOUNDING CHAIRMAN, BOSTON SCIENTIFIC, AND BOARD CHAIR, FIRST

"This important book is a wake-up call for America. For over fifty years, our schools have stayed the same, while the world has changed dramatically. Students memorize academic content, and study for standardized tests, but they never learn how to think, solve problems, or be creative. Wagner's stories about the few remarkable schools that are transforming classroom instruction and pointing the way to the future are compelling. Every parent, teacher, politician, and executive should read this book."

—KEITH SAWYER, AUTHOR OF *GROUP GENIUS*

"*The Global Achievement Gap* offers a simple, readable, intelligent, and compelling analysis of the needs of our schools and the ways to address them."

—DR. ARTHUR E. LEVINE, PRESIDENT, THE WOODROW WILSON NATIONAL FELLOWSHIP FOUNDATION

"It's always an occasion for delight when Tony Wagner writes a new book. He's done it again by provoking us to think about the reasons behind the current furor over school achievement."

—DEBORAH MEIER, AUTHOR OF *THE POWER OF THEIR IDEAS*

"Tony Wagner addresses the most pressing strategic issue facing the United States in the 21st century—can Americans adapt their culture and improve their education system to rise to the challenge of global economic competition on a unprecedented scale?"

—BOB COMPTON, EXECUTIVE PRODUCER, *TWO MILLION MINUTES: A GLOBAL EXAMINATION*

The Global Achievement Gap

Also by Tony Wagner

*How Schools Change: Lessons from Three
    Communities Revisited*

*Making the Grade: Reinventing America's
    Schools*

*Change Leadership: A Practical Guide to
    Transforming Our Schools*

The Global Achievement Gap

Why Even Our Best Schools
Don't Teach the New Survival Skills
Our Children Need—
and What We Can Do About It

TONY WAGNER

A Member of the Perseus Books Group
New York

Published by Basic Books,
A Member of the Perseus Books Group
387 Park Avenue South
New York, NY 10016

Books published by Basic Books are available at special discounts for bulk
purchases in the United States by corporations, institutions, and other
organizations. For more information, please contact the Special Markets
Department at the Perseus Books Group, 2300 Chestnut Street, Suite 200,
Philadelphia, PA 19103, or call (800) 810-4145, extension 5000, or e-mail
special.markets@perseusbooks.com.

Designed by Pauline Brown
Set in 11.5-point Garamond by the Perseus Books Group

Library of Congress Cataloging-in-Publication Data
Wagner, Tony.
    The global achievement gap : why even our best schools don't teach the new
survival skills our children need—and what we can do about it / Tony Wagner.
        p. cm.
    Includes bibliographical references and index.
    HC ISBN 978-0-465-00229-0
    PB ISBN 978-0-465-00230-6
    1. Education, Secondary—Aims and objectives—United States. 2. Educational
change—United States. 3. School improvement programs—United States. I. Title.

LB1607.5 .W34 2008
370.13—dc22
                                                                2009419316

10 9 8 7 6 5 4 3 2

*For PJ
cheerleader, coach, critic—
and best friend*

*"Imagination is more important than knowledge.
For knowledge is limited, whereas imagination
embraces the entire world, stimulating progress,
giving birth to evolution."*
—Albert Einstein

Contents

Acknowledgments

THIS BOOK COULD not have been written without the help of many people. I first want to thank the several hundred people, only some of whom are named in the book, that took the time to answer my questions—often in interviews that took an hour or more. Particular thanks go to the unnamed education leaders of the three school systems I profile in Chapter 2 for their courage and honesty—you know who you are. I am also grateful to the teachers, students, and administrators named in Chapter 6 for allowing me to share their important work.

I especially want to thank several people who helped in invaluable ways. Kirsten Olson—critic, friend, and thought-partner—planted a seed for the idea of this book and read and commented on drafts of every chapter. I am very grateful to Esmond Harmsworth, my literary agent, and to Joanne Wykoff, who works with Esmond at Zachary Shuster Harmsworth. Esmond was an early believer in the book, and both he and Joanne gave me invaluable assistance in the development of the book proposal and critiqued drafts of chapters as I produced them. Particular thanks also go to Amanda Moon, my editor at Basic Books, who did a wonderful job of pushing me to better explain my thinking; to Whitney Casser, her able assistant, who managed all the moving parts of this project; and to Christine Arden, for her fine work copyediting the manuscript. Two others who helped me think through some of the ideas in the book and read very early drafts of the initial chapter are Dwight Gertz and Stan Sharenson. Richard Hersh was also a valuable thought-partner. Ken Kay, president of the Partnership for 21st Century Skills, was enormously helpful in contacting key individuals for interviews, as were Jean Johnson and Ruth Wooden at the Public Agenda Foundation. I also want to acknowledge my collegues at the Change Leadership Group: Bob Kegan, Lisa Lahey, Deborah Helsing, Richard Lemons, and Kati Livingston; my collegues at the Small Schools Project: Rick Lear, Jude Garnier, Harriette Rasmussen, and Kyle Miller; and Steve Seleznow at the Bill & Melinda Gates Foundation. Our regular meetings and ongoing work together have been an invaluable source of new ideas and constructive criticism.

Finally, I thank my wife PJ Blankenhorn, who has been my first reader, strongest supporter, and best friend. More than two years ago, she handed me Thomas Friedman's *The World Is Flat* and told me that I had to read it—and she was right, as usual. Since then, PJ has put up with many weekends that were taken up with my research and work on the manuscript, as well as a few postponed or cancelled vacations, without complaint. Most important, she has helped me clarify key ideas and find better ways of expressing them. It is she to whom this book is dedicated.

Preface

AFTER HAVING SPENT a decade as a full-time high school English and social studies teacher, two years as a school principal, and six years working in the nonprofit world, I returned to Harvard in 1988 to pursue a doctorate in education. For my research, I spent more than a year observing classes and adult meetings in three very different high schools—one private and two public. All three were involved in some kind of change process. I was surprised to learn that the teachers in the two public schools were being told to try new things, such as interdisciplinary studies, team teaching, and cooperative learning, without having any understanding as to why—except that this was what they'd been asked to do by their well-meaning superintendent. As a result, many of their efforts were half-hearted at best. They knew, from years of experience, that the new reform was unlikely to be sustained—that in a few years, there would be another superintendent with a new initiative that would take the place of the current one. And indeed this was the case, as I discovered when I re-studied the same schools ten years later. Reform Du Jour is "business as usual" in most of our schools.

In the sixteen years since I completed my degree, I have been a university professor with responsibilities for teacher training, the president of a nonprofit organization focused on creating school-community partnerships for school improvement, and, for the last eight years, co-director of the Change Leadership Group, a small outfit at Harvard that works to understand what is effective change leadership in education and to support educators undertaking this important work. I have also been an education consultant for more than twenty years and served as senior advisor to the education program of the Bill & Melinda Gates Foundation, where I counseled on grants, strategies, and the challenges of what I call "public engagement"—ways to involve teachers, parents, and community members in discussions of how schools need to change. I've provided professional development for the foundation's program officers and grantees as well. Whatever the formal job description, my passion has remained the same: to help schools and districts improve learning, teaching, and leadership; to better understand the obstacles to change and the most effective strategies for overcoming them; and to share what I'm learning with others through speaking and writing.

I've spent time in schools and classrooms nearly every month for the past twenty years—schools in the United States and in several other countries—and I have learned a great deal about what works and what doesn't when it comes to leading improvement efforts. One of my biggest concerns is that most high school educators do not feel a real sense of urgency for change—perhaps because their work isolates them from the larger world of rapid change and they've lived through too many failed education fads. The result is that course curricula and teaching practices have remained pretty much the same for fifty years or more. Except for increased pressures to get kids to pass the new state tests, "Why change?" remains as unanswered a question for most educators today as it had been when I was doing my doctoral research. In fact, about the only thing that's different is the overwhelming majority of teachers—70 percent, according to the most recent Public Agenda Foundation poll—who think that there is too much testing in schools and that the No Child Left Behind (NCLB) legislation is doing much more harm than good.[1]

Business leaders I talk to are more and more frustrated with our nation's public schools and the people who work in them. Some of them pushed hard for passage of NCLB and new state education laws, in the belief that these efforts would make public education more accountable; but they have seen little or no improvement in this area. Nor have they seen any evidence that students are leaving schools better prepared for the workplace. Many people think the teachers' unions and tenure are to blame because they protect ineffective teachers. Others advocate for more charter schools or vouchers, arguing that the forces of free-market competition are needed to pressure public schools to improve. Based on my review of the research to date, there's no solid evidence to suggest that either strategy significantly improves education outcomes, but business leaders seem determined to find something, anything, to shake things up—whatever it takes to get better results.

Meanwhile, most of us who are parents often don't follow the new education reform laws and don't have many opportunities to talk to either educators or business leaders about education issues. It's all we can do to manage our—and our children's—increasingly frenetic lives. Many of us have a great deal of anxiety about our kids' futures in a world that we see as much more competitive than the one we grew up in. And we are always upset when our child is assigned a teacher whom we consider mediocre—which happens much more often than we think it should. But other than complaining to the principal about our children's teacher, most of us do not know how things ought to be different in schools more generally. Increasingly, though, many of us worry that there's too much testing in schools now—and too many classes that merely "teach to the tests"—where the focus is more on practice tests and test-taking strategies than on learning rich and challenging content.

Schools—especially high schools—aren't changing, then, in part because there is no consensus about what types of changes are needed or might work—or even whether there's a need for change at all. Business leaders (who, many are surprised to hear, have been the primary advocates for education reform), educators, and parents rarely talk to one another and so share little or no common ground. As in the well-known Indian fable, each group is blindfolded, touching just a part of the truth. For some time I've wanted to write a book that would contribute to a dialogue among these three groups about what we want our high school graduates to know and be able to do.

My interest in this problem became more pressing as I began to observe, with a growing sense of alarm, the accelerating pace of change in the twenty-first century and the ways in which this change was leaving our schools and our children further and further behind. Computers and the Internet were becoming essential tools in every workplace—but, from what I saw in schools, students rarely used technology as a part of their learning in classrooms. Students and teachers also continued to learn and work in isolation—whereas the rest of the work world had been organized into teams for decades.

Early in 2006, I read Thomas Friedman's *The World Is Flat.* He makes the case that *any job—blue or white collar—that can be broken down into a routine and transformed into bits and bytes can now be exported to other countries where there is a rapidly increasing number of highly educated "knowledge workers" who will work for a small fraction of the salary of a comparable American worker.* Reading this book deepened my understanding of the profound implications these sudden technological and economic transformations have for our economy and for our children's future. Friedman was talking not just about today's manufacturing jobs—most of which have already disappeared from this country. He was talking about professional jobs for engineers, architects, software code writers, technical support specialists, customer service representatives, accountants, and the like. All of these jobs and many more rely mainly on skilled use of data and other kinds of information that can now be sent or received and processed nearly instantly almost anywhere in the world.

I thought about some recent phone calls I'd made. I'd talked to Dell's technical support several times, because of a computer problem, as well as to AT&T's customer service representatives about a billing issue, and then there was my call to the Quicken software support line. I asked one young man where he was speaking from, and he told me Bangalore. Another woman was in the Philippines. I suddenly realized that, for the last several years, almost all of my various phone calls to customer service or technical support numbers had been answered by someone who was not based in the United States. I thought about my son's job in a technical support unit for a city police department. Could his job be offshored as well?

I began to understand that more and more countries are graduating increasing numbers of young people who not only have basic computational and analytic skills but also are hungry for the middle-class lifestyle we have promoted through media and advertising around the world. In short, our young people are now in direct competition with youth from developing countries for many of what traditionally have been considered our "good middle-class white-collar" jobs. While some of our students are learning skills that enable them to interpret and manipulate information and data, the sheer numbers of students who are learning these skills in other countries and the fact that they will work for much less put our students at an extreme competitive disadvantage. What will American students need to know in order to compete successfully for these jobs? What are the skills that matter most in the world of work today? What will it take for young Americans to get and to keep a "good" job in the coming decades?

Meanwhile, news headlines nearly every day focus on the mounting chaos and deaths in Iraq as well as on new evidence of global warming. Like many of us, I've felt a growing sense of dread—not just about our safety since 9/11 but also about our diminished stature in the world and the looming environmental crisis. But in this context, too, the gap between the "real world" and the world of school is greater than ever. These issues were never discussed in any of the classrooms I observed. Some teachers I talked to wanted to have such conversations with their students, but they felt obligated to spend all available class time covering the content needed to ensure that the students would pass various standardized tests. Others were simply afraid to talk about controversial issues for fear that a parent might complain.

It's not just discussions of current events that make most educators uneasy. They are equally impatient with any talk about the need to focus more on teaching students workplace skills. Many believe that churning out better workers for the corporate world is nothing more than "vocational education" and likely means turning kids into little automatons who know only how to follow orders. Is there any truth to this? Specifically, is there a conflict between preparing students for the world of work and teaching them about their roles as citizens? While educators assume that they are readying students for citizenship as a matter of course, I confess that I'm skeptical about the idea that high school graduates will automatically be better citizens for merely having taken the usual required classes. Teaching kids the history of the Electoral College doesn't prepare them to be more thoughtful voters—or even to want to vote at all. What, then, does it mean in today's world to be an active and informed citizen, and how does a democratic society best educate for citizenship?

Equally important, what would be involved in creating the "challenging and rigorous curriculum for all students" that many are now demanding? What is even meant by "rigor" today, and how do we get more of it in our students' classes? High school students could be required to take more college-prep and Advanced Placement courses, but would they graduate "jury-ready" as a result? Would they know how to distinguish fact from opinion, weigh evidence, listen with both head and heart, wrestle with the sometimes conflicting principles of justice and mercy, and work to seek the truth with their fellow jurors? The overwhelming number of responses I received following an article I wrote in 2006, "Rigor on Trial," in which I explored these questions, indicated to me that there is a great deal of confusion about what rigor really means today.[2] Many people—from superintendents to teachers to parents—wrote me e-mails wanting more information. How was I redefining rigor for the twenty-first century, and what form did it take in classrooms? Could I put them in touch with schools where students were being taught to think? This book project was born out of my urgent need to find better answers to these questions.

I offer this personal introduction so that readers might understand something of my intellectual journey—what my biases are, what drives me, and what I worry most about—all of which have in various ways propelled me to write *The Global Achievement Gap*. This is a book for leaders from all walks of life—business, community, and political leaders as well as parents and educators who lead the way. I hope that it will also be of interest to thoughtful young people like my three children and their spouses, who are emerging leaders. It was written for people who care deeply about how we educate the next generation, and for people who are willing to ask tough questions and say what they think. For this book is not just another intellectual exercise—at least not for me, and I hope not for you, either. Above all, *The Global Achievement Gap* is a call to action.

Introduction

*The formulation of the problem is
often more important than the solution.*

—EINSTEIN

Some Facts We Need to Face

- The high school graduation rate in the United States—
  which is about 70 percent of the age cohort—is now well
  behind that of countries such as Denmark (96 percent),
  Japan (93 percent), and even Poland (92 percent) and
  Italy (79 percent).[1]

- Only about a third of U.S. high school students graduate
  ready for college today, and the rates are much lower for
  poor and minority students. Forty percent of *all* students
  who enter college must take remedial courses.[2] And while
  no hard data are readily available, it is estimated that one
  out of every two students who start college never complete any kind of postsecondary degree.

- Sixty-five percent of college professors report that what is
  taught in high school does not prepare students for college. One major reason is that the tests students must take
  in high school for state-accountability purposes usually

measure 9th or 10th grade–level knowledge and skills. Primarily multiple-choice assessments, they rarely ask students to explain their reasoning or to apply knowledge to new situations (skills that are critical for success in college), so neither teachers nor students receive useful feedback about college-readiness.[3]

- In order to earn a decent wage in today's economy, most students will need at least some postsecondary education. Indeed, an estimated 85 percent of current jobs and almost 90 percent of the fastest-growing and best-paying jobs now require postsecondary education. Even today's manufacturing jobs now largely require postsecondary training and skills.[4] According to the authors of "America's Perfect Storm": "Over the next 25 years or so . . . nearly half of the projected job growth will be concentrated in occupations associated with higher education and skill levels. This means that tens of millions more of our students and adults will be less able to qualify for higher-paying jobs. Instead, they will be competing not only with each other and millions of newly arrived immigrants but also with equally (or better) skilled workers in lower-wage economies around the world."[5]

- The United States now ranks tenth among industrial nations in the rate of college completion by 25- to 44-year-olds.[6]

- Students are graduating from both high school and college unprepared for the world of work. Fewer than a quarter o

for a ma

employe

basic kr

employ

50 per

"deficie

- Only 4

  preside

  74-yea

What are these new skills, an

tant? Why don't our schools

them? What are the best

how do we need to dif

these new challenge

excel in this ne

meeting the

can and

gap?

The conve

these data is simply that our schools are "failing." We've heard this

from Republicans and Democrats alike. We've heard it in the media

and from academics and policy pundits. We've heard it so often that it

has become the accepted wisdom of the day. But what I see in high

school classrooms all over the country suggests a different conclusion.

What I see there is, in fact, not very different from what I saw thirty-

five years ago when I began my career as a teacher—or even what I ex-

perienced as a high school student myself. No better, and no worse. Just

more testing—and more teaching to the tests.

My view is that the numbers cited in the above list, taken together,

point to a new and little-understood challenge for American education:

In today's highly competitive global "knowledge economy," *all students

need new skills* for college, careers, and citizenship. The failure to give all

students these new skills leaves today's youth—and our country—at an

alarming competitive disadvantage. Schools haven't changed; the world

has. And so our schools are not failing. Rather, they are obsolete—even

the ones that score the best on standardized tests. This is a very differ-

ent problem requiring an altogether different solution.

d why they have become so impor-
—even the best ones—teach and test
ways to hold our schools accountable, and
erently prepare and support educators to meet
s? How do we motivate today's students to want to
w world, and what do good schools look like that are
e challenges and getting dramatically better results? What
must we do as citizens about this growing *global achievement*
These are some of the questions I address in this book.

A New Context for Schooling

A little over fifty years ago, Rudolf Flesch wrote a slim volume titled *Why Johnny Can't Read*. More than any other book, this one started the "reading wars"—vehement and often ideologically driven debates about the best way to teach students how to read, which continue to this day—but the nature of the disagreements matters less than the topic. Throughout much of the twentieth century the basic skills of reading, computation, and rudimentary writing were the focus of our attention in schools and at home. For most students, a "rigorous" curriculum meant having to memorize more vocabulary words and do more math problems at night. There were disputes among academics and parents alike over the ways in which various skills were best taught, but there was no disagreement about their importance. Thomas Jefferson first declared literacy to be the key to citizenship. And, increasingly in the twentieth century, the "Three R's" became essential in the workplace as well.

However, in the twenty-first century, mastery of the basic skills of reading, writing, and math is no longer enough. Almost any job that pays more than minimum wage—both blue and white collar—now calls for employees who know how to solve a range of intellectual and technical problems, as we will learn in Chapter 1. In addition, we are confronted by exponential increases of readily available information, new technologies that are constantly changing, and more complex societal challenges such as global warming. Thus, work, learning, and citizenship in the twenty-first century demand that we all know how to *think*—to reason, analyze, weigh evidence, problem-solve—and to *communicate effectively*. These are no longer skills that only the elites in a society must master; they are essential survival skills for all of us.

What I have seen in some of our best public schools over the past decade is that while Johnny and Juan and Leticia are learning how to read, at least at a basic level, they are not learning how to think or care about what they read; nor are they learning to clearly communicate ideas orally and in writing. They memorize names and dates in history, but they cannot explain the larger significance of historical events. And they may be learning how to add, subtract, and multiply, but they have no understanding of how to think about numbers. Not knowing how to interpret statistics or gauge probability, many students cannot make sense of the graphs and charts they see every day in the newspaper. They are required to memorize (and usually quickly forget) a wide range of scientific facts, but very few know how to apply the scientific method—how to formulate a hypothesis, test it, and analyze the results. Yet this way of thinking is at the very heart of many kinds of analysis and research. Finally, I have observed that the longer our children are in school, the less curious they become. Effective communication, curiosity, and critical-thinking skills, as we will see, are much more than just the traditional desirable outcomes of a liberal arts education. They are essential competencies and habits of mind for life in the twenty-first century.

The simplest explanation for the low level of intellectual work and general lack of curiosity found in classrooms—even in our best high schools—is that our schools were never designed to teach *all* students how to think. Since our system of public education came into being at the turn of the last century, the assumption has been that only those in the college-preparatory classes were going to have to learn how to reason, problem-solve, and so on, and historically they comprised only a small percentage of students. And even those few often learned such skills in school more by accident than by design. For the most part, teachers haven't been trained to teach students how to think. The textbooks and tests we used in the past were not designed to teach and assess the ability to reason or analyze—and they remain substantially the same today.

Throughout history and until very recently, most people worked with their hands—not with their heads—and so they didn't need these analytical skills in their daily life. Many generations of the most successful students were often more likely to learn how to think from the conversations they had with parents at the dinner table or during family trips than from their classes. They came to school smart and motivated and left the same, and whatever "value-added" some teachers provided often was and continues to be the result of random acts of excellence—at least in public schools. Private schools were established to educate the elite and so have always demanded more of students, but these schools educate less than 5 percent of the high school student population.

If you doubt my observations about public school classrooms, then those of you who attended these schools should simply ask yourself: How many of your high school teachers demanded that you really think in your oral and written work—as opposed to merely memorizing and regurgitating? How often were you required to write an essay in which you developed your own well-reasoned interpretation of a piece of literature or the significance of an event in history? How frequently did you have to develop and test a hypothesis for a science class or explain your thinking about how you solved a complex math problem? How often were you asked by a teacher, "So what do you think about . . . "? I don't mean just once in a while—I mean every day.

Even students in many private schools aren't asked to do these things nearly as often as I think they should be.

Many of you who are reading this book may have been in a college or honors track in your high school and so could not see the kind of education the majority of your peers were getting in the other classes. Students in the lower academic tracks—a high percentage of whom were poor and minority students—rarely had intellectual challenges of any kind. And this remains true to this day. Boredom continues to be a leading cause of our high school dropout rate—a problem we'll explore in depth later on.

Teaching all students to think and to be curious is much more than a technical problem for which educators, alone, are accountable. And more professional development for teachers and better textbooks and tests, though necessary, are insufficient as solutions. The problem goes much deeper—to the very way we conceive of the purpose and experience of schooling and what we expect our high school graduates to know and be able to do. Those of us who are old enough to have school-aged children had a set of experiences in school that define for us what learning is supposed to look like, and in most cases our past experience still shapes how we think about school. But these preconceptions may also prevent us from clearly understanding how very different the experience of schooling must be for children growing up in a new century. In the coming pages, I will invite you to question your assumptions about what all students should know—what it means to be an educated adult in the twenty-first century—as well as about what good teaching looks like, and how we should assess what students are learning.

I invite you to ask yourself these questions not as a philosophical exercise but, rather, because new answers are needed for our own economic survival—and that of our children. We have learned from the writings of Thomas Friedman, Daniel Pink, and many others that our children must now compete for jobs with increasingly well-educated young people from around the world.[9] Technology has enabled a grow-ing number of routine jobs—both blue and white collar—to be either "off-shored" or automated. These changes compel us to rethink what kind of education all of our young people will need in order to get—and to keep—a good job.

Economic survival is not the only factor that we must consider as we rethink education goals for the twenty-first century. To better under-stand how all of our schools must adapt to new realities, we need to ex-plore three fundamental transformations that have taken place in a very short period of time:

- the rapid evolution of the new global "knowledge econ-omy," with profound effects on the world of work—all work.

- the sudden and dramatic shift from information that is limited in terms of amount and availability to informa-tion characterized by flux and glut.

- the increasing impact of media and technology on how young people learn and relate to the world—-and to each other.

Separately, each of these transformations represents enormous chal-lenges to our education system. Taken together, they compel a funda-mental reconsideration of all of our assumptions about what children need to learn and how learning takes place. In the chapters that follow, I will explore these three forces of change and their implications for teaching, testing, schooling, training educators, and motivating today's students.

In Chapter 1, we'll look at how the world of work is changing and how these and other changes have created an imperative for individuals to master what I call the Seven Survival Skills—the skills that matter most for work, learning, and citizenship in today's global "knowledge economy." Then, in Chapter 2, we'll contrast this New World of Work with the Old World of School—a world that has remained virtually unchanged for more than a half-century. In particular, we'll visit classes in some of our most highly regarded public schools to explore the extent to which these new survival skills are being taught. In Chapter 3, we'll look at the standardized, multiple-choice tests that students must take with increasing frequency and see what they are really like. We'll explore why and how these tests became so prevalent and gauge their influence on education today; we'll also look at some new assessments that have the potential to hold schools accountable for the skills that matter most.

The fact that future educators must be differently trained and supported in their work is the subject of Chapter 4. Chapter 5 explores the ways in which members of the "Net Generation" have been shaped by the very different world in which they've grown up, as well as the challenges involved in motivating today's students and tomorrow's workers. In Chapter 6, we'll take a tour of three remarkable high schools that show how the Seven Survival Skills can be taught and assessed and that point the way toward a new vision for education. And finally, in the Conclusion, we'll consider some questions—questions for me and questions for you—about what we can do to create a very different dialogue about teaching and learning and testing in the twenty-first century.

In *The Global Achievement Gap,* I begin by discussing why today's students must be taught how to think—all students, not just those labeled as "gifted and talented"—and then I explore some of the essential questions that we must answer if we are to take this goal seriously. What changes must be made within the education system to prepare our nation's students for both analytic and creative thinking? What must teachers do differently to stimulate students' imaginations? What kinds of tests must be given to students to show whether we are making progress toward these ambitious goals? Determining the answers to these questions is important indeed; but, as Einstein suggested, "the formulation of the problem" is even more so.

The "problem," simply stated, is that the future of our economy, the strength of our democracy, and perhaps even the health of the planet's ecosystems depend on educating future generations in ways very different from how many of us were schooled. In this book, we embark on a journey together, not only to understand this global achievement gap but also to discover new ways of thinking about education and best practices in schools that are preparing *all* students for learning, work, and citizenship in the twenty-first century.

CHAPTER 1

The New World
of Work and the
Seven Survival Skills

Initial Encounters
with New World "Natives"

In April 2006, I was on my way to give a speech at an educators' conference outside of Minneapolis. On my flight, I happened to sit next to Clay Parker, the president of the Chemical Management Division of BOC Edwards—a company that, among other things, makes the machines and supplies the chemicals for the manufacture of microelectronics devices, including silicon semiconductors and flat-panel displays. It turned out that he had three children and was deeply interested in education issues. I also found out that, as CEO, he chooses to be very involved in his company's hiring of new employees. For the last few years, I'd been reading about the rapidly changing world of work and had grown increasingly concerned that our schools weren't adequately preparing students for today's workplace. I'd decided that I wanted to interview employers about the skills they now look for when they hire young people. So I asked Parker what qualities he most wants in a potential new employee. I expected a list of technical skills—especially since Parker is an engineer by training—but I was way off the mark.

"First and foremost, I look for someone who asks good questions," Parker responded. "Our business is changing, and so the skills our engineers need change rapidly, as well. We can teach them the technical stuff. But for employees to solve problems or to learn new things, they have to know what questions to ask. And we can't teach them how to ask good questions—how to think. The ability to ask the right questions is the single most important skill."

"What other skills are you looking for?" I asked, expecting that he'd jump quickly to content expertise.

"I want people who can engage in good discussion—who can look me in the eye and have a give and take."

"I don't understand," I confessed.

"All of our work is done in teams. You have to know how to work well with others. But you also have to know how to engage the customer—to find out what his needs are. If you can't engage others, then you won't learn what you need to know."

I couldn't quite believe what I was hearing. This guy, who was an engineer and head of a very technical business, said that he most valued employees who could ask good questions and engage others! I was surprised but also a bit skeptical. He didn't fit my stereotype of a CEO—or an engineer, for that matter—with his emphasis on "soft" skills for a hard-edged, high-tech world.

Later, the conversation turned to our children and their schools. Parker happened to mention that one of his children had had a difficult start to his school year when he challenged something a teacher said. It took several months—and some candid conversations between the teacher and the parents—before the teacher finally decided that Parker's child was not a trouble-maker. I made a mental note: *Corporate CEO most values asking good questions; his child gets into trouble at school for asking the teacher a question.* The problem of students getting into trouble for challenging something a teacher says is not new to me, but I found this juxtaposition especially jarring.

I asked Parker what he and his wife were most concerned about when it came to the schools their children attended. "My wife and I fully support the aims of No Child Left Behind," he said, referring to the landmark 2002 education legislation aimed at closing the achievement gap by holding schools more accountable through increased use of standardized tests. "But our children's teachers take more than a month before the testing begins to teach and review the materials that are going to be on the test, so they are clearly teaching to the test, rather than teaching for a deeper understanding of the content."

Only a month of teaching to the test, I thought. Little does he know. His children go to schools in a good suburban district, whereas in schools that serve more economically disadvantaged kids, teaching to the test is the *only* curriculum—not for a month, but for the entire year. But the more important point for me: Here was a man who headed the division of a company that was in direct competition with companies in India and China—a growing company that created good jobs for American youth—and he was very clear about the kinds of skills he needed in employees. He was also quite aware that our current education reform initiatives, while trying to address the problem of the achievement gap between middle-class and poor kids, might not result in all students knowing how to ask good questions. Clay and I agreed to stay in touch, and I went on to my speaking engagement, inspired by this intriguing conversation with a New World "native" who had challenged some of my assumptions about the work world today.

————

For many years, I have traveled to schools and conferences across the country to consult, offer workshops, and give talks. As part of my talks with teachers, principals, and parents, I often show fifteen minutes or so of a classroom video and then ask the audience to grade the lesson given by the teacher. No matter which video I choose, the narrowest grade range I've ever received is *A* to *D*. In other words, even veteran groups of educators have widely differing views on the quality of a lesson. (We'll explore some of the reasons why this is true in Chapter 4.) Back at the conference in Minneapolis, I conducted this exercise with the attendees, and the grades they reported ranged from *A* to *F*, which is quite common. Yet I felt disheartened, as I do at many gatherings that generate similar results when everyone has a different understanding of what a good lesson is all about. It's like trying to bail out the ocean with a bucket. I thought of my conversation with Clay Parker. I wished educators and parents could have listened to him talk about the importance of teaching kids how to ask good questions—how to think, as opposed to merely covering the chapters in the textbooks and preparing for multiple-choice tests. Hearing his ideas might have made it easer for them to reach an agreement on what good teaching really looks like. But then, this was only one interview, and maybe I'd find out that Parker's views on the skills the mattered most for young people today were out of step with those of other business leaders.

Soon after I returned to Boston, I sat down with Christy Pedra, who currently serves as president and CEO of Siemens Hearing Instruments—one of the largest hearing-instrument manufacturers in the world. Siemens is a highly diversified company with 470,000 employees around the globe. Their operations include development and manufacture of technologies for automation and control; information, transportation, and power systems; medical devices; and many more. A business that values innovations in technology, Siemens needs highly skilled employees, and it creates the kinds of jobs we most want and need to keep for our young people here in this country. So I was eager to hear Pedra's perspective on the skills that matter most in her business.

Just five minutes into the conversation, as Pedra was explaining some of the core competencies her company expects of all employees, she said something that took me by surprise, just as the statement from Parker had done just a few weeks before: "I ask questions for a living," she told me.

Pedra went on: "The majority of my years in the corporate world have been in sales. When you're in a sales and marketing environment, it's really important that you understand your customer. I've found that the best way to understand people is to ask questions. I ask questions all day long. If I ask the right questions, I get information that allows me to be more successful in a variety of ways. If I'm talking to customers, I'm more successful because I understand their business and their needs. I understand their perspective on a problem that has to be solved. If I'm dealing with employees and I ask questions, I understand how they think, where they're coming from as they try to solve a problem, what they've done so far to address an issue. So it really comes down to how well you ask questions."

Pedra elaborated: "Questioning techniques that I've learned over the years have actually become very useful in raising my three children—which they'll hate to hear! They call me the head of the CIA—the Child Interrogation Association. They say the real CIA and FBI have nothing on me. But I keep asking them questions like: 'So tell me how this year's history class is different from last year's. What was good and what was bad?'"

Pedra's reference to her children and their classes led me to ask how she assessed the job the public schools were doing for her children. The school system in her community has a reputation for being one of the best in the state, and so I expected a glowing review.

"They're spending too much time getting kids ready to take the MCAS test." (She was referring to the Massachusetts Comprehensive Assessment System, which is widely viewed as one of the most rigorous of all the new state tests.) "And they're not measuring the right things. If you want to encourage young people to be scientists, it's not how much they can retain but how much they can explore. It's how you ask the next question. I can look up anything, but I can't take it to the next level without pushing and exploring. And that's what I want young people to learn to do. I want them to never stop asking questions."

Like Parker, Pedra believed that the ability to ask good questions and engage others were critical competencies for work today. They also expressed the same concern about their children's suburban public schools—schools that many of us consider to be among the best in the country: too much teaching to the test, too much time memorizing, at the expense of spending time on the thinking skills that are more important.

Ironically, the increased emphasis on testing has come about because of a growing fear, shared by many in this country, that if we don't turn out better-educated and more highly qualified students—especially in math and science—then more and more of our best jobs will go to better-prepared students in developing countries. This is a large part of the rationale among business leaders and policymakers for an increased emphasis on testing at all grade levels and requiring more academic courses in math and the sciences, as well as promoting more Advanced Placement courses in our high schools. Yet, both Parker and Pedra told me that the preparation that mattered most for their companies' jobs was less about technical skills and knowledge than about learning how to think, and *their* concern was that time spent on test preparation and memorizing more content knowledge comes at the expense of teaching students to use their minds well.

Who was right? I wondered what a real scientist would say. I set up an interview with Jonathan King, an internationally renowned molecular biologist who teaches a range of biology courses to both undergraduate and graduate students at the Massachusetts Institute of Technology. He also directs a research lab at MIT and has spent nearly fifty years training future scientists for work at universities and the leading bio-tech labs in the country.

King sent both of his two sons through the highly regarded Cambridge Massachusetts public schools, and he described a troubling change that had occurred between the times his first and his second son attended 4th grade. "They went to the same school and had the same teacher," King explained. "My eldest son had a great experience. His class went over to the pond at Mount Auburn Cemetery and took samples from the muck. They brought them back to school and studied what they found. They discovered all kinds of creatures there—ones that even I hadn't seen! It was great, 'hands-on' science, and it really motivated my son.

"But my second son's experience was totally different. Now all the kids had to take the MCAS tests, and the teachers felt they couldn't take the time for 'fun stuff.' They felt they couldn't take the time to collect and study the muck. They had to prepare all the kids for the tests."

"I worry about the future of science in this country," he told me later in the conversation. "For kids to get passionate about science, they have to get their hands dirty—literally. They have to have labs where they study things in depth and learn to observe, instead of just memorizing facts from a textbook. The kids who take my intro lab courses today have gotten top scores on all the Advanced Placement science courses in their high schools, but they don't know how to *observe*. I ask them to describe what they see in the microscopes, and they want to know what they should be looking for—what the right answer is."

Since completing these initial interviews, I've had several hundred conversations with business, nonprofit, philanthropic, and education leaders—from CEOs to college professors, state superintendents, school principals, and teachers. I've talked to senior executives from Apple to Unilever—representing high-tech and retail businesses, basic manufacturing operations, and even the U.S. Army. I've done extensive interviews with senior consultants who work with a wide variety of corporations. And I've conducted numerous focus groups and interviews with high school and college students and young adults. I've also reviewed the research on issues related to "workforce preparedness." Meanwhile, I have continued to spend time in schools working with educators and observing classes nearly every week—and I have to tell you that I've come to see something that has truly frightening implications for the future of our country.

The *Global* Achievement Gap

Increasingly in America today—and in other countries, as well—there are *two* achievement gaps in our education systems. The first of these—well-documented, widely discussed, and the focus of education reform efforts for the past decade or so—is the gap between the quality of schooling that most middle-class kids get in America and the quality of schooling available for most poor and minority children—and the consequent disparity in results. The second one is the *global* achievement gap, as I've come to call it—the gap between what even our *best* suburban, urban, and rural public schools are teaching and testing versus what *all* students will need to succeed as learners, workers, and citizens in today's global knowledge economy. As a country, we've been striving to close the first achievement gap by bringing our poorest schools up to the standards of our middle-class schools—mainly through increased testing and greater accountability for progress, as measured by the tests. However, it has become increasingly clear to me that even in these "good" schools, students are simply not learning the skills that matter most for the twenty-first century. Our system of public education—our curricula, teaching methods, and the tests we require students to take—were created in a different century for the needs of another era. They are hopelessly outdated.

The global achievement gap remains invisible to most of us—in part, because it is fueled by fundamental economic, social, political, and technological changes that have taken place so rapidly over the last two decades that they seem more like static in people's lives than like tangible forces that are shaping our future. But these changes are powerful, and until we understand them and rethink what young people need to know in the twenty-first century and how they are best taught, our future as a country remains uncertain. In this "newly flattened world," to borrow a phrase from Thomas Friedman, the universe in which our children must compete and succeed has been rapidly transformed by groundbreaking and rapidly evolving technologies, as well as by the stunning economic growth of countries such as China, India, Thailand, the Philippines, and many more. Similarly, since 9/11, new threats to our democracy have emerged. And now global warming may threaten the systems that sustain life on this planet.

To deal with these challenges and others that will inevitably emerge, we need to ensure that students are differently educated for the future. If we were "a nation at risk" in 1983—a phrase that comprised the title of a famous education report released that year decrying the "rising tide of mediocrity" in our public education system—we are today far more seriously at risk than most people realize. And while No Child Left Behind (NCLB) was well intended, its implementation is, in fact, putting all of our children further behind in acquiring the new survival skills for learning, work, and citizenship.

I came to understand the concept of the global achievement gap through my research on the competencies that young people need today in order to be prepared for the world of work. I wanted to find out what a high school graduate today would need to know in order to succeed at a "good" job that paid more than minimum wage. I wanted to know how employers assessed the preparedness of our high school and college graduates to compete for good jobs with the rapidly growing number of well-educated young people from other countries. I was also interested in exploring the extent to which adapting to the needs of the workplace might be at odds with being an independent thinker and a good citizen—a disparity that many educators assume to be the case. For I believed then—and still do—that we will have gained little as a country if we solve the problem of preparation for work at the expense of preparing all students to be active and informed citizens in a democracy. We must do both.

In 1988, I read one of the first studies of the changing workplace and the implications for education—*Winning the Brain Race,* by David Kearns and Denis Doyle. The book describes the ways in which work and the skills that today's workers need to succeed are changing in tandem. I have continued to read articles and studies on this topic since then, but I had no idea just how profoundly the world of work had changed when I began my research for this book.

I still believed, at least in part, that aside from the introduction of computers and the Internet, the culture of the workplace and the ways in which work gets done were not that much different from what William Whyte described in *The Organization Man*—his famous study of the nature of work in corporations in the 1950s. It is considered by many to be one of the most important studies of corporate life ever written and is still widely read today. Whyte worried about the degree to which corporations—and most other large organizations in American life—create inordinate pressures to conform and express loyalty to established authority. Whyte was also deeply concerned about the influence of business on education. His apprehension was that businesses' demand for graduates who had practical skills in accounting and math and so on would render liberal arts majors an endangered species. Whyte concluded that what it took to survive and to succeed in modern organizations was a kind of obedience to authority that jeopardized the individualism that had made America great. His solution: Challenge authority "selectively," a rather surprising recommendation from a *Fortune* magazine editor. He never really explained what a selective challenging of authority might look like.

Many critics of the educational system in the 1960s—John Holt, Paul Goodman, Jonathan Kozol, and others—believed that our public schools were little more than assembly lines designed to turn out nonthinking, conformist children who would be well adapted for the organizations Whyte had described. One consequence was that so-called Free Schools, where students called their teachers by their first name and could choose what they wanted to learn, flourished in the late 1960s. But the rhetoric of the Free Schoolers was more about anger at authority than about teaching students to be independent thinkers. Indeed, the education progressives of the era rarely discussed such things as the development of specific academic and intellectual skills or how they should be held accountable for results. Self-expression and the creative process ruled.

Soon there was a strong backlash from parents and education administrators who were concerned that students were showing less and less respect for the rules of school—or even the rules of grammar, for that matter. And so the "back-to-basics" movement swept through our nation's schools in the 1970s. By the 1980s, many education critics blamed the 1960s rebelliousness in schools (unfairly, later research would suggest) for the steady decline in SAT scores.

After the publication of *A Nation at Risk* in 1983, business leaders and policymakers turned their attention to making schools and educators more accountable for results. Thus the Standards Movement was born in the 1990s—an effort to define and test the academic content all students are supposed to master. With the increased "high-stakes" testing that has come as a result of No Child Left Behind, educators have been under more pressure than ever before to attend to the lowest-achieving students—a positive aspect of the law—but also to raise standardized test scores—one of the main problems in schools today, as we'll see. While there is clear evidence that a growing number of teachers and parents are increasingly uneasy with the amount of testing that's going on in our schools, most don't know what to advocate for—other than what's already being done. The only debate taking place about education in America today is simply whether to modify certain provisions of NCLB. Few question what students are being taught or how. And parents and policymakers alike believe that high test scores are the best, most reliable measure of a good school system. Accordingly, test scores are still the most significant determinant of a community's real estate values.

In the world of academics and policy wonks, however, a growing number of alarmist studies have appeared over the last several years about how much more unprepared young Americans are for the demands of work today than was the case twenty years ago. Workers entering the labor force in the United States are less educated than young people in many other countries. The proportion of U.S. students who graduate from high school today—about 70 percent—is smaller than that of their counterparts in most other developed countries, and fewer than half of this group graduate with the skills needed for college and jobs that pay more than minimum wage, as we learned in the Introduction.[1] Other studies show that, overall, students' achievement has not significantly improved as a result of the implementation of NCLB. In fact, 12th graders' reading scores were lower in 2005 (the last reading test year for which we have data) than they were in 1992, and their writing test scores remained unchanged between 1998 and 2002 (the year of the last national writing assessment).[2] These research results rarely reach broad audiences, however, and so most of us go on hoping that the enacted education laws and local reforms are working.

When I ask large audiences of educators at conferences where I speak how many have read the latest business books, sometimes I don't see a single hand go up. From the little they glean in the media, most educators remain instinctively suspicious of the intentions of corporate leaders who claim that today's graduates are unprepared for the world of work. They've been hearing that the competition is getting ahead and "the sky is falling" for more than twenty years, even as the American economy has appeared to be the envy of the world. Like William Whyte in the 1950s, many educators are concerned that preparation for work is a demand to teach only practical skills and blind obedience to employers. But what preoccupies many educators, as we will see, are the growing pressures to prepare all students for the increased number of "high-stakes" standardized tests. They simply don't have time to worry about abstractions like workforce preparedness. They're a lot more worried about their school or district making what's called "adequate yearly progress" so they're not stigmatized as "failing."

Meanwhile, none of us know very much about what's really going on in middle-class classrooms today—not even educators themselves, for reasons we'll explore later. With the exception of one study on interactions in predominantly middle-class elementary school classes,[3] we have no real data about what's being taught in the "good" suburban schools that are supposed to be the models of success—only continuing horror stories about our failing urban schools. So there is no systematic understanding of how all this increased emphasis on teaching and testing more academic content is actually affecting what happens in real classrooms around the country on a daily basis.

This short history may help explain why the global achievement gap has received so little attention. In order to see this gap between what many kids are being taught by competent teachers every day in good schools versus what the world will require of them, you have to spend considerable time understanding what's going on in both the "Old World" of classrooms and in the "New World" of Work.

Moving between these two worlds, I have come to understand that there is a core set of survival skills for today's workplace, as well as for lifelong learning and active citizenship—skills that are neither taught nor tested even in our best school systems. Young people who want to earn more than minimum wage and who go out into the world without the new survival skills I've uncovered in my research are crippled for life; they are similarly unprepared to be active and informed citizens or to be adults who will continue to be stimulated by new information and ideas. Parents and educators who do not attend to these skills are putting their children at an increased risk of not being able to get and keep a good job, grow as learners, or make positive contributions to their community. I believe that opinion leaders and policymakers who do not understand the profound implications of teaching and testing these new survival skills are complicit in an unwitting conspiracy to put our nation at even greater risk of losing our competitive advantage. Unfortunately, the bet that No Child Left Behind will save us is a losing one.

Hyperbole? You be the judge. Come with me as I talk to representatives from the New World of Work and discover what I call the Seven Survival Skills for the twenty-first century.

The First Survival Skill:
Critical Thinking and Problem Solving

In one form or another, the ability to ask good questions has been a recurrent theme in almost all of my conversations about core competencies and skills for success in today's workplace. The habit of asking good questions was most frequently mentioned as an essential component of critical-thinking and problem-solving skills. It turns out that asking good questions, critical thinking, and problem solving go hand in hand in the minds of most employers and business consultants, and taken together they represent the First Survival Skill of the new global "knowledge economy." Equally important, they are skills that our kids need in order to participate effectively in our democracy.

Karen Bruett manages strategic business development in K–12 education at Dell Computer Corporation. She's also the past president of the Partnership for 21st Century Skills—an organization that has emerged as the leading advocate for redefining "rigor" in the knowledge economy. Our conversation helped me to begin to understand why and how critical-thinking and problem-solving skills have become so essential in today's workplace.

"Corporations have changed dramatically in the last twenty years in terms of the ways that work is organized," Bruett explained. "Most companies used to have big hierarchies, and were very top-down in their management styles, and employees were very specialized in their functions. If you look at what's going on in any company today, the organization has been flattened. The way work is organized now is lots of networks of cross-functional teams that work together on specific projects. Work is no longer defined by your specialty; it's defined by the task or problem you and your team are trying to solve or the end goal you want to accomplish. Teams have to figure out the best way to get there—the solution is not prescribed. And so the biggest challenge for our front-line employees is having the critical-thinking and problem-solving skills they need to be effective in their teams—because nobody is there telling them exactly what to do. They have to figure it out."

Soon after talking to Bruett, I had a long conversation with Annmarie Neal, who is vice president for Talent Management at Cisco Systems—a global company that is the leading supplier of network equipment and network management for the Internet. Like Bruett, she argued that critical-thinking and problem-solving skills were the most important competencies at her company. But she offered a slightly different explanation for the significance of these skills:

"Peter Senge's idea of the 'Learning Organization' is on steroids now because organizations today need to deal with all this flow of information. [Senge is the author of *The Fifth Discipline,* a book about the importance of continuous learning and systems thinking in organizations' ability to adapt to change.] Employees need to sift through an overwhelming amount of information in order to figure out what's important and what's not. To do this you have to think critically."

In schools, *critical thinking* has long been a buzz phrase. Educators pay lip service to its importance, but few can tell me what they mean by the phrase or how they teach and test it—in part, because, as we will see, critical-thinking skills are not tested in any of the new state tests or even college entrance tests like the SAT and ACT. So I wanted to hear Neal's definition of *critical thinking*. I was interested to know if she had an operational definition of this term more clearly in mind than many teachers I'd talked to.

Her response was impressive: "Taking issues and situations and problems and going to root components; understanding how the problem evolved—looking at it from a systemic perspective and not accepting things at face value.

"It also means being curious about why things are the way they are and being able to think about why something is important." Indeed, Neal herself went on with a list of questions: "What do I really need to understand about this; what is the history; what are other people thinking about this; how does that all come together; what frames and models can we use to understand this from a variety of different angles and then come up with something different?"

Neal concluded, "One of the biggest issues facing corporations in America today is changing how we think about problems: 'this is the way we've always looked at it' versus understanding the problem from the perspective of a 'flat world.' So we need to approach problems and challenges as a learner as opposed to a knower. We need to be curious versus thinking 'I know the answer.' Yesterday's solution doesn't solve tomorrow's problem."

Neal has spent years teaching at several universities, and so I asked her how she assessed the students she worked with and if they were able to think in the ways she'd outlined.

"I feel strongly that schools don't teach kids how to really think critically," she answered with passion. "When I taught college, I found students just couldn't do it—think critically—and you don't learn that in one semester. I am a psychologist by training, and I know from my child development studies that you need to start teaching critical thinking as soon as children are capable of abstract thinking. It's really tough to teach children how to think differently if they've spent ten years on one level of thinking and then they go to college. Schools need to let kids be much more curious instead of learning to pass tests. They need to learn the inquiry process."

"Any advice for high school teachers?" I asked her.

Once again, Neal's reply was unequivocal: "Throw out the textbooks! The answer isn't in the books. The answer is in everything but the books. Problems change and so approaches to problems need to change. We also need to rethink the accountability system," she added. "We're getting what we measure, but we're measuring the wrong things."

———

There is a remarkable consistency to what corporate leaders have told me about skills and workplace competencies; but then, virtually all of those I spoke to came from the high-tech world. I'd deliberately chosen to sample a disproportionate number of leaders from the technology sector in the belief that these companies often represent the "cutting edge"—not just in terms of technology but also in terms of how rapidly this sector continues to grow and to create new jobs. And not just any kind of jobs. These companies are creating some of the better-paying jobs our economy has to offer—jobs that we want to see stay in this country for our children. So I reasoned that the skills these companies want from young people are particularly important.

But of course not all young people will go to work for high tech-companies. So I broadened my research to include the skills that matter most today for other kinds of jobs as well.

Mark Maddox is human resources manager at Unilever Foods North America. Unilever is the international manufacturer of leading brands in foods as well as home-care and personal-care products. On November 9, 2006, he joined a panel of employers in Daviess County, Kentucky, to discuss workforce readiness at a conference sponsored by the Regional Alliance for Education. What Maddox said about the ways in which work has changed in his blue-collar, assembly-line operations was strikingly similar to Bruett's assessment of how work has changed in the past few decades:

"Twenty-five years ago, management was 16 percent of the labor force, and administrative support was 12 percent; today management is 5 percent, and support 3 percent. In 1991, we began a journey toward 'continuous improvement.' Prior to that, employees reported to work, and supervisors told them what to do. But since then, layers of management have been taken out. That's what the real change has been about. There are lots of reasons—economics, efficiency. Management and administrative support are indirect labor—they're not a part of the manufacturing process. Direct labor is what adds value to your product, so why not just use the intellect as well as the functional capacity of those folks to do the whole job. That's the direction that we, as well as a lot of others in the industry, are headed in today. Today we practice self-direction and continuous improvement and teamwork.

"These changes have led to changing the skill requirements of our work force," Maddox continued. "For our production and crafts staff, the hourly workers, we need self-directed people who either have problem-solving skills or can easily be trained to think on their feet and find creative solutions to some very tough, challenging problems. We no longer have supervisors who take control . . . and so we look for a different employee than a few years ago: one with critical thinking, creativity, mechanical aptitude, and a passion to embrace new ideas. That is what we need for our workforce and our business to succeed in today's global environment. We're not competing for jobs just in neighboring towns. We're competing with Bangalore, India. It's a global competition. That's the challenge we're all going to face."

Speaking to a mixed audience of business, community, and education leaders, Maddox did not say that most high school graduates lack critical-thinking and problem-solving skills, but he did say that Unilever was hiring more and more employees who had some postsecondary education and even B.A.s and M.A.s—for assembly-line work!

I also talked to two senior executives from the retail industry, who asked that their names not be used because they didn't want to disclose to competitors some very innovative employee training practices their company has developed. Their description of the skills that matter most in their business was completely consistent with what others had told me. In response to my question about the skills they look for in managers today, a woman I will call Susan said to me: "The focus for the last five years has been on thinking skills, as well as emotional intelligence—can they interact and relate, can they come up with new ideas, can they bring these new ideas to the table and work with people in the process."

"What do you mean by people with thinking skills?" I asked.

"Individuals who can see past the present, see beyond, think about the future and think systemically, connect the dots." Susan explained. "We're looking for less linear thinking—people who can conceptualize but also synthesize a lot of data."

Susan's comments on the skills most needed today reminded me of a recent national survey of over 400 employers on the readiness of new entrants into the labor force, sponsored by the Partnership for 21st Century Skills and three other national business organizations. Researchers asked many questions about the content knowledge and skills needed by high school graduates, two-year college graduates, and four-year college graduates—about which skills were most valued and how the employers rated young people's mastery of these skills. An especially interesting question had to do with which skills would likely be most relevant in five years. One of the researchers' most important conclusions was based on the fact that nearly eight out of ten employers surveyed said that, in five years, the single most important skill high school graduates would need was "critical thinking/problem solving." Almost 70 percent of the employers in this study ranked the high school graduates they hired as deficient in this area.[4]

Ellen Kumata, who is the managing partner at Cambria Associates, consults to senior executives at Fortune 200 companies. She explained to me the extraordinary pressures on all leaders today, regardless of their product or service. "When I talk to my clients," she said, "the challenge is this: How do you do things that haven't been done before, where you have to rethink or think anew, or break set in a fundamental way—it's not incremental improvement anymore. That just won't cut it. The markets are changing too fast, the environments are changing too fast.

"Fortune 200 companies face all kinds of challenges everyday—globalization challenges, talent challenges," Kumata continued. "The idea that a company's senior leaders have all the answers and can solve problems by themselves has gone completely by the wayside. Leaders expect employees to help them figure out what to do. The person who's closest to the work has to have strong analytic skills. You have to be rigorous: Test your assumptions, don't take things at face value, don't go in with preconceived ideas that you're trying to prove."

Like many of the people I interviewed, Kumata tied critical-thinking skills to the ability to ask good questions: "You have to spend the time to ask the next question. There is something about understanding what the right questions are, and there is something about asking the nonlinear, counterintuitive question. These are the ones that take you to the next level."

Critical-thinking skills have become increasingly important even in the military, as I learned when I spoke with Rob Gordon. He retired from the Army in 2006 to take a position with City Year, a national youth service organization that focuses on giving young people opportunities for community service. Gordon served as a field artillery officer in Germany, completed postgraduate work at Princeton, and was awarded two White House Fellowships in the first Bush and Clinton administrations. His last assignment, prior to retiring as a full colonel, was an eight-year tenure as director of the American Politics Program at West Point. I asked Gordon how the education of Army officers had changed since the time he had graduated from West Point in 1979:

"The environment has changed, and the army's mission has expanded—we're now involved in reconstruction, emergency preparedness, and so on. We began to think of the world as uncertain and changing. This premise has become one of the bedrocks in terms of leadership development at West Point. Leaders need to be able to operate in this new dynamic environment of globalization, the shrinking of distance and reaction time, working in different cultures, new nuclear powers, clash of civilizations. This realization resulted in a major shift in the way West Point developed leaders; a much more adaptive leadership model evolved. We reduced the engineering sequence of courses and added social sciences, humanities, and languages in order to develop cadets' ability to think adaptively and flexibly, as well as critically."

I then asked Gordon what *he* meant by critical thinking. His definition was very similar to Annmarie Neal's, but with an interesting twist: "Critical-thinking skills include the ability to apply abstract knowledge to solve a problem and to develop and execute a solution—the ability to think broadly and deeply. It means having and using a framework for problem-identification—assumptions and facts, acquiring information, viewing alternative solutions. Another part of critical thinking is surrounding yourself with people who have differences of opinion and who can help you come to the best solution: team-based leadership."

Team-based leadership was a term I'd never heard before. It intrigued me. All the people I spoke with stressed the importance of working in teams as a core competency. The idea of teamwork is not new, of course. We hear about its significance all the time, and we know that virtually all forms of work in American life today are based, to some extent, on team structures—all work, that is, except in education. But as I thought about the comments I'd heard concerning teamwork, collaboration, and the need for a different kind of leadership, a second survival skill emerged.

The Second Survival Skill: Collaboration Across Networks and Leading by Influence

My earlier conversation with CEO Christy Pedra at Siemens suggested to me that the concept of teamwork today is very different from what it had been twenty years ago. "Technology has allowed for virtual teams," she explained. "The way some engineering projects in our company are set up is that you are part of a virtual team. We have teams working on major infrastructure projects that are all over the U.S. On other projects, you're working with people all around the world on solving a software problem. They don't work in the same room, they don't come to the same office, but every week they're on a variety of conference calls; they're doing web casts; they're doing net meetings.

"Seven or eight years ago, I was part of a pilot program for the company in creating the virtual office here in New England. We reduced our office footprint, reduced our square footage, and gave people technology so they could work from the road. One of the lessons we learned quickly was that the hardest thing to change was the behavior of the employees. They didn't know how to operate individually and then collaborate from afar, and so we had to provide coaching and counseling on how you communicate via e-mail and conference calls."

Pedra further explained that the creation of virtual offices and teams that communicated electronically made the development of trust an enormous challenge: "I once read that trust is the total number of interactions divided by the number of positive interactions," she explained. "The higher the number of positive interactions, the greater the trust. Knowing that you're not face to face with people, that you don't see them when you're taking off your coat in the morning, or setting up your desk, or grabbing a cup of coffee, how do you provide the opportunity to interact so that they have the ability to develop trust?"

The challenges involved in virtual and global collaboration also came up during my discussions with Annmarie Neal from Cisco. "Collaboration is an essential skill for us," she said. "Command-and-control leadership style is becoming less and less valued in organizations. People have to understand the importance of working fluidly and across boundaries. As organizations become more global, the ability to work fluidly around the world is a competitive advantage: understanding how to leverage the globe, time zones, where the work can best be done, where there are skills that best match the task, either because of the culture or the training."

Being prepared to work globally is a significant issue for the military, too. Rob Gordon told me that military personnel "have to have more of a global consciousness today—we have to interact around the globe with people from diverse cultures and religions. People who have grown up in the U.S. have to go through more steps to better understand what's going on in the world. Both officers and enlisted personnel need to be much more prepared in this area."

A recent lead article in the business section of the *New York Times,* titled "At I.B.M., a Smarter Way to Outsource—Figuring Out What Work Should Be Done Where and By Whom," helped me further understand the changing nature of collaboration in today's workplace:

> Today, the company's global work force is organized in clusters of business expertise and connected by high-speed communications links. Project managers can search worldwide for the right people with the right skills for a job. . . . The utility project I.B.M. is doing in Texas offers a glimpse of the global formula. The far-flung work team includes research scientists in Yorktown Heights, N.Y., and Austin, Tex.; software developers in Pune and Bangalore, India; engineering equipment and quality-control specialists in Miami and New York; and utility experts and software designers like Mr. Taft who have come from Philadelphia, San Francisco, Los Angeles, Chicago, Raleigh, N.C., and elsewhere.[5]

The skillfulness of individuals working with networks of people across boundaries and from different cultures has become an essential prerequisite for a growing number of multinational corporations. A core competency, as both Neal and the *Times* article suggest, is the ability to think strategically: to figure out where the work can best be done from both a talent and a cost perspective. But then comes what may be an even greater challenge: how to forge effective collaborative teams and work with people who come from vastly different cultures.

The Partnership for 21st Century Skills agrees that understanding and appreciating diverse cultures are additional core competencies that all high school graduates need to master and thus has included "Global Awareness" in its "21st Century Skills Framework," which it has been promoting for the last several years to policymakers and education leaders around the country. According to the Partnership, Global Awareness refers to the ability of students to

- [use] 21st century skills [such as critical thinking and problem solving] to understand and address global issues

- [learn] from and [work] collaboratively with individuals representing diverse cultures, religions and lifestyles in a spirit of mutual respect and open dialogue in personal, work and community contexts

- [understand] other nations and cultures, including the use of non-English languages[6]

This list appears fairly simple and straightforward. But Annmarie Neal explained that the mastery of such skills is, in fact, quite difficult for many in the corporations where she's worked. "It's hard for people in the U.S. to work globally because they are used to being in control. It's hard for many to let go and trust people to do the work, to truly empower people to achieve results, not just to complete tasks; to let people in more junior organizations have power—and the resources they need to get a job done."

Neal and many others talked about how "command-and-control" hierarchical leadership is increasingly a relic of the past in corporations, for many reasons. Management's numbers have been radically reduced to save money, and corporations have discovered that the people closest to the work often have a better understanding of how a product or service can be improved. But transitioning to less top-down authority can be very challenging for those accustomed to the old style, as Neal suggested. And not just for the older generation. The "Old World of School" is still run more by command and control than are many companies, as we'll see, and students are accustomed to having teachers tell them what to do. And students almost never work in teams. Hearing these executives talk, I began to understand how ill-prepared today's students are both for working more collaboratively and for exercising a different kind of leadership as team contributors. In the minds of many executives today, teamwork skills go hand in hand with a different approach to leadership. You cannot have one without the other.

Mike Summers, who is vice president for Global Talent Management at Dell Computers, told me that his greatest concern was young people's lack of leadership skills. "Kids just out of school have an amazing lack of preparedness in general leadership skills and collaborative skills," he explained. "They lack the ability to influence versus direct and command." In other words, the only kind of leadership young people have experienced is one that relies on obedience versus the kind of reasoning and persuasion that is the new leadership style demanded by businesses organized in teams and networks.

He went on, "Students have a naiveté about how work gets done in the corporate environment. They have a predisposition toward believing that everything is clearly outlined, and then people give directions, and then other people execute until there's a new set of directions. They don't understand the complexities of an organization—that boundaries are fluid, that rarely does one group have everything they need to get a job done. How do you solve a problem when people who own what you need are outside your organization or don't report to you, or the total solution requires a consortium of different people? How do you influence things that are out of your direct control?"

Mark Chandler, the senior vice president and general counsel at Cisco, shared Summers's concerns and provided me with his definition of the most important kind of leadership in corporations today: "The biggest problem we have in the company as a whole is finding people capable of exerting leadership across the board." When I asked him what he meant by leadership, Chandler replied, "Our mantra is that you lead by influence rather than authority."

————

As I listened to these leaders, I kept thinking about the overlap between what they were describing as core competencies for the twenty-first-century workplace and the skills that many of us believe are essential for active and informed *citizenship* today. Most of us would agree, without question, that all young people today need to learn how to communicate with others both as employees and as citizens. But let's expand this idea: Don't our high school graduates really need to know how to understand another culture or religion, rather than just speak a few phrases of a second language or travel to another country on a study-abroad program for school credit?

I don't necessarily mean that all high school students should take courses in Modern China or Ancient Religions, although that would be fine. But I am more concerned about our kids knowing how to find and make sense of important information about other cultures. How many of our high school graduates today would know how to research the differences between Sunni and Shiite Muslims? More important, how many would know how to make sense, historically, of the bitter rivalry between these two groups and then apply that understanding to current events in Iraq and elsewhere in the Middle East, and so come to an informed opinion about what our country should do about that conflict—or the Arab-Israeli conflict, for that matter? Many older adults may not know how to do this research or understand these ideas either, but today's world is more dangerous than in the past. Without a critical mass of citizens who are capable of thinking in these ways, aren't we headed for even more trouble in the future?

The concept of leading by influence is another example of a skill that's important not just for businesses but for society overall. It's about how citizens make change today in their local communities—by trying to influence diverse groups and then creating alliances of groups who work together toward a common goal. Aren't these the leadership skills we'd want every young person to master in order to be more effective citizens in our democracy?

Increasingly, it seems to me that there is a convergence between the skills most needed for work in the global knowledge economy and those most needed to keep our democracy safe and vibrant. From what I've learned so far, corporations need more young people who are problem solvers—who know how to think critically and how to ask good questions—and sometimes even provocative ones. They also need young people who work effectively with others and understand and respect differences—not just in our own country but around the world. Finally, corporations are increasingly being organized around a very different kind of authority and accountability structure—one that is less hierarchical and more reciprocal and relational. These abilities, in theory, are consistent with the outcomes of a good liberal arts education. Indeed, preparation for the world of work and the role of citizens in a democracy are not as contradictory as may have been the case in the past.

I do not mean to suggest that "what's good for General Motors is good for the country," as Charles Wilson quipped a half-century ago when he was president of the company. GM certainly wants to find more employees who can solve problems and think critically about how to build a better SUV—but not necessarily to question the controversial decision to build more SUVs, which are considered by many to be bad for the environment. And I'm quite sure that questioning some of the business practices at the Houston energy company Enron, or its accounting firm Arthur Andersen, would not have been welcomed in 2001. People who are taught to think critically often question established wisdom or even the authorities who are in charge. If more young people learn critical-thinking skills, to what extent will these skills be welcomed in corporations in the future? Will a generation that has been taught to solve increasingly tough technical problems also ask tough ethical questions and demand more integrity from the companies they work for? Interviews I conducted with young adults and discuss in Chapter 5 suggest that this may be true.

How will corporations respond to workers who add value by creating better products and services, but who also demand more corporate responsibility? Can critical-thinking skills be "compartmentalized"—selectively turned on and off or applied only to certain problems? I doubt it. Or will critical and questioning voices be stifled in corporations, in ways that we do not yet understand? Or might these voices increasingly become the conscience of corporations in the future? If, indeed, GM had encouraged more active discussion of what products it should be making, instead of attending to short-term shareholder returns, it might be in a far more competitive position today. It's interesting to note that Toyota, which is expected to surpass GM in 2008 as the largest car maker in the world, is a company widely known for more actively and intentionally involving employees in decisions about how to improve its products than any other. (Its method is called the "Toyota Production System," which we'll learn more about later.) And Toyota is a global leader not only in profits and quality but also in the development of hybrid cars and other "green" technologies. I wonder if greater employee involvement leads to a stronger sense of corporate citizenship?

These questions must take a backseat for the moment, though, because, as we will see, our schools are not yet producing many graduates who have been taught how to ask good questions, think critically, solve problems, work effectively in teams, or lead by influence—either in our communities or in our companies.

The Third Survival Skill:
Agility and Adaptability

The portrait of the New World of Work that is emerging is a complex one. The shift from a hierarchal authority that tells you what to do to a team-based environment has been both rapid and profound. Similarly, the intensifying rate of change, the overwhelming amount of data, and the increasing complexity of problems that individuals and teams face every day in their work are dramatic new challenges for everyone in the organization. All of these changes illuminate the importance of another set of essential survival skills for work today: agility and adaptability. These skills have been consistently mentioned during all of my discussions with leaders from every kind of organization.

Clay Parker explained that anyone who comes to work at BOC Edwards today "has to think, be flexible, change, and be adaptive, and use a variety of tools to solve new problems. We change what we do all the time. I've been here four years, and we've done fundamental reorganization every year because of changes in the business. People have to learn to adapt. I can guarantee that the job I hire someone to do will change or may not exist in the future, so this is why adaptability and learning skills are more important than technical skills."

Karen Bruett echoed Parker's comments about this rate of change. "People's jobs change very rapidly. I've been at Dell a long time in similar sales and marketing functions—but what I do today versus what I did five or six years ago is completely different. To survive, you have to be flexible and adaptable and a lifelong learner. . . . And so some of the key competencies we hold employees accountable for include the ability to deal with ambiguity, the ability to learn on the fly, and strategic agility." Bruett also worried about the fact that she was seeing no change in schools: "What goes on in classrooms today is the same stuff as fifty years ago, and that's just not going to cut it."

Disruption is the word Annmarie Neal used to explain the importance of agility and being able to deal with new and rapidly changing business environments. "We're right in the throes of launching our new executive competency model here at Cisco," she told me. "We're trying to be very targeted about the skills leaders need. One is about being able to manage disruption: (1) How do leaders deal with exogenous factors that are going to impact the way they think and lead (such as 9/11 and what's going on in other parts of globe)? (2) How do they handle internal disruption—innovation and change management? (3) How do they understand disruptions that are happening in our industry space or in adjacent spaces?"

Mark Maddox described how agility and adaptability are important in improving both quality and productivity in assembly-line jobs as well. "Today's employees must adapt to change; they can't be satisfied with the status quo," he said. "If we did 20,000 cases on the line today, why can't we do 21,000 tomorrow? We have to fight complacency . . . and so we look for employees who have a passion to embrace new ideas."

Rob Gordon explained that at West Point, "We've added an integrative experience where cadets have to demonstrate that they can present leadership skills to solve problems in a changing and uncertain world."

"You have to be able to take in all sorts of new information, new situations, and be able to operate in ambiguous and unpredictable ways," explained Ellen Kumata. "You have to thrive in this environment and deliver results. Our system of schooling promotes the idea that there are right answers, and that you get rewarded if you get the right answer. But to be comfortable with this new economy and environment, you have to understand that you live in a world where there isn't one right answer, or if there is, it's right only for a nanosecond. If you're afraid, you can't think clearly."

The Fourth Survival Skill:
Initiative and Entrepreneurialism

Employees can be good problem solvers and team players, and they can be agile and adapt to new surroundings and ideas, but I learned that mastery of these survival skills is not enough in many companies—and likewise in many communities that face new challenges requiring proactive leadership. In the interviews I conducted, I heard a strong and consistent concern about the ways in which today's workers (and citizens) use or apply these survival skills: Leaders today want to see individuals take more initiative and even be entrepreneurial in terms of the ways they seek out new opportunities, ideas, and strategies for improvement.

In many of the interviews you've already read in this chapter, the importance of individuals and teams being able to take the initiative to solve a problem or come up with a better solution was frequently mentioned in passing. It was Mark Maddox from Unilever who said that "we need self-directed people who . . . can . . . find creative solutions to some very tough, challenging problems." And Karen Bruett explained that the members of her education group, for whom understanding technology has traditionally been their most important skill, "need to shift to understanding the problems of our customer—in this case, in education. They need to help educators figure out how to use technology effectively, and the group is going to have to figure this out for themselves."

Ellen Kumata told a story of how the executives at a large financial firm she had consulted had changed their thinking in just the last few years. "Six years ago I was working with them to figure out what kind of talent they needed. There was a lot of resistance—you can't name it, you know it when you see it, you can't hire for it—all the traditional ways of thinking. Yesterday, we went back to do a full-day working session with all the senior execs on this problem. . . . They've become much more clear about the skills they're looking for: an achievement orientation and a drive for results. Individuals who are self-starters, who take initiative, and who are entrepreneurial. And now they've decided to make finding, growing, and retaining this kind of talent a part of the performance management system for executives. The reason why is because they are expanding rapidly, and their life-blood really depends on coming up with more effective ways of finding and retaining this kind of talent."

Mark Chandler from Cisco was perhaps the biggest proponent of these traits. "Leadership is the capacity to take initiative and trust yourself to be creative," he told me. "I say to my employees if you try five things and get all five of them right, you may be failing. If you try ten things, and get eight of them right, you're a hero. If you set stretch goals, you'll never be blamed for failing to reach a stretch goal, but you will be blamed for not trying. One of the problems in a large company is risk aversion. Our challenge is how to create an entrepreneurial culture in a larger organization."

To recap a bit: The "organization man" of today is very different from the type of person Whyte described years ago. Both white- and blue-collar employees—and military personnel—frequently work in teams or with physical and virtual networks of individuals to solve problems or create better products and services. The most effective way they "lead" teams of peers is through influence, rather than by giving orders. Finally, because of the rapid pace of change, today's successful employees must be highly adaptable and, in a growing number of organizations, even entrepreneurial. In short, more and more individuals in our economy are what business guru Peter Drucker labeled "knowledge workers." Although Drucker coined this phrase in *Landmarks of Tomorrow* as far back as 1959, the skills needed to be a successful knowledge worker today continue to evolve and grow in importance everywhere—except in our schools.

The Fifth Survival Skill:
Effective Oral and Written Communication

During our exploration of the Second Survival Skill, Pedra described one of the first problems she encountered when her group began to work less face to face and in more of a "virtual office." "We had to provide coaching and counseling on how you communicate via e-mail and conference calls," she told me. In fact, her concerns about workers' poor communication skills are widespread among the people I have spoken with, emerging in most of the interviews I conducted. Communication skills are a major factor highlighted in dozens of studies over the years that focus on students' lack of preparation for both college and the workplace, and these skills are only going to become more important as teams are increasingly composed of individuals from diverse cultures. The ability to express one's views clearly in a democracy and to communicate effectively across cultures is an important citizenship skill as well.

When employers were asked about the skills of high school graduates in the Partnership for 21st Century Skills study mentioned earlier, "[m]ore than half (52.7 percent) say [that] Written Communications, which includes writing memos, letters, complex reports clearly and effectively, is 'very important' for high school graduates' successful job performance," and "80.9 percent of employer respondents report high school graduate entrants as 'deficient.'" The study continued with an assessment of two-year and four-year college graduates' writing skills: "46.4 percent of employer respondents report new workforce entrants with a two-year college diploma as 'deficient,' and over a quarter (26.2

percent) report that new workforce entrants with a four-year college diploma are 'deficient.' Almost two-thirds of employer respondents (64.9) say Writing in English is 'very important' for two-year college graduates; almost 90 percent (89.7 percent) say these skills are 'very important' for four-year college graduates."[7]

As Annmarie Neal told me, "The biggest skill people are missing is the ability to communicate: both written and oral presentations. It's a huge issue for us."

When I asked Rob Gordon what advice he had for teachers today, he was emphatic: "Teach them to write! Effective communication is key in everything we do—people need to learn to communicate effectively with each other and with external communities. Even enlisted men need to communicate effectively via e-mail. . . . I saw the importance of this in Iraq when I went back in January of 2004. When we asked a brigade commander what he'd learned, he talked about the importance of relying on soldiers who understood not only what they were seeing on screens that showed near real-time combatant movements but also how to interpret and communicate what they saw."

Mike Summers also spoke forcefully on this issue: "We are routinely surprised at the difficulty some young people have in communicating: verbal skills, written skills, presentation skills. They have difficulty being clear and concise; it's hard for them to create focus, energy, and passion around the points they want to make. They are unable to communicate their thoughts effectively. You're talking to an exec, and the first thing you'll get asked if you haven't made it perfectly clear in the first sixty seconds of your presentation is, 'What do you want me to take away from this meeting?' They don't know how to answer that question."

Listening to Summers's comments as a former English teacher myself, I was surprised by the list of skills he thought important: not only the ability to communicate one's thoughts clearly and concisely but also the ability to create *focus, energy, and passion.* Summers and other leaders from various companies were not necessarily complaining about young people's poor grammar, punctuation, or spelling—the things we spend so much time teaching and testing in our schools. While it's obviously important to write and speak correctly, the complaints I heard most frequently were more about fuzzy thinking and the lack of writing with a real *voice.* What business leaders don't understand, however, is that most teachers aren't trained or encouraged to teach this kind of writing. Instead, as we'll see, they are often asked to teach 120 or more students a day a simplistic formula style of writing that will enable the students to pass standardized tests, and they have very little time to do anything more.

The Sixth Survival Skill:
Accessing and Analyzing Information

Employees in the twenty-first century have to manage an astronomical amount of information flowing into their work lives on a daily basis. As Mike Summers told me, "There is so much information available that it is almost too much, and if people aren't prepared to process the information effectively it almost freezes them in their steps." Annmarie Neal pointed out that organizations need to be able to understand how people deal with the flow of information. She also stressed the importance of critical thinking in the context of how an employee receives and uses information. Rob Gordon said that all high school graduates need to learn how to access and analyze different kinds of information. And Susan, the woman who works in the retail industry, talked about needing "people who can conceptualize but also synthesize a lot of data." As she mentioned: "There's so much more data that people have to synthesize. And they can't just produce a bunch of reports. They have to find the important details and then say 'here's what we should do about it.'"

In writing about the growing importance of the knowledge worker in the 1960s, Peter Drucker explained that it was the increasing availability of information and the need to know how to analyze it that, in fact, enabled and even required more and more employees to become knowledge workers. In other words, the ability to analyze information in order to discern new challenges and opportunities had become, even in Drucker's time, a vital core competency in the workplace. Today, this is even truer. In a very short period of time, with the advent of the Internet and the increasing availability of fast connections, we have evolved from a society where only a few people had limited information to one where all of us experience information flux and glut—and can look up almost anything imaginable on our computer in a search that takes nanoseconds.

It's not just the sheer quantity of information that represents such a challenge but also how rapidly and constantly the information is changing. Quick, how many planets are there? While I was at Harvard in the early 1990s, I heard the then president of the university, Neil Rudenstine, say in a speech that the half-life of knowledge in the humanities is ten years, and in math and science, it's only two or three years. And that was fifteen years ago! I wonder what he would say it is today.

Obviously, this information revolution has profound implications not just for work but also for citizenship and lifelong learning. To be active and informed citizens today, knowing how to read the newspaper is no longer enough. We have to be able to access and evaluate information from many different sources. Indeed, all this access to information is of little use—and may even be dangerous—if we don't know how to evaluate it. Thus the immediate availability of information places an even greater premium on critical-thinking skills. Recently, a teacher told me a story that clearly illustrates this new challenge and unfortunately reflects quite a common occurrence. She had assigned students the task of researching Martin Luther King, Jr., near the time of the national holiday in his honor. But what many of them found during their Internet searches was scary. It turned out that a white supremacist group had prepared for this important holiday and figured out how to manipulate Internet searches in such a way that their website was listed among the top five or so when an individual typed Dr. King's name into a search engine. Their home page provided some factually accurate biographical information, so the site may have appeared legitimate at first glance, but when students went any further into the site, they encountered every kind of racist belief—all presented as facts.

Instant access to overwhelming amounts of information raises fundamental questions about the nature of the curriculum in our schools today. But before we can explore this issue, we have one more survival skill to consider.

The Seventh Survival Skill:
Curiosity and Imagination

The words *curiosity* and *inquisitiveness* are almost always mentioned when I ask leaders to tell me what skills matter most today. Creativity and innovation are key factors not only in solving problems but also in developing new or improved products and services. And so today's employees need to master both "left-brain" skills—such as critical thinking and problem solving, accessing and evaluating information, and so on—and "right-brain" skills such as curiosity, imagination, and creativity. It's not enough to just be trained in the techniques of how to ask questions—as lawyers and MBAs often are, for example. Employees must also know how to use analytical skills in ways that are often more "out-of-the-box" than in the past, come up with creative solutions to problems, and be able to design products and services that stand out from the competition. In other words, they have to be new and improved knowledge workers—those who can think in disciplined ways, but also those who have a burning curiosity, a lively imagination, and can engage others empathetically.

Clay Parker stressed the importance of hiring employees who are more than just smart. "I want people who can think—they're not just bright, they're also inquisitive. Are they engaged, are they interested in the world?" Bear in mind that analytical and creative capacities are closely related but different. As Mark Summers told me: "People who've learned to ask great questions and have learned to be inquisitive are the ones who move the fastest in our environment because they solve the biggest problems in ways that have the most impact on innovation."

Annmarie Neal described curiosity as an essential element of critical thinking. She told me that curiosity is about "taking issues and situations and problems and going to root components; understanding how the problem evolved—upstream and downstream components, looking at it from a systemic perspective; not accepting things at face value but being curious about why things are the way they are." In other words, the ability to do a "systems analysis" is important, but it is the habit of curiosity that allows an individual to begin to wonder how a system might be substantively improved or even reinvented. As I've heard time and time again, new employees straight out of high school and even college do not know how best to think about problems and how to approach them. We need to be curious.

Daniel Pink, the author of *A Whole New Mind,* sees more white-collar jobs being automated or "offshored"—an issue that is at the heart of the questions I'm asking about the skills young people most need today. But he also observes that, in this era of increasing abundance, people want more distinctive products and services. Plain vanilla won't cut it anymore in today's crowded marketplace: "For businesses it's no longer enough to create a product that's reasonably priced and adequately functional. It must also be beautiful, unique, and meaningful. . . . In an age of abundance, appealing only to rational, logical, and functional needs is woefully insufficient. Engineers must figure out how to get things to work. But if those things are not also pleasing to the eye or compelling to the soul, few will buy them. There are too many other options."[8] Pink also notes that developing our capacities for imagination, creativity, and empathy will be increasingly important to our competitive advantage in a future he describes as being dominated by "high concept and high touch": "High concept involves the capacity to detect patterns and opportunities, to create artistic and emotional beauty, to craft a satisfying narrative, and to combine seemingly unrelated ideas into something new. . . . High touch involves the ability to empathize with others, to understand the subtleties of human interaction, to find joy in one's self and to elicit it in others, and to stretch beyond the quotidian in pursuit of purpose and meaning."[9]

Michael Jung, who holds a Ph.D. in economics and an M.A. in economics/business administration, would agree with Pink. But he takes Pink's analysis a daring leap further as he looks to the future from his vantage point at McKinsey and Company as a senior consultant to multinational corporations all over the world. Jung is working on a new generation of approaches to large-scale change management in the private and public sectors, and he is leading a new McKinsey Office dedicated to developing and applying such programs.

According to Jung, "In the knowledge economy we have lots of highly idiosyncratic niches not only with products or businesses, but also within companies. I think the most successful worker will not merely adapt to working conditions that are given to him but be able to adapt in a way that creates a position that fits his own profile—active adaptiveness. *We still think that work is given to people; whereas I think people actually are increasingly taking the work.*

"Our old idea is that work is defined by employers and that employees have to do whatever the employer wants," Jung went on to explain. "That has not been true in professional jobs for a long time because people have so many ways to influence what they do and how they do it that, if they are good, they actually create their work space. . . . If you go to your hairdresser, he is supposed to give you exactly the cut you tell him to do, but actually you would like him to come up with an interpretation that you like—he's adding something personal—a creative element. The same is true for the guy who is writing code, the same is true for the sales rep who combines the company way with his personal style so that he is more authentic and credible. Authenticity pays."

———————

Charlie Chaplin's silent movie *Modern Times* is a classic parody of the "Old World" of blue-collar work. As an assembly-line worker, Chaplin's character is always getting into trouble with the bosses and ends up getting caught in the cogs of the machine. He's simply another replaceable part. What I've come to learn is that the most successful companies in the emerging economy need a new and very different kind of worker who teams with others to continuously reinvent the machine as well as the products and services it creates. And I've discovered that, for some of us at least, our stereotypes of both white- and blue-collar work are badly out of date. As out of date, perhaps, as our beliefs about what constitutes an adequate education. As out of date, we shall see, as the schools we created to meet the needs of a very different era.

In a seminar I was leading recently, an administrator from one of the country's most prestigious private schools suddenly asked: "Why is it that the longer our kids are in school, the less curious they seem?" The room fell silent. No one challenged her assertion; nor did anyone offer an explanation. This was happening at one of the country's best private schools! If *they* can't cultivate curiosity, then how can we expect public schools to do so? What is it about the way we school our children that seems to be stifling curiosity, and what can we do about it? Should we find a way to hold schools accountable for developing the Seven Survival Skills for the New World, and can we test such skills?

These are critical questions to consider because, as we've learned in this chapter, it's no longer the case that curiosity and imagination and all of the other skills I've described here are habits of mind for just the elites of our society—the ones who can afford to send their children to private schools. Indeed, the Seven Survival Skills are for future generations what the "Three R's" were for previous generations. They are the "new basic skills" for work, learning, and citizenship in the twenty-first century.

CHAPTER 2

The Old World
of School

I REMEMBER THE first time I began to realize that there might be a second hidden "achievement gap"—or what I've to come to call a global achievement gap—between what our more academically able students are being taught versus what they will need to succeed in today's world. I was accompanying a group of program officers from the Bill & Melinda Gates Foundation on visits to several "early colleges" funded by the Foundation (programs that combine high school and community college courses so that students can get college credit while still in high school). They wanted some assistance in determining what "rigor" should look like in classrooms and in assessing the progress their grantees were making as they strived to ensure that all students were "college-ready."

We visited a total of eighteen classes over three days at three schools. Debriefing our school visits, we concluded that only one class out of the eighteen appeared to be adequately preparing students with the skills and level of intellectual challenge they'd need to succeed in college.

We all came away from our visits feeling sobered and somewhat dis-heartened. But it was a conversation with some students in an Ad-vanced Placement chemistry course that especially upset me. Let me describe what I saw and heard:

Students are in groups of two and three, mixing chemicals according to directions that are written on the blackboard. Once the mixtures are prepared, they heat the concoction with Bunsen burners. According to the directions on the board, they are supposed to record their observa-tions on a worksheet. I watch a group of three young men whose mixture is giving off a thin spiral of smoke as it's being heated—something that none of the other students' beakers are doing. One student looks back at the blackboard and then at his notes. Then all three stop what they are doing—apparently waiting for the teacher, who is sitting at her desk, to come help them.

"What's happening to your mixture?" I ask the group.

"Donno," one mutters. "We must have mixed it up wrong."

"What's your hypothesis about what happened—why it's smoking?"

The three look at one another, and then the student who has been doing all the speaking looks at me and shrugs.

"Do you know what a hypothesis is?" I press.

My question is greeted with blank looks. Finally, their spokesperson says, "We had it on a test as a vocab question. Isn't it—like—an idea of what's supposed to happen?"

These kids—who have to be among the most academically able in the school to be allowed to take an AP class—were taking a course where they were supposed to be learning college-level skills and con-tent. But what I'd seen barely qualified as an introductory cooking class. All they were doing was following the "recipe" that the teacher had copied onto the board. When their cake flopped, so to speak, they had no idea what to do. What were these students supposed to be learning? It certainly wasn't how to apply the scientific method to the study of a problem or the analysis of a phenomenon—arguably one of the most important skills all high school graduates need to master.

Remember my conversation in the first chapter with Jonathan King, the MIT scientist? He told me that MIT freshman coming out of high school AP classes know how to pass all the tests, but they don't know how to observe, and they want to be told what the right answer is. I understood his words, but now I had really seen for myself what he'd been talking about. How are we supposed to compete with the growing numbers of well-educated young people from India and China and elsewhere, if we're getting results like these, I asked myself as I left the class.

The work that teachers and students are doing in the suburban public schools we consider to be the best in the nation is supposed to be the gold standard for all of our nation's children. When business leaders, policymakers, and educators call for a "challenging and rigorous education" for all of our students, they're saying that every adolescent in America should take the kind of college-preparatory curriculum that only some of our students have the opportunity to take today. When *Newsweek* creates its list of the best high schools in America, all it looks at is the percentage of students taking the rapidly growing Advanced Placement program—courses for which the Educational Testing Service offers an exam that is considered to be as rigorous as what would be expected of college freshmen—or the much smaller International Baccalaureate program (an honors academic program that originated in Europe). The high schools with the greatest number of students taking the most AP and IB courses are considered to be the best. It's as simple as that. Many of the most selective colleges also weigh the number of AP courses a student has taken in the admissions process. (As we'll see, however, the number of colleges that actually allow students to place out of freshman-level courses on the basis of having taken AP courses in high school has declined significantly.)

Are these the right measures of success—the gold standard that we should hold up for all teachers and children? To what extent are students who are currently taking what we consider rigorous courses in our high schools learning the Seven Survival Skills? From powerful books written by Jonathan Kozol and others, we've known for some time that many poor and minority kids leave school barely knowing how to read or write—and this is truly a national disgrace and a catastrophic problem. But how are some of our most academically well-prepared students doing (or at least the students we consider to be prepared)? Are they learning how to think critically, solve problems, work collaboratively, take initiative, communicate effectively, access and analyze information, be curious and imaginative? To answer these questions, we're going to visit some classrooms together in this chapter.

A Tale of Two Cities

"It was the best of times, it was the worst of times." Remember this opening line to the classic novel by Charles Dickens? It sums up what I've seen in the years that I have spent observing and working in some of our country's most highly regarded suburban public school districts. You walk into the main entrance of most suburban high schools, and the first thing you usually see are glass cases on the wall filled with trophies—celebrations of various sports championships. School spirit in most of America's high schools still ebbs and flows according to how well the sports teams are performing. Walking through the hallways, you are struck by how clean and well-maintained the buildings are—unlike what you'd find in our crumbling urban schools. There is little or no graffiti on the walls, no cigarette smoke or butts in the bathrooms, and only an occasional piece of trash on the floor. When the bells ring for the change of classes, the corridors quickly fill with crowds of neatly dressed students who are talking to friends or listening to their iPods as they make their way to their next class. No fights and rarely an angry word. Except for the ubiquitous white earbuds and changes in fashion, you might think you'd been transported back to the 1950s.

By all outward appearances, it is the best of times for these students and their teachers and administrators. But the real question is not about how the sports teams are doing or how well-maintained the building looks or even how well the students are behaving. The important question is What's going on in classrooms? Sure, sports are important, but why don't we see more public celebrations of *academic* achievement in our high schools? Parents and community members and even educators sometimes forget that the real purpose of high school is to produce students who will be capable citizens and participants in our democracy—students who know how to solve problems and add value, both in their communities and in the workplace. It's not just about winning teams. Only a small number of students play varsity sports—usually 10 percent or fewer—and only a tiny fraction of those will ever have a career in sports. By contrast, all students' futures are profoundly affected by the quality of teaching and learning in a high school.

In order to really understand what's happening in classrooms, you need to observe teaching and learning in lots of schools. I'm going to take you on a "learning walk" in some schools across the country. This learning walk is one way to essentially audit what's taking place in a group of classes in a given period of time. If you spend ten minutes or so in eight to ten classes over several hours (along with district or school administrators and teacher leaders who may accompany you), you have a snapshot of the teaching and learning that take place in that school. It's obviously not a way to evaluate individual teachers or an entire course, but this kind of sampling detects patterns within and across schools. If we know what to look for and what questions to ask students, learning walks can be a very accurate way of assessing the purpose of a lesson and the skills that students are learning in their classes—especially when augmented by other clues and evidence, such as students' written work and the kinds of homework assignments students are given.

Like any sampling process in research, learning walks are not a 100 percent reliable means of assessing all that goes on in a school. But the idea is that every minute in class is precious—especially in the typical forty-five-minute high school class period—so observing ten-minute slices from a representative sample of classes can tell you a great deal about the students' learning experiences in a school. Over the last decade or so, I've led over 100 learning walks in dozens of school districts in order to train administrators to be instructional leaders—leaders who know that improving instruction is their most important job—and to help them determine priorities for strengthening the work of the teachers in their schools.

Before we go into some classrooms, though, I need to explain the context and my ground rules. First, we will not visit the stereotypical urban high schools—which we know have been failing to educate students for years. My intention, rather, is to look at what goes on in schools that are considered to be "high-performing" models of successful education. Both of the schools we'll visit are *ranked among the best in the state* where they are located—according to their state's standardized test scores. Second, what I found in my learning walks in these two high schools was consistent with what I've seen in similar "good" suburban high schools all over the country. I choose to profile what was going on in these schools because they are representative of the kind of teaching and learning that's taking place for our college-bound students in our best public high schools. My purpose is not to offer a muckraking exposé; indeed, it would be unfair to the hard-working professionals in these school districts to single them out in some way, so I use pseudonyms for the schools and their administrators. In fact, in both of the districts where these schools are located, the administrators were particularly interested in developing strategies for improving teaching and learning. What makes these districts unusual, then, when we compare them to many middle-class schools in this country, is not what's going on in their classrooms but, rather, their leaders' willingness to admit that, despite the good reputation of their schools and districts, they nevertheless need to improve.

The first high school, which I will call Jefferson High, is located in a southern state that was among the first to take on the problem of improving student achievement. Beginning in the late 1980s, a succession of governors has proclaimed education reform to be the state's top priority, and their legislature was one of the first to create new curriculum standards and new tests. Indeed, the problem of test scores was the reason I was asked to consult to one of their top-performing school districts.

This district—let's call it Ashland—boasted some of the highest test scores in the state. Ordinarily, this would be cause for celebration in the community—and especially among the school and district leaders. Accustomed to being constantly criticized in the media and having their district's test scores compared to those of other districts, most superintendents who had test scores like Ashland's would, understandably, be quite complacent. But most superintendents aren't like the man whom I call Frank. He'd quit a successful career in business because he wanted to do something more meaningful. Although he was new to the job and to the field of education, Frank had been trained to truly analyze the numbers, and what he learned as he compared the district's state test scores to other data concerned him.

Ashland's elementary schools were among the highest-ranked in the state, according to their test scores, but Frank discovered that a national test of students' reading abilities, which the district had administered in addition to the mandated state tests, revealed that almost one-third of his students were leaving 5th grade with reading abilities that were a

year or more below grade level. Ashland was understandably proud of
the fact that more than 80 percent of their high school students graduated. The problem, Frank learned, was that very few graduates ever
completed a college degree—fewer than 20 percent!

Frank knew that there was a relationship between these two findings—
that students who leave elementary school reading well below their
grade level are at risk of dropping out of high school or, if they do complete their diploma, are unlikely to succeed in college. But Frank
wanted to know what else might be wrong. To what extent, he wondered, were the high school teachers adequately preparing their students for college?

I went to visit some classes with the high school principal, who was
also committed to understanding this problem. Jefferson, like most of
our nation's high schools, is organized on the basis of "tracks." Students
are put into groups according to their academic abilities—as determined
by test scores and recommendations from previous years' teachers. While
many American high schools have four or even five groups or tracks, this
one had only three—one for students designated as college-bound, one
for those who need only a "general" education (which, today, is an absurd
idea), and one for those who need some kind of remediation. To better
understand the problem of the low college completion rate, we visited
only classes in the first track. Here is a sampling of what we found:

Honors Geometry.   Students are filling in worksheets with problems.
One student tells us it's the homework for tomorrow. The teacher remains at his desk, grading papers.

12th Grade English.   Students are working in groups to translate different scenes from *Macbeth* into contemporary English. I ask a student
to share with me what the longest paper was that he's had to write so far
this year.

"We've written two papers so far," the student tells me. (This was late fall.) "The longest one was a two-page 'How To' essay."

"What about last year?" I ask.

"I had to do a five-page research paper."

9th Grade Global Studies.   Students are at their desks, using colored pencils to fill in blank maps of Europe. They all have their textbooks open in front of them and are using the map in the text as reference.

10th Grade World Civilization.   Teacher: "Adam Smith was for free trade. Can anyone tell me why?"

A student in the front row mutters a reply that is barely audible.

Teacher: "Right. Now, what were the six reasons for British success in 1700?"

No hands go up. The teacher answers his own question and then asks, "How was geography an advantage for England during this time?" Not waiting for a student to reply, the teacher goes on to answer the question. After several similar questions, students are directed to fill out a worksheet that is on their laptops.

12th Grade Economics.   The class is watching a faded color film about a prospector in the Old West who can't get the food and mining supplies he needs. The tape is so old that the words on the sound track can barely be heard. There are no questions on the board, and no students are taking any notes.

9th Grade Integrated Science.   Students are taking a mid-term test on electricity and magnetism. I ask for a copy of the test and observe that all of the questions on the test are multiple choice.

———

Reading this description, you may be tempted to conclude that the trouble with this school is the teachers—that they seem to be just going through the motions or are not giving students enough challenge. Many business leaders I talk to think that the number-one problem in public education is powerful teachers' unions and tenure laws. They believe that the quality of teaching is mediocre in many schools because unions are protecting tenured teachers who are ineffective for whatever reason. I'm certainly not a fan of tenure, but I view the problem differently. First, the quality of teachers' preparation, continuing professional development, and supervision is very low in our nation's schools—a problem I explore in Chapter 4. In addition, almost all of the state tests for which teachers have to prepare students are computer-scored, multiple-choice assessments of factual recall. So most teachers are doing the best job that they know how to do, and they are teaching what they have been told are the subject-content standards that their students will be tested on. The majority of teachers I meet go to work every morning *wanting to make a difference* for at least some kids. They're certainly not in it for the money.

Most teacher evaluation systems are checklists of teachers' techniques, which must be filled out periodically by school administrators. Is the purpose of the lesson and the homework assignment on the board? Are the content standards to be covered in the lesson made clear to students? And so on. Rather than look only at what *teachers* are doing, I try to assess what *students* are being asked to do: the *specific skills and knowledge* that students are expected to master and the level of *intellectual challenge* in the lesson. What the teacher does is the means by which the students learn—not the end.

Thus, for example, I listen for the nature of the questions that students are asked during class or in written assignments, while also observing how much a teacher probes students' thinking with follow-up questions or insists that students supply more detail or supporting evidence for their answers. I have consistently found that the kinds of questions students are asked and the extent to which a teacher challenges students to explain their thinking or expand on their answers are reliable indicators of the level of intellectual rigor in a class. If the questions require only factual recall—which is most often the case—then students are probably not being asked to do very much in the way of reasoning, analysis, or hypothesizing—and the primary skill being taught is memorization. If I see this pattern in a number of classes, then I can reliably predict how well a school's students might perform on an essay exam or how well prepared they are for college.

Next, during class discussions, I look at who's answering the teacher's questions. If only one or two hands are going up in response to questions—and they are usually the same hands in the front row—the implication is that few students are engaged in the lesson, and that the teacher is accustomed to calling on the "usual suspects" or, even worse, is focused only on those students whom he or she considers willing or able to learn.

Then I ask myself two questions:

1. What is the difference between what I saw in this high school class versus what I'd see being taught in, say, a 6th grade class? In other words, do I see evidence that students are being progressively intellectually more challenged as they move into higher grades?

2. What is my level of confidence that, with more classes like the ones I've just seen, these students will be adequately prepared for college or for today's workplace?

When the principal and I concluded the learning walk after observing these classes and a number of others, our answers to my two questions will likely not come as a surprise to you. We were concerned. We came away from our time in classrooms with data that suggested why so few Jefferson high school graduates were completing college. They simply weren't being taught the skills they'd need to succeed. This problem is hardly unique to Jefferson: As we learned in the Introduction, *40 percent of all students who start college need some form of academic remediation.*[1] Yes, there are many reasons why students don't finish college—lack of direction in their lives and financial burdens are serious problems for many—but too often students simply lack the skills that are essential for success in college: the ability to think critically, read complex material, apply knowledge to new problems, and write well. Lacking these skills, they become frustrated, discouraged, and lose all confidence that they can succeed.

Why weren't the educators at Jefferson teaching these skills—the ones that matter most? They've been told that teaching subject content is more important than teaching skills. And they're being held accountable for getting students to pass the state test rather than for ensuring that their graduates do well after high school. So if you want to point a finger, save it for the next chapter when we look at the kinds of tests for which these teachers have to prepare their students.

———

Lincoln High, the name I'll give to the second school I've chosen for our learning walk, is located in a New England state that has long enjoyed a reputation for having some of the best public schools and highest standardized test scores in the country. This high school is one of the highest performing in the state, and it's been named by a national publication as one of the top fifty public high schools in the country. It's located in a district I'll call Zenith. Zenith would hardly be considered a middle-class school district. In fact, the *median* family income in this district is approaching $175,000. Those who can afford to buy homes here and pay the high property taxes choose to live in communities like Zenith in lieu of having to pay private school tuitions. Indeed, many of the executives' children whom I interviewed in the first chapter go to high schools just like Lincoln. Lincoln graduates nearly all of its students, and almost all who graduate go on to college—including many who are accepted at some of the country's most selective universities. High schools like Lincoln, then, think of themselves as incubators for the future leaders of our country.

Grace is the name I've given the superintendent who asked me to evaluate Zenith. She had read one of my articles in which I questioned whether Advanced Placement courses were the best standard for academic rigor today. Although she led a school district that was already considered to be outstanding by every measure, Grace was a "teacher's superintendent" and very aware of the importance of good instruction. She was concerned that the district's teacher evaluation system, which it negotiated with the union, didn't give classroom teachers actual feedback that they could use to improve. (This is nearly a universal problem, as we'll see.)

Grace wanted me to work with her administrators and teacher leaders to develop a common definition of *excellent teaching* that might eventually be used to improve the formal evaluation system. I agreed on the condition that she accompany me for a learning walk at Lincoln. I wanted us both to have some "baseline" data about the quality of teaching on an average day. Grace had never observed any classes unannounced—a common problem in education—and she was curious about what we'd see. We discussed our observation criteria before starting our walk and agreed that we'd look for evidence that students were exhibiting skills such as reasoning and critical thinking in their oral and written work. We also agreed that a working definition of *excellent teaching* would include challenging all students to think every day in every class. Here's what we saw:

Advanced Placement English.   It is the beginning of class, and the teacher explains that the students are going to review their notes on the literature they will use to answer questions on the Advanced Placement exam, which will be given next week. There are seven students in the room, and all of them are deeply slouched in their chairs, which are arranged in a semicircle around the teacher's desk.

The teacher is seated at her desk, as she asks: "Now what is Woolf saying about the balance between an independent versus a social life?"

Students ruffle through their notebooks. Finally, a young woman, reading from her notes, answers, "Mrs. Ramsey sought meaning from social interactions."

"Yes, that's right. Now what about the artist, Lily? How did she construct meaning?"

"Through her painting," another student mumbles, her face scrunched close to her notes.

"And so what is Woolf saying about the choices these two women have made, and what each has sacrificed?"

No reply. The teacher sighs, gets up, goes to the board, and begins writing.

Social Issues Honors Seminar.   Students are watching a segment from *60 Minutes*. There are no questions on the board, and none of the students has any paper in front of them. In response to my whispered question, a student tells me they watch a selection from *60 Minutes* once a week.

"Why?" I ask. "Is there an assignment?"

"No" is the reply. "It's just to be better informed, I guess."

The video clip ends, and the teacher chooses a student to do his presentation in front of the class. He presents a three-minute, seven-slide PowerPoint on Karl Rove, which includes a political cartoon, Rove's biography, and a description of his duties in the Bush administration. It is completely unrelated to the *60 Minutes* segment they'd just watched. As soon as the presentation is finished, and without any questions or discussion of the PowerPoint, another student is called up to present.

9th Grade Honors English.   A student is standing in front of the class giving a two-minute presentation on subject-verb agreement. Another student's presentation on comma use in dependent and independent clauses follows. The apparent goal of the assignment is to have students teach one another the rules of grammar.

Advanced Placement U.S. Government.   The teacher is finishing up reviewing answers to a sample test that the class took the previous day, which contains eighty multiple-choice questions related to the functions and branches of the federal government.

When he's done, he says, "Okay, now let's look at some sample free-response questions from previous years' AP exams." He flips the overhead projector on, turns out the lights, and reads from the text of a transparency: "Give 3 reasons why the Iron Triangle may be criticized as undemocratic."

"How would you answer this question?" the teacher asks. No one replies. "Okay, who can give me a definition of the Iron Triangle?"

"The military-industrial-congressional complex," a student pipes up.

"Okay, so what would be three reasons why it would be considered undemocratic?" The teacher calls on a student in the front row who has his hand half-raised, and he answers the question in a voice that we can't hear over the hum of the projector's fan.

"Good. Now let's look at another one." The teacher flips another transparency onto the projector. "Now this question is about bureaucracy. Let me tell you how to answer this one. . . . "

Honors Geometry.   The teacher is reviewing material for an upcoming test.

"Now, what are the similarities between triangles and polygons?" the teacher asks. No one answers. "Come one, we've studied this," she pleads. "Okay, then, so what does 'proportionality' mean?" No hands. The teacher waits and then finally asks, "Do you remember when we talked about proportionality when measuring the human body—like the ratio of waist to hip measurement or height to weight?"

Several students nod. "Okay, then," the teachers smiles. "That's proportionality. Now on the test, I'll probably give you problems where you have to use polygon congruence to solve them and also use triangle congruence to prove that parts of triangles are congruent."

Advanced Placement Chemistry.   We learn that half of the class is out of school on a field trip. The remaining students are milling about and talking or sitting at their desks. Some are doing homework. The teacher is at his desk attending to paperwork.

Advanced Placement Environmental Studies.   Students wander in slowly and take their seats. They continue to talk, while waiting for the class to start. After more than five minutes by the clock on the wall, the teacher gets up from his desk and speaks.

"Okay, we're starting a unit on alternative energy today. So I have a question for you: How is charcoal made?"

No students raise their hands.

"Mesquite should tell you," the teacher continues. "How is mesquite made? Basically it's carbon—a clean version of coal that you find underground. Now, what do we mean by 'sustainable'?" Without waiting for a reply, the teacher continues, "Wind and solar are sustainable, right? How about some other examples?"

"Muscle power," a student answers.

———

Grace and I continue through the school and observe five more classes—none substantively different from those I've just described. All of them were designated as honors or Advanced Placement courses. Eventually, we call it quits and head to her office to debrief. During the short car ride back to her office downtown, Grace is silent.

Once we're seated in her office, she finally speaks. "I just can't believe it," she says, shaking her head. "When I do scheduled visits for the purposes of evaluation, it's nothing like what we saw today."

"Based on the criteria we discussed before our learning walk, in how many of the twelve classes we observed did you think there was evidence of student thinking?" I ask.

Grace replies in a subdued voice: "I'd say we went zero for twelve."

In fact, in the majority of the classes that we observed, teachers had a common purpose—a "core curriculum," if you will—just as they did at Jefferson. It's often referred to as "test-prep," and a growing number of people believe—and studies suggest—that teaching for the sake of succeeding on the state and national standardized tests is quickly becoming an epidemic in our nation's schools—one that is profoundly infecting our students and their ability to become critical thinkers. Before we discuss this problem further, I want to take you on one more learning walk.

You're in the Army Now

The Department of Defense runs its own school system, which, in 2002, served more than 100,000 students in over 200 schools located on or near military bases all over the world. A major study of these

Department of Defense Education Activity (DoDEA) schools, released in 2001, revealed that the system consistently outperformed most public school districts in America. At the time the study was done, DoDEA schools enrolled a minority population that averaged 40 percent of the total, nearly half their students qualified for free or reduced-price meals, and their annual mobility rate was 35 percent due to transfers— and yet these schools graduate 97 percent of their students, and the majority go on to college.[2]

The National Education Goals Panel sponsored the DoDEA study. Its press release on these intriguing results quoted the Indiana governor at the time, Frank O'Bannon, who was chairman of the Panel: "The Department of Defense education formula may be one of the best-kept secrets in education, until now. We recognize that the DOD school system is unique in some ways, but there are important lessons for all schools. Educators across the nation should take a close look at these recommendations for improving the academic achievement of all students and closing the achievement gap."[3]

The eight recommendations that followed were a general list of good education practices such as "high expectations for all," "small schools," "staff development," "sufficient financial resources," "organizational coherence," "parental involvement," and so on that go a long way toward explaining how these schools get better results when compared to many urban school districts. In addition, I observed that the DoDEA schools are better funded, their staff members are better trained, their schools are smaller so that students get more individual attention, there is far less leadership turnover, and, most important, they have the same high expectations for all students.

I was immediately curious when I learned about the DoDEA schools. It appeared that they were doing a dramatically better job of closing the achievement gap between low-income students and middle-class students—a significant accomplishment. It was exciting news. But what would I actually find in the classrooms, I wondered? Would the teaching and learning look any different from what I'd seen in conventional public schools?

Five years later, I had a chance to find out.[4] Although the educators in Department of Defense schools are all civilians, their leaders are quite influenced by military culture, and to a greater extent than in most school districts, they are very committed to the idea of continuous improvement. Since the study was released, this school system that serves military parents had implemented a five-year plan in which they trained all of their principals to focus on what they called "standards-based" instruction and to make "data-driven" decisions. (I'll explain these terms in a moment.) Several of their leaders had attended a summer institute at Harvard where I had taught, and they subsequently approached me there to ask if I'd help them think about how to evaluate this initiative.

Eventually, I was on a flight to another country, where I would live on a military base for a week, visit schools, and train educational leaders to use an assessment tool I developed to measure the effectiveness of their principals. This evaluation consisted of a number of components, but the most important was observing lessons and interviewing principals on *their* assessment of teaching and learning in their schools. What follows is a sampling of the lessons we observed in several middle schools and high schools over the course of the week:

7th Grade Language Arts.   Students are at their desks, filling out worksheets. Looking over a student's shoulder, I find that the sheets highlight different sentences and that the task here is to put commas in the right places within the sentences.

7th Grade Science.   The teacher is teaching a lesson on gravity. "Okay, let's review your textbook reading from last night. Who was Isaac Newton?"

A girl in the front row waves her hand frantically, and the teacher calls on her. "He discovered gravity," she says proudly.

"Okay," the teacher replies. "When was he born?"

No hands.

"Look it up in your text," the teacher advises.

While the students are opening their books, the girl in the front row who'd answered the first question speaks, "What's a galaxy and what's a universe and are we going to learn about the stars?"

"Have you found the date yet?" The teacher asks the class, ignoring the student's question.

9th Grade U.S. Honors History.   Students are working in groups of three. Judging from the animated conversations taking place, they appear to be very engaged in their group activity. According to the directions on the board, each group is supposed to use song, dance, and pantomime to illustrate a portion of a chapter of the history text that they've been assigned.

I talk to a group of three girls who, they tell me, are doing a skit from a part of the textbook that describes the life of the Plains Indians. They are planning a pantomime about the tribe's use of buffalo and the farming of squash. "What are you learning from this activity?" I ask.

"We're learning to get out of our comfort zone," one girl replies.

"What about history?"

"We're learning some vocabulary," the same girl answers.

"What vocabulary—can you show me some of the new words you're learning?"

The girl who's been answering the questions hesitates a moment, until admitting, "Well, they're not new exactly. It's more of a review. We studied Indians in 5th grade."

11th Grade World History.   Students are filling out a worksheet that requires them to answer questions on colonization—which countries colonized what areas when. They are using the maps in their textbooks as reference.

Advanced Placement Art.   Students are working at tables or easels all around the spacious studio, focusing on a wide variety of drawing and painting projects. I randomly pick a student to ask about her project. She tells me that she's working on a charcoal portrait of a young woman, which will go into the portfolio that's a part of the AP requirement for the course.

"How do you assess your work—how do you know how good it is?" I wonder.

Her face takes on a puzzled expression. Finally, she answers, "Well, I can see that the work I'm doing now is much better than what I did last year."

"So can you explain to me how this drawing is better than one you might have done a year ago?"

She smiles slightly and shrugs. "I don't know. . . . "

———

In the week we spent observing classes, the pattern rarely varied. With the exception of one math class, which I will describe in a moment, the purpose of nearly every lesson was for students to memorize factual content. The reason for this became clear as I explored with the team what training the principals had received and what was meant by the terms *standards-based* and *data-driven,* which were the key concepts in the five-year plan and subsequent professional development that all principals had received. It turned out that for a school system that serves children of military dependents and, indeed, for nearly every state education agency in the United States, *standards-based education* has come to be defined as the ability to ensure that every teacher's lesson focuses on a particular academic content standard—out of a list that has been developed by academics and curriculum specialists and then incorporated into textbooks and promulgated through ongoing professional development sessions for teachers. Indeed, all over the country, education "experts" have determined that the way to improve the academic "rigor" of high school classes is to teach more academic content.

These academic content standards are all organized by grade level and subject. So, for example, every 7th grade Language Arts teacher is expected to teach kids the proper use of commas so that they'll pass the standardized tests on grammar and punctuation. (Why do you suppose they also teach them again in 9th grade, as we saw at Lincoln? Why do even 12th grade English teachers complain that students can't punctuate their sentences correctly?) Similarly, all of the 7th grade science teachers are required to teach specific "units of study" like the one we saw on gravity. It is only in an occasional honors or arts class where someone may see deviations from the standard lesson. Likewise, what *data-driven* really means is simply that principals are trained to use the results from standardized tests to determine the extent to which teachers are, in fact, teaching the required content. The more the teachers cover the required content, the better the test scores will be for a school—and the effectiveness of principals is assessed by the progress they make in steadily improving the test scores of their school.

There is no agreement—in schools that serve children of military parents or in any other school district I know of—that all teachers should be teaching every student how to think. Teachers are expected only to cover the specified academic content. The proliferation of content standards actually makes it much more difficult for teachers to focus on inquiry and analysis and even writing. In addition, teachers have not been trained to teach all students how to reason, hypothesize, analyze, and so on. Most have never even seen lessons illustrating how this would be accomplished.

The exceptions to the rule—the teachers who use academic content as a means of teaching students how to communicate, reason, and solve problems—are rare, fewer than one in twenty in my experience. Their lessons stand out in stark contrast to what you see in most classrooms. I was lucky enough to witness one such lesson while visiting a school on the base that week, which I'll briefly describe here:

Algebra II.   It is the beginning of the period, and the teacher is finishing up writing a problem on the board. He turns to the students, who are sitting in desk-chairs that are arranged in squares of four that face one another. "You haven't seen this kind of problem before," he explains. "And solving it will require you to use concepts from both geometry and algebra. Each group will try to develop at least two different ways of solving this problem. After all the groups have finished, I'll randomly choose someone from each group who will write one of your proofs on one of the boards around the room, and I'll ask that person to explain the process your group used. Are there any questions?"

There are none, and the groups quickly go to work. There is a great deal of animated discussion within all of the groups as they take the problem apart and talk about different ways to solve it. While they work, the teacher circulates from group to group. Occasionally, a student will ask a question, but the teacher never answers it. Instead, he either asks another question in response, such as "Have you considered . . . ?" or "Why did you assume that?" or simply "Have you asked someone in your group?"

What are some of the design elements that make this an effective lesson—a lesson in which students are, in fact, learning a number of the Seven Survival Skills, while also mastering academic content? First, students are given a complex, multi-step problem that is different from the ones they've seen in the past and, to solve it, they have to apply previously acquired knowledge from both geometry and algebra. Mere memorization won't get them very far in this lesson; critical-thinking and problem-solving skills are required. Second, they have to find two ways to solve the problem, which requires some initiative and imagination. Just getting the correct answer isn't good enough; they have to explain their proofs—using effective communication skills. Third, the teacher does not spoon-feed students the answers; he uses questions to push students' thinking—as well as the limits to their tolerance for ambiguity. Finally, because the teacher has said that he'll randomly call on a student to show how the group solved the problem, each student in every group is held accountable. The group can't rely on the work of one or two students to get by, and the teacher isn't going to just call on the first student to raise a hand or shout out an answer. Teamwork is required for success.

These students weren't the only ones learning that day. For the team of educational leaders who accompanied me on the learning walks and then interviewed the schools' principals, it was a remarkable week. They discovered that their principals could usually name their weakest teachers, but they had little to say about what they had done or might do to help their teachers become more effective. They could also usually name several of their stronger teachers, but none of them had any ideas about how those teachers could improve. The principals, the team concluded, did not have a clear idea of what elements constituted effective instruction, and they did not know what they might do to improve instruction, beyond continuing to emphasize teaching to the standards. They didn't know because their training in these areas was, to use their leaders' own words, "a mile wide and an inch deep." Indeed, none of our nation's principals in any of our school districts have received adequate training in these areas. Nor have our teachers. This is a problem we'll explore in Chapter 4.

The most important goal identified by the educational leaders at schools that serve children of military parents, then, was the need to train their principals to be instructional leaders—individuals who know what good teaching looks like and can help all teachers improve continuously. Being *standards-based* and *data-driven* wasn't good enough. They also came away with serious questions about the kinds of tests used to assess learning. These computer-scored, multiple-choice tests measure what students have memorized, but not whether they can apply what they have learned to new situations and problems. The tests are simply not designed to assess reasoning and analytic skills. To the great credit of these leaders, their report back to headquarters was an unflinching analysis of such weaknesses, as well as a call for a new and very different five-year plan.

The Hidden "Gap" Exposed

Here's a short list to summarize the Seven Survival Skills before we move on:

- Critical Thinking and Problem Solving

- Collaboration Across Networks and Leading by Influence

- Agility and Adaptability

- Initiative and Entrepreneurialism

- Effective Oral and Written Communication

- Accessing and Analyzing Information

- Curiosity and Imagination

I focus my observations on high schools for this chapter because students are most developmentally ready to learn what we call critical-thinking skills in high school, and it is a time when they must prepare for the demands of careers and college. By this time, they have matured enough to reflect on their own thinking processes and to begin to understand what skills they will need to succeed as adults. However, elementary schools can and should be teaching thinking skills, as well as how to collaborate and be curious and take initiative. So, how are our nation's middle-class elementary schools doing on teaching the Seven Survival Skills?

Rather than take you on learning walks through elementary schools where I've spent time, let me summarize some key findings from scholars at the University of Virginia whose study of elementary classrooms was recently published in *Science*.[5] Funded by the National Institutes of Health, this is one of the largest studies of its kind. Researchers observed more than 2,500 1st, 3rd, and 5th grade classes in more than 1,000 schools, spread across 400 predominantly middle-class public school districts. Here are some of the things they learned:

- Fifth graders spent more than 90 percent of their time in their seats listening to the teacher or working alone and only about 7 percent of their time working in groups. Findings were similar in 1st and 3rd grades.

- In 5th grade, more than 60 percent of students' time was spent on improving basic literacy or math skills, while less than 25 percent of their time was devoted to science and social studies.

- The average 5th grader received five times as much instruction in basic skills as instruction focused on problem solving or reasoning; this ratio was 10:1 in 1st and 3rd grades.

The researchers summarized the kind of instruction they saw across all three grades:

> Typically, over the course of a 20-minute period, instruction involved only one method or mode (e.g., vocabulary worksheet or watching the teacher do math problems), and teachers gave generic feedback on correctness rather than encouraging extension of student performance or discussing alternative solutions. . . . Opportunities to learn for this sample of mostly middle-class students proved highly variable and did not appear congruent with the high performance standards expected for students or for teachers as described by most state teacher certification and licensure documents. Rather, experiences in 5th grade, although highly variable, were geared toward performance of basic reading and math skills, not problem-solving or reasoning skills or other content areas. Few opportunities were provided to learn in small groups, to improve analytical skills, or to interact extensively with teachers.[6]

The elementary teachers observed in this study were almost exclusively focused on teaching the reading and math basics. Why? As a result of the No Child Left Behind law, their students are being tested every year after 2nd grade on these skills—and these alone. No school wants to be publicly shamed with the brand of "needs improvement," which is what happens if its students do not make "adequate yearly progress" two years in a row. Indeed, because of NCLB, the curriculum in both elementary and secondary schools all across the country is being limited only to what's being tested, according to a study conducted by the nonpartisan Center on Education Policy.[7] Among this group's findings:

Increased time for tested subjects since 2002. About 62 percent of districts reported that they have increased time for
English language arts (ELA) and/or math in elementary
schools since school year 2001–02 (the year NCLB was
enacted), and more than 20 percent reported increasing
time for these subjects in middle school since then.
Among districts that reported increasing time for ELA
and math, the average increase in minutes per week since
2001–02 was substantial, amounting to a 46 percent
increase in ELA, a 37 percent increase in math, and a
42 percent increase across the two subjects combined.

Reduced time for other subjects. To accommodate this increased time in ELA and math, 44 percent of districts
reported cutting time from one or more other subjects or
activities (social studies, science, art and music, physical
education, lunch and/or recess) at the elementary level.
Again, the decreases reported by these districts were relatively large, adding up to a total of 141 minutes per week
across all of these subjects, on average, or nearly 30 minutes per day. These decreases represent an average reduc-
tion of 31 percent in the total instructional time devoted
to these subjects since 2001–02.

Greater emphasis on tested content and skills. Since 2001–02,
most districts have changed their ELA and math curricula
to put greater emphasis on the content and skills covered
on the state tests used for NCLB. In elementary-level
reading, 84 percent of districts reported that they have
changed their curriculum "somewhat" or "to a great ex-

tent" to put greater emphasis on tested content; in middle school ELA, 79 percent reported making this change, and in high school ELA, 76 percent. Similarly, in math, 81 percent of districts reported that they have changed their curriculum at the elementary and middle school level to emphasize tested content and skills, and 78 percent reported having done so at the high school level.

The Center on Education Policy study illustrates just what we saw in our learning walks. Increasingly, there is only one curriculum in American public schools today: test-prep. But perhaps this is a justifiable change if more of our students are at least becoming better readers and mathematicians as a result. But here, too, the evidence is troubling. There is a new phenomenon in public education: kids known as "bubble children." Jennifer Booher-Jennings at Columbia University was one of the first researchers to describe a test-score improvement strategy that focuses on borderline students—students who might pass the tests with some additional instruction.[8] She describes a consultant to a school district giving the following advice:

Using the data, you can identify and focus on the kids who are close to passing. The bubble kids. And focus on the kids that count—the ones that show up [transfer in] at Marshall [the fictional name of the school] after October won't count toward the school's test scores this year. . . . Take out your classes' latest benchmark scores and divide your students into three groups. Color the "safe cases," or kids who will definitely pass, green. Now, here's the most important part: identify the kids who are "suitable cases for treatment." Those are the ones who can pass with a little extra help. Color them yellow. Then, color the kids who have no chance of passing this year and the kids that don't count—the "hopeless cases"—red. You should focus your attention on the yellow kids, the bubble kids. They'll give you the biggest return on your investment.

Booher-Jennings's findings were recently confirmed by University of Chicago researchers who found that, among Chicago's 5th graders, students in the middle of the academic range have made the most academic progress in reading and math, as measured by the standardized tests. However, those who were among the lowest-scoring students had made no progress or had even fallen further behind. And the results for the most gifted students were very uneven, with some making no gain whatsoever.[9]

To summarize: There is no strong evidence that any of the Seven Survival Skills are being taught at any grade level in American public schools. Instead, class time is narrowly focused on teaching only the skills and content that will be tested. (We'll explore the quality of these tests in the next chapter.) Even worse, there is mounting evidence that, as a nation, we are not making any progress toward solving the very problem the No Child Left Behind law was designed to address—the achievement gap between predominantly white middle-class students and economically disadvantaged minority students.[10] Indeed, the most significant impact of NCLB may be its contribution to the growing gap between what's being taught and tested in even our better schools versus what today's students will need to succeed and be productive citizens in the twenty-first century—the global achievement gap.

What About the Competition?

The Organisation for Economic Co-operation and Development (OECD) was founded in 1961 in order to promote economic growth and world trade. It sponsors the Programme for International Student

Assessment (PISA), which was launched in 2000. PISA develops and administers standardized assessments of reading, mathematical, and scientific literacy to a sample of between 4,500 and 10,000 15-year-olds in participating countries. However, the OECD leaders were concerned about the extent to which these subject-content skills translate into the kinds of skills adults need in life. So in 2003, they administered a remarkable test of problem-solving skills, in addition to other assessments, in all forty-one of the countries then involved in the program. The goal was to measure what they call "cross-curricular competencies"—that is, to directly assess life competencies that apply across different areas of the school curriculum. The assessment measured students' problem-solving abilities in three areas:[11]

- Making decisions under constraints

- Evaluating and designing systems for a particular situation

- Trouble-shooting a malfunctioning device or system based on a set of symptoms

When I heard about the assessment, I was fascinated. At first blush, it sounded like a test of the First Survival Skill: critical thinking and problem solving. When I looked at the test items, I was impressed. Together, they comprised a challenging assessment of a variety of problem-solving skills that adults have to use on a regular basis, such as planning the best route for a trip while taking numerous factors into consideration; designing an automated check-out system for a library; and trouble-shooting a malfunctioning irrigation system. So what did the OECD learn in this first-of-its-kind international comparison? Here is a summary of the overall findings from the test:[12]

About one in five 15-year-olds in OECD countries can be considered a
reflective, communicative problem solver. These students are able not
only to analyse a situation and make decisions, they are also capable of
managing multiple conditions simultaneously. They can think about
the underlying relationships in a problem, solve it systematically, check
their work and communicate the results. In some countries, more than
a third of students reach this high level of problem-solving competencies. In other countries, however, the majority of students cannot even
be classified as *basic problem solvers,* a level at which they are required
to deal with only a single data source containing discrete, well-defined
information.

How did the "home team" do? you may ask. Badly. Very badly, indeed. Our overall score put us behind twenty-eight other countries—
just after the Russian Federation and barely ahead of Portugal.
According to a summary of the results prepared for the U.S. Department of Education by the National Center for Education Statistics,
nearly one-quarter of U.S. students scored below level 1—a level far
lower than that achieved by students in the OECD countries. A lower
percentage of U.S. students than OECD students scored at levels 2 and
3. And in four countries (Finland, Hong Kong–China, Japan, and Korea), 30 percent or more of students performed at level 3 in problem
solving, compared to only 12 percent of U.S. students.[13] This analysis
reveals that even the kids we consider to be our most academically talented are not even close to the competition: "On average, U.S. high
achievers for problem solving (those scoring in the top 10 percent in
the United States) were outperformed by their OECD counterparts. To
be in the top 10 percent of students in the United States, students
needed at least a score of 604 . . . but 675 or better in Japan."[14]

Let me explain one implication of these findings as we think about
our children's future. Put simply: If I'm an employer of a multinational

corporation, and I need to hire lots of employees who can solve problems, all other things being equal I'm likely to locate my new facility in a number of other countries before I'd consider coming to the United States. We are simply not developing our intellectual capital to the extent that many other countries are.

Perhaps our real competitive advantage as a country in the future will be in those areas requiring innovation—which in turn relies on curiosity and imagination, the Seventh Survival Skill described in Chapter 1. Indeed, America has historically excelled in those areas where innovation has been important, though no one is quite sure why. Is it the openness of our political system that encourages the free exchange of ideas, or the nature of our free-enterprise economy that is a stimulus for entrepreneurship? If these are sources of our competitive advantage, how much longer will they continue to be so as more and more countries move toward greater free expression and less government regulation of their economies?

Our nation's public schools are not contributing significantly to this country's capacity for creativity, imagination, and innovation—any more than they are developing the problem-solving skills of our students. You saw the evidence with your own eyes in our learning walks earlier in this chapter. Meanwhile, countries such as India, China, and Singapore are trying to transform their education systems so as to produce more creative students.

Thomas Friedman quotes Azim Premji, the chairman of Wipro, one of India's premier technology companies in one of his columns: "We need to encourage more incubation of ideas to make innovation a national initiative." Friedman goes on to cite Nirmala Sankaran, the CEO of HeyMath, an India-based education company: "If we do not allow our students to ask why, but just keep on telling them how, then we are only going to get the transactional type of outsourcing, not the high-end things that require complex interactions and judgment to understand another person's needs. . . . [W]e have a creative problem in this country."[15]

Yong Zhao, the director of the U.S.-China Center for Research on Educational Excellence at Michigan State University, wrote the following in an *Education Week* commentary:

> Despite China's stunning improvements in everything from gross domestic product to student performance in international comparative studies and talent contests, the country has not been happy with its education system and has launched a series of reforms over the past two decades. The most significant government statement came on June 13, 1999, when the Central Committee of the Chinese Communist Party and the State Council, China's highest decision-making bodies, jointly issued "The Decision to Deepen Education Reform and Comprehensively Implement Essential-Quality-Oriented Education."
>
> This landmark document reflects the deep concern of China's leaders over the negative consequences of traditional test-oriented education. Its policy goals are straightforward: to emphasize sowing students' creativity and practical abilities over instilling an ability to achieve certain test scores and recite rote knowledge.[16]

The motto of Singapore's education reform movement is "Thinking Schools, Learning Nation." According to its Ministry of Education's website:

> Thinking Schools will be learning organizations in every sense, constantly challenging assumptions, and seeking better ways of doing things through participation, creativity and innovation. Thinking Schools will be the cradle of thinking students as well as thinking adults and this spirit of learning should accompany our students even after they leave school.

A Learning Nation envisions a national culture and social environment that promotes lifelong learning in our people. The capacity of Singaporeans to continually learn, both for professional development and for personal enrichment, will determine our collective tolerance for change.[17]

And as Tharman Shanmugaratnam, Singapore's minister of education, explained in a speech: "One of the key adjustments under way is in the way we educate our young so as to develop in them a willingness to keep learning, and an ability to experiment, innovate, and take risks . . . . Our ability to create and innovate will be Singapore's most important asset in [the] future."[18]

It would seem that education reform in India, China, and Singapore is moving in a direction that is exactly the opposite of ours. As we work to close the achievement gap between white middle-class students and economically disadvantaged minority students by requiring more and more multiple-choice tests and measuring the success of our schools and our students on the basis of test scores alone, the risks of not attending to the *global* achievement gap increase every day.

CHAPTER 3

Testing,
1 2 3

WELCOME BACK TO high school. Take out your Number 2 pencil. I'd like you to answer some questions from actual state tests that all 10th graders were required to take recently. I gathered this sample of questions from the 2006 Texas Assessment of Knowledge and Skills (TAKS)—given in the state that claims to have invented educational accountability in the 1990s under then-Governor George W. Bush. It was the governor's experience raising test scores in Texas that, according to many sources, inspired the proposal and subsequent passage of No Child Left Behind in 2002. So are you ready?

Texas 10th Grade English Test Sample Question[1]

Lydia has written this report for her U.S. history class. As part of a peer conference, you have been asked to read the report and think about what suggestions you would make. When you finish reading the report, answer the questions that follow.

The American Red Cross

(1) The American Red Cross is an organization that aids people all around the world. (2) It started as a result of the efforts of a dedicated woman. (3) That woman was named Clara Barton. (4) It was during the Civil War that Barton began the work that lead to the establishment of the American Red Cross. (5) She assisted on the battlefield by nursing injured soldiers and helping transport supplies. (6) Eventually the Government of the United States selected her to serve as superintendent of nurses for the army.

1. What is the most effective way to combine sentences 2 and 3? (Circle your answer.)
    A. It started as a result of the efforts of a dedicated woman, that woman was named Clara Barton.
    B. It started as a result of the efforts of a woman who was dedicated and named Clara Barton.
    C. It started as a result of the efforts of a dedicated woman named Clara Barton.
    D. It started as a result of the efforts of a dedicated woman she was named Clara Barton.

2. What change, if any, should be made in sentence 4?

  A. Change **was** to **is**

  B. Insert a comma after Civil War

  C. Change **lead** to **led**

  D. Make no change

Texas 10th Grade Math Test Sample Questions[2]

1. Which lists the functions of the form $y = ax^2$ in order from the widest to the narrowest graph? (Circle your answer.)

  A. $y = \frac{7}{3}x^2$, $y = \frac{2}{3}x^2$, $y = \frac{1}{2}x^2$, $y = 2x^2$

  B. $y = \frac{1}{2}x^2$, $y = \frac{2}{3}x^2$, $y = 2x^2$, $y = \frac{7}{3}x^2$

  C. $y = \frac{7}{3}x^2$, $y = 2x^2$, $y = \frac{1}{2}x^2$, $y = \frac{2}{3}x^2$

  D. $y = 2x^2$, $y = \frac{7}{3}x^2$, $y = \frac{1}{2}x^2$, $y = \frac{2}{3}x^2$

2. Lee, Kelly, Linda, and Madison all took the same math test. Linda earned a lower score than Kelly, but she did not earn the lowest score. The highest test-scorer's name does not begin with an L. Madison earned a higher score than Kelly. Which person earned the lowest score on the math test? (Circle your answer.)

  A. Kelly

  B. Lee

  C. Linda

  D. Madison

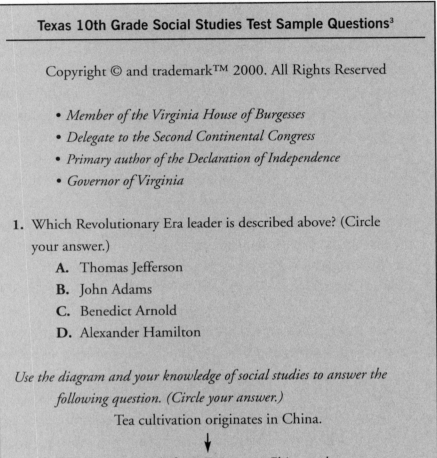

Texas 10th Grade Social Studies Test Sample Questions[3]

Copyright © and trademark™ 2000. All Rights Reserved

- *Member of the Virginia House of Burgesses*
- *Delegate to the Second Continental Congress*
- *Primary author of the Declaration of Independence*
- *Governor of Virginia*

1. Which Revolutionary Era leader is described above? (Circle your answer.)
   A. Thomas Jefferson
   B. John Adams
   C. Benedict Arnold
   D. Alexander Hamilton

Use the diagram and your knowledge of social studies to answer the following question. (Circle your answer.)

Tea cultivation originates in China.

↓

Marco Polo travels from Europe to China and returns.

↓

Tea becomes the favorite drink in Great Britain.

2. These three statements best reflect the results of
   A. cultural diffusion
   B. technological innovation
   C. the socialist system
   D. the feudal system

I bet you aced the English and social studies items, right? Indeed, you were probably thinking that most 7th graders would know the right answers to those questions, and you might have been a bit shocked at the simple-mindedness of the questions being asked. But if (like most of us) you remember and use very little algebra, you probably flunked the math question, which means that you are unlikely to get a high school diploma in the state of Texas. This test is very similar to the test all Texas students must take and pass in 11th grade in order to graduate from high school; in effect, it's a practice test. You get to take it a few times—but if you haven't received a passing grade by the end of 12th grade, you don't graduate, even though you may have completed all the required courses for a diploma.

The state's accountability system is currently considered "middle of the road" in its level of academic difficulty relative to other states, according to research from the Thomas B. Fordham Foundation, a conservative education research and advocacy group. The Foundation's 2006 report of education reform practices in all fifty states praises the state's charter school laws but gives Texas a *C–* in "Quality of State Standards" and a *D+* in "Rigor of State's Definition of Proficiency in Reading & Math."[4] But what does a state's test look like that rates an *A* on both of these measures, as assessed by the same Fordham report? Sharpen up those Number 2 pencils: You're going to answer some sample questions from the 10th grade Massachusetts Comprehensive Assessment System (MCAS). Passing this test sometime before the end of your 12th grade year is also required in order to receive a high school diploma.

Massachusetts 10th Grade English Test Sample Questions[5]

How much of what we learn adequately explains the world around us? Read the poem "When I Heard the Learn'd Astronomer" to learn what the poet has to say about this question. Answer the questions that follow. (Circle your answer on this sheet.)

When I Heard the Learn'd Astronomer

When I heard the learn'd astronomer,   **1**

When the proofs, the figures,
were ranged in columns before me,   **2**

When I was shown the charts and diagrams,
to add, divide, and measure them,   **3**

When I, sitting, heard the astronomer where
he lectured with much applause in the lecture room,   **4**

How soon unaccountable I became tired and sick,   **5**

Till rising and gliding out I wander'd off by myself,   **6**

In the mystical* moist night air, and from time to time,   **7**

Look'd up in perfect silence at the stars.   **8**

—*Walt Whitman*[6]

*Mystical—mysterious   *continued on next page*

1. Which of the following statements represents the **main** theme of the poem?
     A. Science cannot fully express the wonder of the world.
     B. Nature is one's best source of recreation.
     C. Technology causes more problems than it solves.
     D. Learning causes one to become ill and fatigued.

2. In line 5, what is conveyed by the phrase "tired and sick"?
     A. the speaker's sorrow and loss experienced in his life
     B. a sense of approaching danger
     C. a sense of the speaker's poor health
     D. the speaker's boredom and disappointment with the lecture

3. What is the **main purpose** of the phrase "perfect silence" in the last line of the poem?
     A. to explain why he has to leave the lecture room
     B. to convey a sense of loneliness and sorrow
     C. to contrast with the sounds in the lecture room
     D. to highlight the pleasure of science and learning

4. What do the last three lines of the poem suggest?
     A. the importance of personal experience with nature
     B. the dangers of losing track of time
     C. the importance of learning about astronomy
     D. the dangers of wandering off alone

5. Which of the following is the **best** synonym for the word
learn'd as it is used in line 1?

    A. aware

    B. remembered

    C. knowledgeable

    D. invented

The next question is an open-response question.

    • *Read the question carefully.*

    • *Explain your answer.*

    • *Add supporting details.*

    • *Double-check your work.*

*Write your answer to question 19 in the space provided in your Student
Answer Booklet.* (Use the back flyleaf of the book, if you like.)

19. In the poem, a shift occurs at the end of line 4.

    A. Explain what happens before and after the shift.

    B. Explain what causes the shift.

*Use relevant and specific information from the poem to support your
answer.*

Massachusetts 10th Grade Math Test Sample Question[7]

*Write your answer to question 21 in the space provided in your Student
Answer Booklet.* (Or on the back flyleaf of this book, if you like.)

continued on next page

21. The distance, d, in feet, that a dropped rock falls in t seconds can be estimated using the formula below.

$$d = 16t^2$$

Use the formula to answer the following questions.

   A. What is the distance, in feet, that a dropped rock will fall in 10 seconds? Show your work.

   B. What is the ratio of the **distance** a dropped rock will fall in 30 seconds as compared to the **distance** a dropped rock will fall in 10 seconds? Show your work.

   C. How many seconds will it take a dropped rock to fall 144 feet? Show your work.

   D. To the nearest tenth of a second, how many seconds will it take a dropped rock to fall 80 feet? Show your work.

Massachusetts 10th Grade U.S. History Test Sample Questions[8]

This session contains fifteen multiple-choice questions and one open-response question. [I offer only the first three questions as samples.] *Mark your answers to these questions in the spaces provided in your Student Answer Booklet.* (Or circle your answers on the page.)

   1. Why was the Bill of Rights added to the United States Constitution?

   A. to ensure rights of foreigners

   B. to ensure slaves' right to vote

   C. to protect the federal government from the states

   D. to protect the individual rights of citizens from government abuse

continued on next page

2. When people purchase shares of stock in the stock market, they are investing in

    A. corporations.

    B. labor unions.

    C. governments.

    D. political parties.

3. The excerpt below is from Frederick Douglass's "Independence Day" speech in 1852.

The rich inheritance of justice, liberty, prosperity and independence, bequeathed by your fathers, is shared by you, not by me. The sunlight that brought life and healing to you has brought stripes and death to me. This Fourth of July is yours, not mine.

        —Frederick Douglass, "Independence Day" speech (1852)

In this speech, Frederick Douglass was speaking on behalf of which group?

    A. exiled American Indians

    B. deported American Jews

    C. oppressed Irish Americans

    D. enslaved African Americans

So what did you think of this test? Did you find it a little more challenging? To an extent, I would agree. But being the "recovering" high school English teacher that I am, I can't help but raise some issues about the first set of questions relating to the Whitman poem. Were you a little bothered by the arbitrariness of the first question about the

Whitman poem—the one about the theme of the poem? I suppose the right answer might be A—*"Science cannot fully express the wonder of the world."* But I wonder how many students answered D—*"Learning causes one to become ill and fatigued"*—because there's certainly evidence of that in the poem, and it's exactly how many students feel when they spend four years of their lives studying the materials that will enable them to pass these kinds of tests, as we'll discover.

What did you think of the definition of *mystical* offered on the test ("mysterious")? Here are some dictionary definitions of the word, ordered from most to least commonly used:[9]

1. **with divine meaning:** *having a divine meaning that is beyond human understanding*

2. **of mysticism:** *relating to, involving, or associated with mysticism or mystics*

3. **with supernatural significance:** *having supernatural or spiritual significance or power*

4. **mysterious:** *mysterious or difficult to understand*

Why do you suppose the test makers used the least common definition? Perhaps because it was the safest? Anyone who has read and studied Whitman knows that he had the more common religious definition of the word in mind when he wrote the poem. To suggest otherwise is to distort the meaning of the poem. Why didn't the test makers quote the most widely used definition of *mystical*—and the one closest in meaning to Whitman's beliefs—and then ask students to interpret the poem using this definition? The reason test makers don't ask questions like this involves both politics and money, as we'll see later in the chapter when we explore how these forces combine to shape the tests that students take.

How about the rest of the test? Once again, you probably managed to get the right answers on the English and history items, but I bet you struggled with the math questions. Given enough time, you might have figured them out—but in tests like these, there is a premium on answering as many questions as quickly as possible. Once again, I suspect that you may not be eligible for a high school diploma. In 2007, 13 percent of all 10th graders in Massachusetts did not pass the MCAS. (The eventual pass rate will likely go up as students may take the test again in 11th and 12th grades.) Results varied widely by community. In the city of Lawrence, for example, nearly half of all students failed the math portion of the exam, whereas in Wayland and in many other wealthy suburban communities, all students passed.[10]

However, the number of students who pass the MCAS does not reflect the actual high school graduation rate, as many high school students, when faced with the reality that they are unlikely to pass the test no matter how many times they take it, drop out. According to *Education Week*'s 2007 special report on high schools, the Massachusetts high school graduation rate is 73 percent.[11] Nor is passing this test an indication that students are ready for college. A recent *Boston Globe* article reported that about 80 percent of the state's high school graduates go on to college, but the first state "school-to-college" analysis found that 37 percent of those students lacked the skills and knowledge needed for college. Nearly 65 percent of the students who were enrolled in a community college had to take at least one remedial course.[12] We'll explore what it takes to be "college-ready" later in this chapter, but the question now is: If the MCAS test requirement is increasing the dropout rate and a passing score is not a reliable indicator that a student has mastered the skills needed for college (or for work), then what purpose does the test serve?

A Way to Think About NCLB
and High School State Tests

No Child Left Behind and the new state testing requirements that are at the heart of the law continue to be a hotly debated topic—both nationally and locally. As I've said, the fact that schools and districts are now being held accountable at all—and accountable for the success of all of their students—is a new and very important concept in public education. But a growing number of critics now argue that the initial benefits of the law are greatly outweighed by its many flaws, including the following: an unrealistic goal of 100 percent proficiency in reading and math for all students by 2014; a highly punitive approach toward students, teachers, and schools in terms of the consequences for poor performance on the tests; the lack of any assistance for schools that are not making "adequate yearly progress"; a weak definition of the requirement to have "highly qualified teachers" in all subjects; and, most significant, the highly varied standards that individual states use for determining whether students are "proficient" and schools are making "adequate yearly progress."[13]

I agree with these criticisms. But I believe it's also important to look at how state tests influence what happens in high school classrooms today. As we saw in the last chapter, almost every single class we visited focused on preparation for a test of some kind. Some say, and I agree, that teaching to the test isn't necessarily bad—as long as it's a good test! So, for the purposes of this chapter, I want to raise two questions that are less frequently explored in the debates about NCLB and the "high-stakes" state tests that all students are now required to take as a result of the 2002 law:

- To what extent do these state tests assess the skills that matter most for work, citizenship, and college?

- What is the impact of teaching to these tests on students' motivation to learn and to stay in school?

Is Math Really "Problem Solving"—and What About Science?

Many business leaders today—Bill Gates among them—claim that our high school graduates lack adequate preparation in science and math; others say that for the United States to remain globally competitive, we need to produce more engineers and scientists. As a result, beginning next year, the NCLB law adds science to the list of subjects that must be tested in elementary, middle, and high school. In addition, in August 2007, Congress passed new "competitiveness" legislation, which establishes federal grants to improve teacher recruitment and training in science and math. Yet employers across a wide range of businesses, including high-tech companies, appear to place comparatively little value on content knowledge in either math or science as a prerequisite for work today.

Clay Parker and others talked about the relative importance of technical knowledge versus critical thinking and people skills in the first chapter. In the major study of 400 employers' expectations for new employees who are high school grads, two-year college grads, and four-year college grads that I cited in that chapter, knowledge of mathematics did not even make the top-ten list of the skills employers deemed most important for any of these groups. Indeed, it ranked only 14th or 15th on the list of the most essential knowledge and skills needed for success—just ahead of science and foreign language comprehension. What the report referred to as "applied skills" dominated the top-ten list of the most important skills for all three groups of students, a list quite similar to the Seven Survival Skills: "professionalism and work ethic, oral and written communication, critical thinking and problem-solving, teamwork and leadership, reading comprehension, and ethics and social responsibility." All of these came ahead of knowledge of both science and math in the survey rankings.[14]

Here's a possible explanation for this finding: While all employers need workers who can solve problems, they do not find that students who have taken the *usual* math and science courses and passed the tests can apply this content to solving real problems. Yet we continue to teach the same tired content in the same old ways because it is supposed to be developing students' "problem-solving skills."

So-called advanced math is perhaps the clearest example of the mismatch between what is taught and tested in high schools versus what's needed for college and in life. It turns out that knowledge of algebra is required to pass state tests, as you saw, because it is a near-universal requirement for college admissions. But why is that? If you are not a math major, you usually do not have to take any advanced math in college, and most of what you need for other courses is knowledge of statistics, probability, and basic computational skills. This is even more evident after college. Graduates from the Massachusetts Institute of Technology were recently surveyed regarding the math that this very technically trained group used most frequently in their work. The assumption was that if any adults used higher-level math, it would be MIT grads. And while a few did, the overwhelming majority reported using nothing more than arithmetic, statistics, and probability.[15]

No one whom I've interviewed has been able to explain to me why advanced math is a college admissions requirement whereas probability and statistics are not. The implication seems to be that advanced math trains us to become better problem solvers. Back when I was in high school, I was told that Latin should be studied because it trained the mind, too! But what is the evidence to support either claim? Some educators point to studies showing that students who take advanced math in high school do better in college. But this conclusion actually ignores one of the essential laws of statistics: the importance of distinguishing between results that show cause and effect versus a mere association. There is absolutely no evidence that knowledge of calculus *causes* greater success in college; there is only an association. I'm willing to wager that if we required four years' study of the Greek language, we could show it had at least as high an association or correlation with success in college. Taking *any* academically challenging course in high school will show an association with success in college.

I am not suggesting that math and science aren't important subjects (or that all students should be required to study Greek). The question is not whether to teach math and science but, rather, what to teach and how. How many students graduate from high school today knowing how to solve algebra problems by rote, but do not understand math as a way of thinking about how to solve problems? Similarly, how many high school students take three years of science—including biology, chemistry, and physics—but do not know what the scientific method is and how to use it, as we saw in the AP chemistry class described at the beginning of the last chapter? We keep hearing that all students need more math and science courses, but I believe that all students need more *engaging and relevant* math and science courses. The question is: What should all high school graduates know in order to be *literate* in math and science as disciplines of problem solving?

The most recent Programme for International Student Assessment (PISA) tests of scientific and mathematical literacy, developed by the Organisation for Economic Co-operation and Development, show how woefully unprepared American adolescents are in these vital subjects when compared with the youth of fifty-five other countries. Of particular interest is the goal of these tests, which is "to determine the extent to which young people have acquired the wider knowledge and skills in *reading, mathematical* and *scientific literacy* that they will need in adult life," rather than mere recall of specific content knowledge.[16]

The PISA test makers define *scientific literacy* as "[a]n individual's scientific knowledge and use of that knowledge to identify questions, to acquire new knowledge, to explain scientific phenomena, and to draw evidence-based conclusions about science-related issues, understanding of the characteristic features of science as a form of human knowledge and enquiry, awareness of how science and technology shape our material, intellectual, and cultural environments, and willingness to engage in science-related issues, and with the ideas of science, as a reflective citizen." U.S. students ranked 25th on the science test out of the fifty-six countries participating, just ahead of Latvia and just behind the Slovak Republic.[17]

PISA defines *mathematical literacy* as "[a]n individual's capacity to identify and understand the role that mathematics plays in the world, to make well-founded judgments and to use and engage with mathematics in ways that meet the needs of that individual's life as a constructive, concerned and reflective citizen."[18] U.S. students performed even more poorly on this test, placing 35th out of the fifty-six nations participating, just behind the Russian Federation and ahead of Croatia.[19] (The reading test had to be scrapped in the United States, due to a printing error in the test booklets.)

On December 4, 2007, Andreas Schleicher, head of the Indicators and Analysis Division, OECD Directorate for Education—the organization that sponsors the PISA tests—gave a briefing on these results for educators, policymakers, and the media at the National Press Club in Washington, D.C. The program was titled "Losing Our Edge: Are American Students Unprepared for the Global Economy?"[20]

In the question-and-answer segment of this program, Stuart Gibson, a member of the Fairfax County Virginia School Board, asked Dr. Schleicher about the importance of moving away from the paper-and-pencil, multiple-choice tests that dominate American education and toward what the questioner called more "relevant, authentic assessments." He replied:

Across countries, there are very different styles of assessment. I would put the United States at one end of the extreme, largely driven by efficient multiple-choice tests, versus other countries like Italy, Spain, and Sweden which have open-ended interviews. You do see these differences reflected in the results. United States students tend to be rather good in multiple-choice tasks, when four choices are clearly laid out. They have a much harder time when they're given open-ended tasks.[21]

What Schleicher was saying, in other words, is that our students often cannot apply what they have learned to a new problem or context they haven't seen before. That's what an "open-ended" task requires. You're not given a list of answers to guess from but instead have to construct one, using previously acquired skills and knowledge.

We have to ask ourselves: What are the hidden costs and consequences to our country of having adopted an accountability system that relies extensively on inexpensive, "objective" multiple-choice tests versus more complex and expensive open-ended tests that demand real thinking and a deeper understanding of concepts, which many other countries use? To what extent is the type of tests we use one of the root causes of our poor performance on these international math and science assessments, as Schleicher seemed to suggest? We'll look at some better kinds of tests later in this chapter. And in Chapter 6, we'll spend time in a high school that is doing a remarkable job of preparing and motivating students to become mathematicians, scientists, and engineers with very different teaching and assessment strategies.

Writing by Formula

Regarding the two tests you just took: At least the written communication skills that employers say are essential for work were being assessed, right? Both the Texas and Massachusetts 10th grade state tests do require a composition from students—which is unusual, because many states are cutting this requirement out of their testing program due to the cost and time involved in scoring each individual paper. To assess the extent to which students are learning effective written communication skills, let's look at a sample student essay from the 2006 Massachusetts Comprehensive Assessment System exam—one that earned a score of 3 out of a possible 6. In other words, it represents an average essay in the state that is reputed to have the most rigorous assessment system.

2006 MCAS Grade 10 English Language Arts[22]

Writing Prompt: Composition

Works of literature often feature characters with the ability to inspire or lead others.

From a work of literature you have read in or out of school, select a character with the ability to inspire or lead others. In a well-developed composition, identify the character, describe how the character inspires or leads others, and explain why this character's ability is significant to the meaning of the work of literature.

2006 MCAS Grade 10 English Language Arts Composition
Topic/Idea Development—Score Point 3[23]

This composition shows rudimentary topic/idea development. Ideas are clustered in brief paragraphs, leaving little opportunity for development. Organization follows an obvious plan. Details used to support the central idea that "Harry Potter is an inspiring person" are basic and lack development.

In the fictional novel "Harry Potter and The Sorceror's Stone" by J.K. Rollings, Harry Potter is an inspiring person. Harry inspires us by his courage, hope, and determination.

Harry's courage is shown through the changes he had to make going from a normal boy's life into a wizarding life. One such change was his ability to catch the Golden Snitch. Also, Harry had inspired many of his fellow classmates To have the courage to try out for the quittage Team.

Harry Potter shows the inspiration of hope through his perseverence in the Sorceror's stone challenge. Hope is shown when Harry defeats the villain Lord Baltimore and the school feels safe again.

Finally, Harry inspires when he shows how determined he can be by overcoming the hardships in his life growing up. Harry's uncle was constantly abusing him verbally, Harry was determined not to let it bother him. Again the defeat of Lord Baltimore is also an example of Harry's determination. Harry was determined not to give up the stone.

Harry Potter's courage, hope and determination in J.K. Rollings' "Harry Potter and the Sorceror's stone are an inspiration to anyone in and out of the novel.

Not bad, right? The ideas are clear, and the punctuation and spelling are generally okay—though the misspellings of the antagonist's name (Lord Voldemort) as "Lord Baltimore" and the author's name (J. K. Rowling) as "J. K. Rollings" make me wonder whether this student actually read the book—or perhaps just saw the movie. But to paraphrase one of my questions from the learning walks: What is my level of confidence that a student who produces this quality of work in 10th grade is likely to be ready for college or the workplace in two years? This student chose to write about a book that is at about a 6th grade reading level—not a good sign. (According to Amazon's website, the Harry Potter books are meant for children ages 9–12.) J. K. Rowlings's books are immensely entertaining and have helped transform many elementary school students from nonreaders to readers, but they entail very little of the complex reading all high school students should be doing—or will have to do in college. How might this student fare with a book that is at a high school student's reading level?

And what about the writing? Sadly, what we see here is formula writing—sort of like painting by the numbers: introductory paragraph, three paragraphs of supporting evidence, and a concluding paragraph. To the extent that students are completing any writing assignments at all in high schools, they are being taught to follow a regimented five-paragraph formula in order to pass not only the state tests but also the new SAT exam, which in 2005 began requiring that all students complete a writing section.

The introduction of the new SAT writing test was what led one prestigious college—Sarah Lawrence in New York—to *drop* the requirement that applicants take the SAT as part of the admissions process. (Did you know there are now over 750 colleges and universities that do not rely on either the SAT or the ACT to make most of their admissions decisions?[24]) According to a *New York Times* article explaining Sarah Lawrence's decision: "In announcing that all standardized admission tests would be optional, beginning with the high school graduating class of 2005, Sarah Lawrence said the SAT writing test, while well-intentioned, would 'not be helpful' in assessing applicants for 'a writing-based curriculum such as ours.'. . . At Sarah Lawrence, Ms. Briggs [then dean of admissions] said, such an essay is 'not at all reflective of how our students are going to have to write' many lengthy papers based on long-term research, analysis and discussion. 'They are never given a topic they've never seen and asked to write spontaneously for 25 minutes,' she said."[25] Four years later, the *Boston Globe* reported that "[h]undreds of universities, including several top schools, ignore or pay little heed to students' scores on the writing section of the SAT in admissions decisions, skeptical about how well the essay reflects writing skills."[26]

Citizenship-Ready?

How about readiness for citizenship, based on the questions that students were asked in the U.S. history portions of these tests? While the primary purpose of studying U.S. history is not preparation for citizenship, it is nevertheless fair to ask to what extent the content that's being taught in these classes will help students understand the roots of some of the issues we face as a country, while also developing the analytic skills students need to come to their own conclusions about the important questions of our time.[27] Here, it is worth noting that the U.S. Citizenship and Immigration Service has recently revamped the civics test that all immigrants must take to become naturalized citizens. According to a recent *New York Times* article, "Immigration officials said they sought to move away from civics trivia to emphasize basic concepts about the structure of government and American history and geography." Applicants for citizenship no longer have to memorize who said "Give me liberty or give me death" or who wrote "The Star-Spangled Banner." But they *do* have to know what Susan B. Anthony did.[28]

Contrast the low level of the questions students were being asked in the history test samples above with what is now required to become a U.S. citizen, or with what some effective U.S. history teachers I know require of all their students: to identify and explain the first ten Amendments to the Constitution and then to write an opinion essay on which one of the amendments in the Bill of Rights is most important and why, using evidence from both history and current events.

It's certainly important for our students to have a basic knowledge of major events in our history and to demonstrate understanding of the key principles of our democratic form of government. But I am equally concerned about teaching and testing the skills or *competencies* required to be an active and informed citizen. When I taught 9th grade English, I required all of my students to research an issue of concern to them; summarize the arguments, both pro and con; write a letter to the editor of the area newspaper; and mail it. My focus was on developing the research, communication, and critical-thinking skills that I think are essential for students to become active and informed citizens—to be able to debate the issues thoughtfully and vote intelligently—so I developed this "Letter to the Editor" test to assess these skills.

What does it take, though, for all high school graduates to be "citizenship-ready"—or "jury-ready," for that matter? Imagine that you were on trial for your life for a crime that you did not commit, and the jury that would decide your fate consisted of people who had completed high school having studied what was required to pass state tests. How confident would you be that your jurors would know how to analyze an argument, weigh evidence, recognize bias (their own and others'), distinguish fact from opinion, and balance the sometimes competing principles of justice and mercy? Could they listen with both a critical mind and a compassionate heart and communicate clearly? Would they know how to work with others to seek the truth? While our jury system may always be compromised by the presence of individuals who cannot distinguish fact from opinion, I still believe it is as important to prepare students for this critical role in adult civic life as it is to prepare them for work or college. In Chapter 6, we'll learn about how some schools use mock trials in classrooms to teach these skills.

The Seven Survival Skills are as important for citizenship as they are for work. Looking at the state tests in this chapter, did you find evidence that any of the skills I outlined in the paragraphs above were being assessed? Most of the sample questions, as well as those comprising the rest of the tests, were assessing students' knowledge of *facts*. Some readers may be thinking that these facts and the other content knowledge we saw being taught in the previous chapter are what all students will need to do well in college. So let's explore this question.

College-Ready?

A few years ago, I was asked by the leaders of one of the most highly regarded public high schools in New England to help them with a project. They wanted to start a program to combine the teaching of English and history because they thought that such a program would give their graduates an edge in college—and more than 90 percent of their students went on to college. They thought that teaching the two subjects together would help students gain a deeper understanding of both history and the literature of an era. Yet when I asked them how they knew that this would be the most important improvement they might make in their academic program, they were stumped. They'd just assumed that this innovation would be helpful to students.

Personally, I think interdisciplinary studies make a great deal of sense, but I also know that schools have very limited time and resources for change and so must choose their school and curriculum improvement priorities with great care. I proposed that we conduct a focus group with students who'd graduated from the high school three to five years prior, in which I would ask the alums what might have helped them be better prepared for college—a question rarely asked by either private or public high schools. The group readily agreed, though, and worked to identify and invite a representative sample population of former students who would be willing to meet for a couple of hours when they were back at home during their winter break.

The group included students who attended state colleges and elite universities. My first question to them was this: "Looking back, what about your high school experience did you find most engaging or helpful to you?" (I would ask the question differently today: "In what ways were you most well prepared by high school?") At any rate, they found the topic quite engaging and talked enthusiastically and at length about their high school experiences.

Extracurricular activities such as clubs, school yearbooks, and so on topped the list of what they had found most engaging in high school. Next came friends—there were no cliques in this small high school, they claimed, and so everyone got along well. Sports were high on the list as well: Because the school was small, nearly everyone got a good deal of playing time.

"What about academics?" I asked.

"Most of our teachers were usually available after school to help us when we needed it," one young man replied. Several nodded in agreement, and then the room fell silent.

"But what about classes?" I pressed.

"You have to understand," a student who was in his last year at an elite university explained to me somewhat impatiently. "Except for math, you start over in all of your courses in college—we didn't need any of the stuff we'd studied in high school."

There was a buzz of agreement around the table. Then another student said, with a smile: "Which is a good thing because you'd forgotten all the stuff you'd memorized for the tests a week later anyway!" The room erupted in laughter.

I was dumbfounded, not sure what to say next. Finally, I asked: "So how might your class time have been better spent—what would have better prepared you for college?"

"More time on writing!" came an immediate reply. I asked how many agreed with this, and all twelve hands shot up into the air. And this was a high school nationally known for its excellent writing program!

"Research skills," another student offered and went on to explain: "In high school, I mostly did 'cut and paste' for my research projects. When I got to college, I had no idea how to formulate a good research question and then really go through a lot of material."

"And time management. I was clueless when I had to figure out how to work on a project that was due at the end of the semester, instead of the end of the week," a student across the table added.

"Learning to work with other students in study groups" came the final answer. "You can't understand all the material by yourself. If you don't learn to prepare for exams in study groups, you're dead."

Needless to say, my report back to the leaders at the school was not what they had expected. Their curricular improvement efforts went in a very different direction, as a result. But more than the particulars of this consulting project, the words of the students have stayed with me. Was this just an unusual group, I wondered?

In the last several years, there has been a growing interest in pushing more students to go to college as one way to increase the skill level of our nation's workforce. As part of this effort, new research has been conducted on what it means for students to be "college-ready." Achieve, a nonprofit education organization created by the National Governors Association, recently interviewed 300 instructors who taught first-year students in two- and four-year colleges. One of the most striking findings of the report is what these college teachers said students entering college were unprepared to do:[29]

- 70 percent say students do not comprehend complex reading materials

- 66 percent say students cannot think analytically

- 65 percent say students lack appropriate work and study habits

- 62 percent say students write poorly

- 59 percent say students don't know how to do research

- 55 percent say students can't apply what they've learned to solve problems

What was surprising about this study was the fact that college teachers said students most lacked *competencies,* rather than knowledge of specific subject content—which is exactly what the students in my focus group had said years earlier. The work of David Conley sheds further light on this subject. He has studied the skills and knowledge that matter most for success in college by looking at the kinds of assignments first-year college students are given and comparing his results to what he finds in high school classrooms and on state tests like those we just explored. And his conclusions are clear:

> The success of a well-prepared college student is built upon a foundation of key habits of mind that enable students to learn content from a range of disciplines. Unfortunately, the development of key habits of mind in high school is often overshadowed by an instructional focus on decontextualized content and facts necessary to pass exit examinations or simply to keep students busy and classrooms quiet. For the most part, state high-stakes standardized tests require students to recall or recognize fragmented and isolated bits of information. Those that do contain performance tasks are severely limited in the time the tasks can take and their breadth or depth. The tests rarely require students to apply their learning and almost never require students to exhibit proficiency in higher forms of cognition.[30]

Conley lists the core "habits of mind" that matter most for success in college: "intellectual openness; inquisitiveness; analysis, reasoning, argumentation and proof; interpretation; precision and accuracy; and problem solving." He then goes on to identify the most important "Overarching Academic Skills": writing and research. Knowledge of subject content ranks third behind this list in his typology.[31]

Despite the comparative lack of importance of studying more academic content for college-readiness, Advanced Placement courses have grown rapidly in popularity—in part, perhaps, because they *appear* to be the only way to increase the level of rigor in high school classes. So we need to take a more careful look at the AP program overall to see if, in fact, it does a better job of preparing students for college and thus deserves its reputation as the new gold standard for rigor in high school, as some now claim. (The International Baccalaureate program has also become more popular and demands more thinking from students in both coursework and assessments, but it is far less prevalent than AP.)

Enter Advanced Placement

Advanced Placement course syllabi and exams are developed and administered by The College Board, a national nonprofit organization that also administers a number of other national tests, including the SAT. According to its annual report from 2006, over 1 million students took more than 2 million AP exams, up from about half that number of students taking the tests in 1995. AP exams are offered in twenty-two subject areas, and while any student who pays the hefty $83-per-test fee may take any of these exams, the overwhelming number of students who take AP exams every year enroll in the prescribed high school AP courses that are designed to prepare them for specific exams.[32]

AP courses were originally designed in the 1950s as a way for the most academically advanced students to take a college-level course while still in high school. Many colleges began to offer credit to students who scored at the higher levels on the AP exams. But that trend is changing rapidly. According to a 2006 *USA Today* article, a growing number of colleges no longer offer credit for AP courses.[33] The main concern of the colleges is that too many students who have passed AP exams lack either the academic skills or the depth of understanding required for true college-level work in the subject. The article goes on to cite several studies indicating that *success on AP exams is not a good predictor of success in comparable college courses.*

In the previous chapter, we visited a number of AP classes and came away disappointed with what we saw, as you'll recall. But to better understand the pros and cons of AP, I talked with three experts from the field: two students who have taken the courses and exams and one teacher who has taught the AP US History course and served on a national panel of scorers for the corresponding AP exam.

Our first expert is a teenager whom I will call Julie. (She didn't want her real name used for fear that her AP teacher would interpret her comments as a criticism of him.) For the first two years of high school, Julie attended a highly regarded public school in the Northeast. She has since transferred to an independent (private) school. Julie took AP U.S. History in 10th grade.

"It had been cracked up to be a really challenging college-level course," Julie explained. They said: 'Don't do this unless you have talked to your 9th grade history teacher and are sure you can handle the workload.' But the summer reading, which was the introduction and first chapter in the textbook, *Nation of Nations* by Davidson, wasn't that challenging. It took awhile, though, because you had 100 terms per chapter that you had to take notes on—important people, dates, battles, places, whatever they thought was going to be on the test. The book was really dry to read. No thinking involved in it whatsoever. Also, this guy (Davidson) doesn't like to analyze any event, just likes to give you the facts—people who won the battles. He didn't even look at patterns.

"During the year, we had a test or a paper due every three weeks," Julie continued. "The tests were really boring—we just had to memorize the terms from the chapters we'd read. The papers were interesting, but we didn't have enough time to discuss them. It really was a course that was led by the textbook. Everything had to be within the bounds of the book. . . . My teacher was great and tried to get us to think in our papers. I really liked the challenge of analysis. But by the end of the course, we were cramming to get all of the terms in our head so it made the study of history go from being very analytical to pure memorization. For the extended response parts of the exam, we found out that what got the best score was repeating as many facts as possible while you answered the question."

"So what was the impact of the course on your interest in history?" I asked.

Julie replied, "It neither enhanced nor hurt my love of history—it was just a speed bump I had to get over." Julie was sick for three weeks prior to the exam but nevertheless managed to get a "4," which is the second-highest score possible.

Alec Resnick was a junior at the Massachusetts Institute of Technology when I spoke with him about his AP experience. He was focusing on a double major in math and history. He should have been a senior, but he took a year off to take humanities courses at Harvard. Alec transferred to a public school "AP Academy"—a small program that was set up to prepare gifted students for a wide range of AP exams—in his sophomore year of high school, where he took a total of ten Advanced Placement courses and received all 4s and 5s on the exams. I asked him how he would summarize his experience.

"They were a refreshing change from being bored in my regular classes," Alec said, "but after a year it struck me that too much of the wrong kind of work can be just as bad as not enough engaging work. The AP classes, by standardizing curricula, made all students' experiences

and discussions the same. Teaching to these standardized curricula
made students into passive receptacles because the teachers have these
boxes full of facts and information that you need to master, and they
spend the term pouring it into you. By my junior year, I realized that
this wasn't what I was looking for in an education."

"What does it take to do well on AP tests?" I wondered.

"There are two classes of people who do well on AP tests: people
who follow directions well and people who are intuitive test takers. In
both cases, they develop the same set of skills, which is guessing what
the test makers want. The AP program makes lots of claims: that the
courses present you with lots of data, ask you to interpret it, and as a result that you develop critical-thinking skills, but I think that's complete
BS. What I saw in the actual classes was that you ended up learning lots
of strategies for approaching the tests—recipes for how to get a 5.
When you ask people to think critically within very narrow bounds,
you get way more information about the bounds than about their ability to think critically. . . . It's entirely possible to master AP tests and
learn very little, if anything. That's what dissatisfied me most."

"Did the AP courses prepare you for college?" I asked.

"They did in the sense that some of my college classes were more
of the same—especially in science. But college doesn't have to be more of
the same—and it shouldn't be. That's why I decided not to be a physics
major—too many required courses where you just sit passively in your
classes and then go memorize stuff for the tests. Math is great because
there are so few requirements. I'm taking some elective graduate courses
now, and they're completely different. We're doing real research and
having great discussions. People are exploring questions instead of
canned answers. High school and college should be more like that."

Interviewing Alec, I had very mixed feelings. He has been deeply demoralized by his disappointing school and test-taking experiences and

so has given up his dream of being a scientist. Alec now wants to be a teacher and to start a school. I'm sure that he will make important contributions to education, but I wonder if both he and our society might have been better off if he'd had a very different set of experiences in his high school classes or had encountered a different kind of teaching in his college science courses. We may have gained an educator, but we have lost a promising young scientist.

Ten-year veteran teacher Dina McArdle has taught AP U.S. History at Ballard High in Seattle for five years and is the third "AP expert" whom I interviewed. Two years ago, she was chosen to be an AP U.S. History Exam scorer and spent eight days learning how to score and then scoring the essay portions of the exam (which comprise about half of the total exam). For Dina, learning how to score the essays was a wonderful professional development experience. She had never before had the opportunity to discuss how to grade history essays with other knowledgeable teachers sitting around a table. But once she had been trained by the AP supervisors, "there was an underlying assumption that you were supposed to read a lot of exams in the time you were given," Dina explained. "I read maybe 1,000 essays over eight days. In a typical ninety-minute period, I'd read 25 to 50 essays."

I asked Dina to assess the rigor of the test. "It is old-fashioned," she told me. "It tests robotic memorization of well-established facts, plus essays on discrete topics for which there is supposed to be one right answer. I want to see more opportunities for students to have more topics to write about and to have to do more research and analysis—link issues, see patterns, follow ideas over time."

Redefining Rigor

All three of the AP experts here found something of value in being associated with the Advanced Placement program, and their responses are consistent with the views of many others whom I've interviewed. Students and teachers alike find elements of AP to be significantly more challenging than teaching and taking courses aimed at preparation for state tests. No wonder the program has become the gold standard for rigor. But ultimately, all three found that the tests were much too focused on mastery of factual content—at the expense of research, reasoning, and analysis. I believe that the AP system—and, indeed, much of what passes for academic rigor in college, which the courses attempt to mimic—is not merely "old-fashioned," as Dina suggested. It is hopelessly obsolete.

We have long defined *rigor* in schools as mastery of more and more complex academic content. Many parents who demand more rigor in their children's schools want to see more homework—more math problems and vocabulary to memorize. And many teachers who are considered more rigorous demand that students move at a faster pace and cover more material in their classes. This definition of *rigor* was institutionalized early in the last century when "Carnegie units" became the way college entrance requirements were defined and standardized—four years of English, three years of math and science, two of a foreign language, and so on. Taking more academic (as opposed to vocational) courses, in which students were required to "cover" (i.e., memorize) more academic content, became the widely accepted definition of *rigor* for both high school and college and has remained unchallenged for at least a century.

But consider how different that era was compared to today's era of information flux and glut. A hundred years ago, there were comparatively few public libraries, most people didn't have access to encyclopedias, and Bill Gates hadn't even been invented yet. Memorizing material made some sense. You couldn't just go look it up, and what you memorized was likely to still be true ten or even twenty years later.

Today, though, we're faced with radically different circumstances. Most Americans now have Internet access, which gives all of us a growing tidal wave of information, and that information is constantly changing and increasingly exponentially. This fundamental revolution in the nature of information has given rise to the "knowledge worker" and demands for a very different set of skills for work and citizenship, as I've explored. The most important skill in the New World of work, learning, and citizenship today—the rigor that matters most—is the ability to ask the right questions. Old World rigor is still about having the right answers—and the more, the better.

Let's make it simple. Which is more important: memorizing the parts of speech or writing an effective essay? (By the way, there is no research which shows that knowing the parts of speech is necessary for learning to write well!) What is more critical: memorizing the periodic table, which is constantly changing, or knowing how to get relevant information when you need it and being able to explain what it means? We can't teach and test everything. Teachers today are trying to do it all—cover it all—and this is a recipe for frustration and failure. In fact, Hawaii commissioned a study to find out how much of a teacher's time would be required to teach all of the state academic content standards in 5th grade. The answer: 3,000 percent of the allotted time.[34] We have to decide what's most important. Here's my stand:

The rigor that matters most for the twenty-first century is demonstrated mastery of the core competencies for work, citizenship, and life-long learning. Studying academic content is the means of developing competencies, instead of being the goal, as it has been traditionally. In today's world, it's no longer how much you know that matters; it's what you can do with what you know.

Of course, I'm glad I know my times tables and so don't have to carry around a calculator to figure out the tip for dinner at a restaurant.

Some facts are very important and useful to memorize. In addition, there is obviously a certain kind of core knowledge that students ought to know in the various academic disciplines as well as specific content that students need to know to be literate and effective citizens. But serious efforts to discuss and agree on what kind of knowledge is truly foundational across academic disciplines for high school graduates are exceedingly rare in the highly compartmentalized world of academia. In fact, the avalanche of "content standards" that teachers feel compelled to cover today is due in part to the academics who were consulted by many states' education experts in the early 1990s about what state academic content standards should be. These academics couldn't agree on what the most important knowledge was, and so the compromise was to say that everything was equally important.

My purpose in criticizing the state and AP tests is not to make the case against testing but, rather, to ask some basic questions. I believe in accountability in education, but what do we think we should hold people accountable for—what's most important to learn? In the first chapter I attempted to answer the question of what skills matter most—and, indeed, the development of real competence with the Seven Survival Skills will only become increasingly important in the future. But we must also consider who should be held accountable if students fail to meet certain standards. Should the students be punished, as is increasingly the case today? Finally, how will we *measure* what it is we decide is most important?

Business, political, and education leaders who call for more rigor in classrooms and advocate for more accountability in public education have not been anywhere near as rigorous as they need to be in considering these questions. Nor have they considered what the impact of all of these tests really is on student motivation for learning. You heard two students speak about how the AP courses had affected them, but what other data do we have?

Student Motivation: The Holy Grail

In my interviews with business executives, I've heard as much concern about young people's lack of work ethic as I have about their lack of skills. The most frequent complaint I hear from veteran teachers—aside from comments about having to teach to inane high-stakes tests—is that today's students seem much less *motivated* to do well in school than earlier generations were. Yet, despite the depth of concern and frequency of such comments—and although they come from business execs and teachers who often don't agree on much—there is precious little discussion of the problem of student motivation in all of the debates about education reform today. The assumption seems to be that if there's a problem with motivating students, then the threat of not passing the tests and not receiving a high school diploma will take care of it. All stick and no carrot.

I'll explore the topic of motivating the younger generation at length in Chapter 5. But for now, let me just observe that a hidden cost of the teaching and testing that dominates high schools today is its negative impact on student motivation to learn for pleasure or even to continue in school at all. Students have far less time for extracurricular activities and electives in high school today, compared to even a generation ago. Many more academic courses are required for graduation now in most states, and school districts are insisting that more class time be spent on test preparation, as we've seen. Schools also have less money in their budgets for elective courses. The combined effect has been to squeeze most art, music, and other elective courses out of the curriculum. While observing a high school last week, I talked to Sierra, a bright, engaging young woman in the 11th grade, and she told me that she did well in all of her courses, but hated her last school and decided to transfer to an alternative school. Why? Because they had eliminated all the arts from her schedule—and these classes were the reason she was excited to go to school to begin with.

Motivation and our nation's dropout rate go hand in hand. There has been much debate about the problem of the dropout rate in American high schools in the last few years, ever since Manhattan Institute scholar Jay Greene and others determined that the true graduation rate for American public high schools is much lower than what had been reported by many states. Only about two-thirds of all American public school students graduate in four years with a regular high school diploma—a number far lower than that in other industrialized countries.[35] Many people had assumed that the primary reason students dropped out of high school was because they lacked the skills to do the work—especially reading and writing skills. While this is true for a number of students, a recent study funded by the Bill & Melinda Gates Foundation found that poor basic skills in reading, writing, and computation were not the main reason for the high dropout rate: It turns out that *will*, not *skill*, is the single most important factor.[36]

In a national survey of nearly 500 dropouts from around the country, about half of these young people said they left school because their classes were boring and not relevant to their lives or career aspirations. A majority also said that schools did not motivate them to work hard. More than half dropped out with just two years or less remaining to earning a high school diploma, and 88 percent had passing grades at the time that they dropped out. Nearly three-quarters of the interviewees said they could have graduated if they had wanted to.[37]

It isn't just the dropouts whose motivation to learn is being affected by the relentless focus on testing and memorization. It's nearly all students. You saw for yourself, in the previous chapter, how incredibly boring most classes are. In countless focus groups I've conducted with high school students, "boring classes"—which include so-called advanced classes—are among their main complaints about school.

Are there better tests out there—tests that measure the skills that matter most for work, citizenship, and college? Tests worth taking? Tests that even students find worthwhile? Yes.

Toward a More Meaningful
Accountability System

In the last half-decade, some extremely important work has been done in the field of assessment that points to exciting new answers to the right ways to test for so-called higher-order thinking skills. One of the most influential pioneers in this revolution in testing is Dr. Richard Hersh, who some years ago found that he had a serious problem during the time he was a liberal arts college president.

"I would greet parents or contributors during events, and we'd all agree about the value of a liberal arts education," Hersh told me. "But once in a while, someone would ask, 'Dr. Hersh, just what *exactly* is the value of a liberal arts education, and how do you know your college is delivering it?' I always had a smooth answer at the ready, but I'd go home and be thinking, 'I wish I had a better answer.'"

So Hersh set out, with support from several major foundations and the help of Steven Kline and Roger Benjamin, both at the Rand Corporation at the time, to see if it was possible to measure the "value-added" of a college—how much students actually learned between their freshman and senior years. First, they met with college professors to seek agreement on the subject content all college seniors should master. "They couldn't even agree on the important content within their own departments, let alone across the campus or between colleges," Hersh noted. "But they all did agree on a core set of competencies that colleges should teach all its students: critical thinking, analytic reasoning, written communication, and problem solving. This consensus allowed us to design a content-neutral assessment that we could give a sample of students in freshman and senior year and then measure growth in the four areas."

Because, as Hersh says, "life is not a multiple-choice test," students can now take what is known as the Collegiate Learning Assessment (CLA), an open-ended, ninety-minute "performance assessment" in which the students have to demonstrate their reasoning, problem-solving, and writing skills while attempting to solve a "real-world" problem. In the sample test that I took (there are at least a dozen different versions of the test), I was asked to advise someone running for mayor in a town with a high crime rate about which of several proposals for reducing the rate might be most effective. First, I had to evaluate eight documents that were posted online. They ranged from newspaper stories about crime patterns to studies of the value of adding additional police to a report on a drug treatment program, and they were all based on real examples. Having read them, I then had to write two memos online: one comparing the pros and cons of adding more police versus bringing in a specific drug treatment program and another that was a position paper for the candidate. The test was challenging, and the results from the test tell us a great deal about the Seven Survival Skills.[38]

Introduced in 2003 after several years of development, the CLA has gained national recognition as a model assessment for "value-added," and more than 250 colleges and universities are using this system as a way to help them assess what their students are learning between their freshman and senior years. Hersh and the other developers of the CLA are now exploring its use as an assessment of high school students' college- and work-readiness. The new program is called the College and Work Readiness Assessment, or CWRA. A number of very prestigious private schools—including Hotchkiss, Holland Hall, St. Andrew's, and Lawrenceville—are using it to test *all* of their students, not just a sample. Teachers say it is the best test, by far, of the skills that matter most for college. Plus, the CLA is less than half the cost of an AP exam—or about $40 per student—and so there is no reason public schools couldn't use this test as a way of determining whether their students are college-ready.

Students were interviewed about their test-taking experience as part of the pilot tests of this assessment in the private high schools, and here is a sample of what they said:[39]

"thought the test was an incredible assessment; the problems were engaging and challenging."

"test was better than any other standardized test I have ever taken in my high school career. I felt I could really utilize what I have learned here in this test."

"I thought the test was original, thought provoking, and an interestingly different approach to testing."

"This test was different in that it was an evaluation of one's analytical skills, use of evidence, and writing abilities, as opposed to the more generic demands of the SATs."

"I actually had to think critically, and assess the problems given. I was not guessing anything, but investigating from the reports given to us."

"This test asked me to utilize my critical thinking skills rather than just memorizing methods and words."

Other than in these small private schools, where every student was tested, the primary use of the CLA is as an institutional audit. In these instances, the test is given only to a representative sample of a college's freshmen and seniors—not to every student. It tells a college (or, potentially, a high school or school district) the extent to which a sample population of students has mastered core competencies for thinking and communication. "Individual teachers can then use the CLA as a model for developing performance assessments of their own that they can give to assess all of their students," Hersh explained.

From the CLA and from the National Assessment of Educational Progress (NAEP)—a federally funded program that similarly tests sample populations of students on key academic skills and some limited subject content on a rotating basis—we learn several important lessons about fixing the public education accountability system.[40] First, instead of requiring each state to spend large sums of money on developing new tests every year and giving them to all students, we can use the money to develop higher-quality open-response, competency-based tests that can be given less frequently to a representative sample of the student population. Second, by testing only a sample of students, the "unit of accountability" would become the institution—the school, college, or school district—rather than the individual student or teacher. The beauty of the CLA is that it tests skills *all* teachers should be accountable for teaching in every class. Indeed, an endless battery of state tests is neither the most effective nor the most efficient way to hold individuals accountable, and they undermine the morale of both students and teachers. Teacher accountability is a subject we'll take up in the next chapter, and we'll explore better methods that some schools are using to hold both teachers and students more accountable a little later in this chapter and in Chapter 6.

Several other new kinds of standardized tests have been developed in recent years and are worth mentioning. For instance, there is the new cross-disciplinary PISA problem-solving test, developed by the Organisation for Economic Co-operation and Development, which I described in the last chapter.[41] And the Educational Testing Service has developed an Information, Communication, and Technology Literacy Assessment that it calls the "ISkills Test." This seventy-five-minute online test requires students to use a variety of technologies to perform a number of tasks, including acquiring and assessing information online, searching databases for specific data, creating a graph that supports a point of view, and developing a PowerPoint presentation using the information that has been researched.[42] Neither of these tests are currently being used by any states because they are more expensive to administer than existing tests, and there has not yet been a public demand for better assessments.

Collectively, however, these assessments have the potential to tell us much more than the state tests or AP exams can about students' competencies in most of the Seven Survival Skills: critical thinking and problem solving, accessing and analyzing information, effective oral and written communication, and perhaps even agility and adaptability. But what about some of the others: initiative, curiosity, and imagination?

The pioneering work of Robert Sternberg, who believes that there are three kinds of intelligence—creative, analytic, and practical—illustrates that tests like the SAT tell you only something about a person's analytic skills, at best. Therefore, Sternberg has been developing ways to assess students' creative and practical intelligences—which he views to be at least as important for success in life. In 2006, Sternberg left Yale University to become dean of arts and sciences at Tufts University, which is now committed to using assessments of all three intelligences in the college admissions process. Because he thinks the university will begin to attract a very different kind of applicant as a result of this new approach to admissions, Sternberg is also training college teachers in ways to develop all three intelligences in their courses.[43]

Sternberg's work is groundbreaking and has gained national attention, but let's not leap to the conclusion that there will eventually be standardized tests for all of our Seven Survival Skills. To assess some of the so-called soft skills, such as teamwork, leadership, initiative, and curiosity, you need to know a student well and to look at his or her work over time—as a movie, if you will, rather than as a single snapshot. Invariably, human judgment is involved, and corporate folks will tell you that they rely on human judgment far more than on paper-and-pencil assessments for most of their hiring and promotion decisions. But not just on one individual's judgment, either. Many companies require a job applicant to talk to five or ten people as a part of the interview process, and "360 reviews"—in which a number of co-workers' assessments of an individual are sought—are a very common form of employee performance review. What would this kind of collaboration look like in the area of assessing students' work?

The New York Performance Standards Consortium is a fascinating example of schools working together to define and assess both the hard and soft skills that matter most for high school students—and then holding one another accountable for quality results. Founded in 1997, the Consortium is a network of twenty-eight high schools that have collaborated to develop what they call "performance tasks," which they require all high school students to complete successfully before they graduate: an analytic essay, a research paper, a science experiment, and a demonstration of applied mathematical concepts—academic "merit badges," if you will. Teachers have also collaborated on how these tasks should be assessed and what the standard is for a student to be labeled as proficient in particular areas. Finally, experts from universities and the business world, who are not connected to the schools, participate in reviews of student work as well.[44]

Nebraska's pioneering work in assessment also deserves mention here. Under the courageous and inspired leadership of Doug Christensen, Nebraska's State Department of Education has evolved a unique and radically different state accountability system, called the School-based Teacher-led Assessment Reporting System (STARS). Nebraska is the only state not to give multiple-choice standardized tests. Instead, there is a writing test as well as the requirement that every district develop its own assessment system based on state standards. These local assessments must be approved by the state and may include student oral presentations, demonstrations, and projects. Most of the district assessments are developed and scored locally by teachers, thus creating a culture of competence and commitment rather than one of mere compliance, according to researcher Chris Gallagher, who has studied the Nebraska system.[45]

"Ours is a bottom-up model," Christensen explained. "It begins in the classroom with instruction that's aligned to our standards and extends to assessments developed locally that are tied to how well students apply concepts and problem solve, rather than simply memorize facts and figures and dates that they can't remember 10 minutes later."[46]

These examples tell us that we have proven models of dramatically better accountability systems—systems that focus on assessing the skills that matter most in ways that both teachers and students find more motivating and engaging. Indeed, a little-known fact about the education reform movement is that many states began to develop accountability and testing systems very similar to these in the early 1990s. But in every single state except Nebraska, these efforts were derailed. To better understand why, we'll take a look at Kentucky as an example of a state whose education reforms started out moving in the right direction but then went off track. Helen Mountjoy tells us what happened.

The Politics and
Finances of Testing

Helen Mountjoy was a mom with two young children in the local public schools in 1980 when the superintendent in her district was removed by the local school board. So Helen and two others decided to run for the school board on a reform ticket. She served eight years, including four as board chair.

"At the time, Kentucky's public schools were some of the worst in the nation," Helen told me. "We ranked 48th in high school completion and about the same on test scores. We spent less and we expected less of our children."

Sixty-six school districts sued the state in 1985, challenging the funding formula for their schools. The state supreme court found in favor of those who had sued and issued a sweeping opinion—the chief justice even went so far as to threaten to hold legislators in individual contempt, if they did not act swiftly. Accordingly, the Kentucky Education Reform Act (KERA) was signed into law in 1990, calling for far-reaching changes in school governance, funding, curriculum, testing, and other areas.

The legislation set forth extremely challenging and rigorous education goals for all students—including requiring the testing of several of the Seven Survival Skills. The legislation also abolished the state education board, and Helen was appointed to the new board. This time, she served for fifteen years, including six as chair of the board. Here is part of her remarkable story in her own words:

"According to the law, we had to create a new state test within one year of taking office. The statute called for primarily a performance-based assessment, but nobody knew what that meant. (*It is assessment based on authentic tasks such as activities, exercises, or problems that require students to show what they can do—as with the Collegiate Learning Assessment.*) . . . We started out with true performance events where students worked in teams and solved a problem of one sort or another, but these were extraordinarily expensive to create and to pilot, and they had to be changed every year, plus people were concerned about the subjectivity that crept into scoring—so we had to ditch those after five years.

"We were totally unprepared for the kind of response we got from our right-wing brethren. . . . For example, it was said that these open-response tests would measure students' values, and that students would be kept in school until they could answer 'the right way.' 'Critical thinking skills' means teaching your children to be critical of you and your church.

"And those are the arguments [the cost of the tests and their objectivity] that are still within our state," Helen explained. "People on one side of the room who don't want to do anything but a norm-referenced (multiple-choice) test because you know you can trust that kind of test, and all the people on the other side of the room saying, 'You know they test basic skills, but they don't call them 'basic' for nothing.' I'm nervous about what the outcome is going to be."

Helen noted that the state's assessment system still requires both "on-demand writing" and student writing portfolios. But she also pointed out that "the disconnect between policy-setting and what actually happens in classrooms is so dramatic—between what the board envisioned and the way it's implemented (by teachers). All you have to do is go in and watch some of our teachers teach writing. And it would make your hair curl. Very formulaic and incredibly repetitive so as to drum any glint of creativity from a child's heart. Teachers keep making corrections and keep making corrections until there's nothing left of the student's work."

Helen ended our conversation on a note of sadness: "We had the formula for doing the right things. And there are some places where the right things are being done, but even in the best districts the focus is always on test scores, not student learning. They don't seem to understand that the two aren't necessarily the same thing. That's the tragedy of what's happening in Kentucky and what's happening all over the nation with NCLB."

Since we last spoke, Helen has been given another leadership opportunity to address these challenges. In January 2008, Ms. Mountjoy was named the secretary of education for Kentucky!

And So Goes the Nation . . .

With minor variations, the Kentucky story is a typical tale of education reform in too many of our states. During the 1990s, many states—Vermont, Massachusetts, Minnesota, and Oregon, to name just a few—began to create rigorous assessments to measure the skills and habits of mind that were becoming increasingly important in the new global economy: the ability to think critically, solve problems, do research, write well, work in teams, and so on. Since then, however, all such efforts have been abandoned, for the combinations of reasons that Helen described: the comparatively higher costs of such tests and the politicization of learning. For some in this country, the only things that should be tested are facts, and nothing else matters. Factual recall tests are also about ten times cheaper to develop and to score—which is another obvious reason for their popularity with state legislators.

No Child Left Behind has put the final nails in the coffin of the states' development of more rigorous and authentic assessments, according to Robert Tobias, director of the Center for Research on Teaching and Learning at NYU's Steinhardt School of Culture, Education, and Human Development. A former math teacher–turned–testing expert, Tobias worked for thirty-three years in the New York City public schools and served for thirteen years as executive director for the Assessment and Accountability division until his retirement in 2001.

"There seemed to be a real concern [for a brief period in the early 1990s] for higher standards, better instruction, and aligning assessments with higher standards, meaning that the assessments themselves had to be more demanding," Tobias explained. "The tests went from strictly multiple-choice to open-ended formats. There was a real improvement. Then came NCLB, with its sanctions and stringent demands on states for evidence of improvement on standardized tests. So the states were on the line to show that all kids were learning and would be 'proficient' by 2014. It was essentially a gun held to their head."

Tobias went on: "So, given that circumstance, and given what I think any statistician would recognize as an unreasonable goal of 100 percent of students meeting proficiency, the only reasonable response on the part of the states was to dumb down the assessments. And now everyone is trying to 'game' the system by teaching to the tests. In New York City today, students take anywhere between six and fifteen standardized tests a year! They try to claim that some of it is 'diagnostic' testing—but, really, they're all just practice tests."

Final Questions

Our current accountability system primarily tests how much students have memorized and can recall at a given moment in time, and there are fifty different state standards for what it means to be proficient—none of which meet the standards for work, college, or citizenship in the twenty-first century. This system is shaped by obsolete notions of academic rigor and by political and financial considerations. It is clear that we have the knowledge and the models we need to create a dramatically different and better accountability system: one that looks at students' growth over time by means of both national and local assessments of the competencies that matter most. The question is: Are we willing to embrace a new definition of rigor—to rethink what high school graduates should know and be able to do? Apparently, the American public already has begun to do so. According to a recent study sponsored by the Partnership for 21st Century Skills, "80 percent of voters say [that] the things students need to learn today are different than 20 years ago." And "almost nine in 10 voters (88 percent) believe 21st century skills can and should be part of the curriculum."[47]

Two equally important questions follow: Are we willing to confront the academic and financial conservatives who are holding our states' testing systems hostage—and perhaps our students' futures as well? And can we agree that students in every state should be tested for mastery of a few core competencies using a uniform assessment system, in addition to locally developed assessments? We have the skill; indeed, the new assessments are far more challenging and demanding than what currently exists. But *do we have the political will?*

CHAPTER 4

Reinventing the
Education Profession

L ET'S SAY YOUR name is Greg, and you are a high school principal who also teaches a social studies class. You are part of a talented, veteran team of school and district leaders from a very good suburban public school district who have come to Harvard for an intensive, three-day executive education program. Walking from your hotel through the brick and ivy Cambridge campus in the cool, crisp fall air, you are both nervous and excited. Laughing, you say to yourself, "Well, I finally made it to Harvard!" You and your colleagues find the seminar room, where a dozen or so other teams similar to yours are taking their seats at round tables.

The instructor—whose name is Tony Wagner—asks the members of each group to introduce themselves and talk briefly about the "problem of practice" they plan to work on together over the next three days. The problem your team brought to work on is the lack of "buy-in" from your veteran teachers. They're good people, but they don't see the need for the "curriculum alignment" project the superintendent has made one of her top priorities for the year.

Soon after Wagner begins the session, he suggests that "the district that has ten priorities really has none" and presses your team to think about your "theory of action"—a way of thinking more systematically, using questions such as What is the real problem you're trying to solve, and how do you know it's the most important problem you should be working on? What is your strategy, why did you choose this strategy, and what evidence will tell you whether it's working? And, finally, Who is accountable for what, and what will they need to make the strategy work? Your head is spinning. You and your team have never been asked to think about questions like these before.

In the team discussion time, your group talks for a while about the curriculum alignment project, but very hesitantly, because the superintendent is sitting right there, and everyone knows this project is her baby. No one really dares touch the issue about districts having too many priorities—even though you and everyone else around the table know it's true. This superintendent is sharp, but she's really just like all the rest of them. With all these superintendents, it's always "Reform Du Jour" or education "Fad-of-the-Month Club," you and your colleagues like to joke. They come in with a bunch of initiatives and priorities, and then they go to a conference and hear a speaker and come back with three new priorities—in addition to the ones that were already in place. And, for all that, they usually move on to another district after three or four years, and then some new guy comes in with all the "answers."

"Maybe we need to communicate more clearly to teachers why this curriculum initiative is important to the district, and what our other priorities are, and how they all relate" you finally offer in a quiet voice. All eyes at the table dart to where the superintendent is sitting.

She frowns slightly and responds with a cool tone of firmness and finality: "This will reduce the overlap in the curriculum, and everyone will know exactly when each of the state academic content standards are supposed to be covered and how the curriculum map aligns with the tests. We should see a clear improvement in our test scores, as a result." End of conversation. Does she really think she can cure the skeptics with two sentences about tests?

Wagner is speaking again, and he declares that if your goal is to improve student learning—and that is the only goal that really matters—the first problem that you have to work on is to improve teaching and the coaching of teachers. It sounds so obvious, the way he says it. Your district has a teacher evaluation system as required by law, but it's a complete waste of time. It takes forever to do all those observations and to fill out lengthy forms every year, and it often takes several years to get rid of even one teacher. It's a hoop-jumping exercise, really, and everyone knows it. The system is simply not designed to help all teachers improve. And your district is hardly unique in this respect—every district's evaluation system is pretty much the same.

The instructor says that if you want to improve instruction, you have to first agree on what good teaching is all about. He turns on a video of a 10th grade English class, shows the first third of the lesson, stops the tape, and asks you to grade the lesson—on a scale of *A* through *F*. You put your grade on a 3 x 5 card and pass it forward. You talk about the lesson at your table with your teammates while the instructor and his colleagues tabulate the results. You are surprised to find how much disagreement there is around the table about the quality of the lesson. You gave the lesson a *C–*, while your assistant principal, who also evaluates teachers in your building, gave it an *A–*. You glance over to your superintendent, and she's frowning. You're dying to know the grade she gave the lesson, but you don't dare ask, and she's not offering.[1]

Now Wagner drops a bombshell. He puts up a slide showing the overall grade range for the lesson. You and others in the room gasp in astonishment. It goes from *A* to *F*! And worse, there are about as many people who give the lesson a *B+* or above as who gave it a *D* or below! How could that be? The instructor tells you that he gets pretty much the same result with every group who sees the video, and then he asks, "How do you make sense of this?"

"Some people expect too little of African American kids," one woman suggests with an edge in her voice. (The students in the tape are mostly African American.)

"That may well be true," the instructor says, "but we've also used a video with mostly Caucasian kids and have gotten the same grade range."

"We're all looking for different things in a lesson," someone across the room says. "It depends on what our experiences are, what we value most."

"Let's test that assumption," the instructor tells the audience. He asks for three volunteers who had rated the lesson a *B+* or above to explain their reasoning. And then he asks three who had given it a *D* or below to do the same.

You can't believe it. The six people who speak use practically the same words. They all talk about the rigor and relevance of the lesson for the kids and the relationships the teacher seems to have with them—but they come to totally different conclusions!

"So, in fact, we are often looking for the same things—but we do not agree on what we see," the instructor observes.

Then he says, "I'd like to suggest another explanation for why you all graded the lesson so differently. In education, we talk about all kinds of things—theories of learning and classroom techniques, and so on. But we never actually look at and talk about teaching together. And if we want to improve instruction, the first thing we need to do is make the classroom walls transparent. We have to do 'learning walks' together and talk about what we see. We have to videotape ourselves and one another—not just in our classrooms but in our coaching sessions with teachers and even in our meetings. We need to talk about elements of good practice and then strategies for helping everyone in the system improve every year.

"And as we discuss and agree on what is 'good instruction,' we need to start with a clear definition of *rigor*," Wagner says. "We can have debates among our teachers about what *rigor* is, but the world—employers and colleges—have a very clear definition of *rigor*—of what they expect your students to know and be able to do. They're demanding a set of skills that are not subject to debate." He shows several slides with survey data about the skills the college professors and employers expect high school graduates to master. The data are powerful and not exactly what you expected: The professors and employers want skills—and essentially the same skills, such as critical thinking. They want high school graduates who know how to think critically? But you wonder to yourself, How many of our teachers even know how to teach critical thinking?

You squirm in your seat. You can't wait for the break. In your gut, you know there's a lot to what he's saying. And maybe you'll try a "learning walk" back in your building—that is, if the superintendent thinks it's a good idea. You know you should spent more time in classes, and you keep meaning to. . . . But, Jeez, you don't want your own classes or faculty meetings videotaped! Teachers are a critical bunch. . . . And, besides, they'd hate this idea! Not even worth bringing up.

All those data he presented about what rigor really is today and how subject content is less important than it used to be make a lot of sense, but the parents and Advanced Placement teachers aren't going to buy it—not for a second! They want all of their kids to get "5s" on all the tests so they can get into Harvard, and that means memorizing everything for the tests. . . . Heck, doesn't he realize that the AP teachers practically run the school? Why doesn't Wagner talk to the admissions people here at Harvard about different criteria for judging kids' applications—criteria other than the numbers of AP courses they've taken?

And then there were all those questions he asked about strategy. Who has time to figure any of that out? It's all you can do to answer your e-mails, return parents' calls, and get the central-office forms filled out and sent back on time before your have to rush out to some evening or weekend event where you're expected to put in an appearance— it's an 80-hour-a-week job. And he says we have to have a "theory of action" and a strategy for improving instruction. How about a strategy for survival?

At the end of the three days, as you fill out the seminar evaluation form, you're thinking that this has been one of the most challenging in- tellectual experiences of your career, and you're committed to trying to get into classes more often—though you have no idea about what to look for or how to really talk to teachers about their instruction. You worry about how they'll react to the idea of your coming into their classrooms.

Just before you doze off on the plane ride back, you're thinking: Maybe you don't have to do everything they suggested—after all, your kids are all doing well on the state tests and the APs. What's the saying— "If it ain't broke, don't fix it!" Besides, nobody else in the country is doing any of this. . . .

———

For the past eight years, my colleagues at the Change Leadership Group and I have put on more than a dozen three-day "learning labs" in Cam- bridge, which are based on our research of the issues related to change leadership in education, and we have conducted hundreds of similar workshops all over the country. "Greg" is not an actual person, of course, but rather a composite of many of the educators who have attended our programs. His thinking reflects how a majority—though certainly not all—educators have responded to some of our ideas. The grade range in the lesson assessment exercise is quite real. I've also done this exercise with private school educators and gotten the same results—so it's not just a public school problem!

Why can't competent, veteran educators even come close to agreement on the assessment of a lesson, even in private schools? Isn't that their core business—teaching? Doctors and lawyers and engineers and architects seem to have at least some agreement on what constitutes "good practice" in their professions; not only that, they appear to be committed to making their practice better. So what's going on with educators?

Even the most talented and experienced education leaders struggle with questions that business leaders take for granted and deal with every day, questions like: what's the problem you are trying to solve, what do the data tell you, what's your strategy, how do you know it's working, who's accountable for what, and so on. Similarly, business leaders would have a difficult time understanding Greg's and his team's deference to his superintendent, and the outdated, compliance-based "command-and-control" mindset that still seems to characterize many of our public education bureaucracies. Greg's uneasiness about assessing his own teachers would baffle them as well.

A better understanding of how educators are prepared for their profession and how they learn and interact with colleagues in their work is a precondition for transforming public education. I use my own story in the coming pages to shed light on the complexities that surround the task of improving what goes on in every classroom.

Preparing to Be a Teacher

Walking to my first class in my Masters of Arts in Teaching program, I wondered what I was doing here. I felt that I'd gotten into Harvard by luck and that other students were a lot smarter than I was. But I didn't let these feelings overwhelm me because I knew that I wanted to be a teacher—and Harvard was supposed to be one of the best schools of education in the country. So I would just have to work as hard as I could and hope that it was good enough.

After a few months, my anxiety gave way to a growing sense of excitement in my elective courses, which, fortunately, were more than half of all the courses that I had to take. At the time, I thought I wanted to be a social studies teacher, so I took several anthropology seminars and found them both challenging and engaging. Then I took a sociology course called "Character and Social Structure in America" in which we read Alexis de Tocqueville's *Democracy in America* and other classics. It was a large lecture course, but I had a wonderful section leader by the name of Jay Featherstone.

Jay also offered a noncredit seminar on education that soon became my favorite class. We poured over all of the books by the education reformers of the day—John Holt, Jonathan Kozol, Herbert Kohl, and many others—and we talked about our beliefs about education and how schools needed to be improved. Jay would throw out a question about the week's reading and then just sit back—only occasionally jumping back in to ask another provocative question. Sadly, it was the only education class that I felt I derived any benefit from—and it was an extra class that wasn't even offered for credit! All of the required courses, which included "Psychology: The Learning Process" and "The Teaching of Social Studies," seemed totally unconnected to everyday issues of teaching and learning, and students in my classes—myself included—were never really engaged by the content or teaching methods of these classes.

At the time, Harvard sponsored a summer academic enrichment program for suburban public school students, so I was placed with a social studies teacher in a class of middle school students. This was a component of the "practice teaching" portion of my degree program, which was required for teacher certification. I thought the teacher was dull and that many of his lessons bombed with the kids, who truly didn't seem very interested in being there. Watching him all summer, as I was required to do, was painful. I found out later that he'd decided to leave the classroom to become an administrator. In my opinion, it wasn't hard to understand why.

At the end of the summer, I took the initiative to seek out a better "master teacher" for my academic-year practice-teaching experience, rather than wait for Harvard's placement. With a bit of searching, I found a high school social studies teacher in an urban alternative school program—a small autonomous school-within-a-school situated within a large comprehensive high school, which was much more like the kind of school I hoped to teach in—and the Harvard officials acquiesced to my urgent request for a placement they considered to be unconventional. Most of my fellow students were being placed in suburban schools. (This is no longer true today.)

Once again, I was required to spend almost all of my time in the school just watching this man teach. I thought some of his lessons seemed pretty good. But we never really talked about what *he thought* about his lessons. I wanted to know his views on what worked and what didn't, and why. In the spring, he finally let me design and teach a five-day unit on my own. I don't remember what I taught—just how nervous I felt. He said that I was doing fine, but he wasn't there very often and rarely gave me much feedback or constructive criticism. And that was it—all of the discussions I remember about teaching and the sum total of the feedback that I received as a wannabe teacher boiled down to a lot of unanswered questions on my part.

I graduated in June and felt completely unprepared for my new profession. I was now a fully certified and credentialed teacher, with a framed degree and a state certification paper to prove it. Today, by the standards of the No Child Left Behind law, I would be deemed "highly qualified" because of my degree and subject-content preparation. The trouble was, I really didn't know the first thing about teaching. I felt I'd learned absolutely nothing about how to be a good teacher in my master's program. And they were going to set me loose on a bunch of high school students? It sounded a little bit dangerous to me.

Teaching in Public School

With my family I moved to the Washington, D.C., area for a job heading up a new alternative school program in a suburban public high school. I worked with the most disaffected students, trying to understand what might motivate them to learn or even to stay in school. Because I was spending much of my week working with students one-on-one, and in small groups, I volunteered to teach a regular English class so that I could better understand what teaching conventional classes was all about. I also wanted to be part of a department and not to be working all alone. The head of the English department gave me a class of thirty-nine students, whereas most other English classes had only about twenty-five and his own AP English class had thirteen. Did he want me to fail, I wondered?

I still vividly remember the first time someone actually came into my class to observe me. It was the principal, and he was there to complete my annual evaluation. I tried not to look at him, and to focus on the kids, but it was hard. I felt naked—on display. Aside from having my master teacher in the classroom at Harvard pop in while I was teaching my five-day unit, no adult had ever actually watched me teach before. He sat in the back of the room for ten minutes, as we discussed a short story students had read for homework, and then quietly slipped out.

We were to meet in his office a week later to discuss my evaluation. Though nervous, I found myself actually looking forward to the meeting.

As the principal showed me into his office, he smiled and motioned me to a seat in front of his massive mahogany desk. Once I took a seat, he handed me a piece of paper and said, "Look this over." Taking it from him, I remember my hand shaking slightly. Finally, someone was going to give me some feedback on my teaching.

Looking down, I saw four pages of checklists with perhaps forty items grouped into five or six categories. There were only two columns running down the length of the pages, one labeled "Satisfactory" and the other "Needs Improvement." Quickly scanning the sheets in front of me, I saw that the Satisfactory box was checked for every single item.

"If you agree with this, then all you have to do is sign at the bottom," the principal told me. I certainly didn't feel that my teaching was satisfactory in all respects, but who was I to argue and what questions would I ask? Besides, after almost a year of teaching every day, I still had no idea—other than sheer gut instinct that was mostly based on whether the kids seemed engaged—when I'd taught a good or bad class or even what were the elements of an effective lesson. I clearly wasn't going to get any feedback in this conference. I signed, picked up my copy, and left—the knot in my stomach replaced by an empty ache. The conference had lasted less than five minutes.

A year later, the exact same scene played out—same principal, same checklist, same result. The same thing happened again in year three. But now, having completed the required three years of "successful" teaching, I was not just certified—I was tenured! A teacher for life, if I chose to be.

I took no pride in this apparent achievement. In fact, I felt embarrassed for my chosen profession. I knew that I was a better teacher than when I'd started. I'd at least figured out the classroom management part, and I saw some evidence that many of my students were really learning to write. They seemed to enjoy our writing workshops, where students read their work aloud for discussion, as well as our seminar-style discussions of literature and current events. But I also knew that there were lots of times when I felt confused about why a lesson had gone poorly or how to reach an especially withdrawn student. I didn't know what I needed to do to be a better teacher. I felt I was way out on a limb, trying new things, with no safety net. I began keeping a teaching journal and writing some articles about what I was learning.

More than anything, I longed to talk to other teachers about the craft of teaching and to get feedback on my work in the classroom. The head of the English department had never observed any of my classes, despite my invitations. Teachers never visited one another's classes—it almost seemed like some kind of unspoken taboo, symbolically enforced by the heavy wood classroom doors that stayed firmly closed all day, except for the periodic comings and goings of students. Nor did we ever talk about teaching and learning in our monthly faculty meetings. They were mostly times for announcements and the like and rarely went more than twenty minutes. I dreaded going into the faculty lounge, where a few veteran teachers were always holding forth with opinions and gripes—mostly about how poorly paid they were. Once or twice a year, we had a professional development in-service day, during which we sat and listened to someone lecture us on some hot topic in education. It was a different topic every time, and there was never any follow-up. We all vied for seats in the back of the auditorium where we could at least get some papers graded.

Private School Teaching

After five years of teaching in public schools, I took a job at one of the leading independent schools in Washington, D.C., where I hoped to find a greater sense of professionalism and colleagues who were interested in learning from one another. I formed a little education discussion group, which met a few times for a potluck dinner and conversation about some article on education. Pretty soon, though, it was more about the dinner and the wine than about the articles we were supposed to discuss. I asked if I could observe some of my fellow English teachers and was welcomed into their classes. Though they never asked any questions about what I'd observed, I was fascinated by the opportunity just to watch others teach and to see the great variety of approaches, as well as a surprisingly wide variance in skillfulness.

During my third year at the school, I helped initiate a faculty meeting during which we watched several videotapes of instruction and discussed what we witnessed. Nine years after starting my master's degree program at Harvard, this was the first time that I remember ever talking about teaching with other teachers! But the meeting was over after an hour, and we never did anything like it again.

In my own teaching, I was constantly trying new things to get students to take more initiative and responsibility for their own learning. I had pairs of students take charge of the beginning of discussions on a rotating basis and would meet with them ahead to help plan how they'd engage the class. I used my planning periods to conference with students about their writing and discovered that I could teach writing far more effectively this way, especially when students chose the writing we were to discuss from their folder of work.

By now, I could figure out the right "architecture" for a course after teaching it a couple of times—the right combination of engaging literature and writing assignments that required both analysis and creativity, but once I did, the classes seemed to almost teach themselves. According to the students, word in the school was that I was considered one of the top English teachers, and my Expressive Writing class turned out to be one of the most popular elective courses, but I still didn't really know what I was doing right as a teacher and what I needed to do to improve. Teaching was totally trial and error, guided only by my instincts about what worked and what didn't. I had students in all of my courses fill out end-of-semester evaluations, which were very helpful, but I wanted to know what a veteran teacher might say about my classes. After four years of teaching in this school, not one person had ever come to visit any of my classes.

The good news about teaching in private schools is also the bad news: The principal and dean of faculty assume you're competent, and they leave you alone to do essentially whatever you like. There was no formal teacher evaluation system—only word of mouth from parents and students. If the administration heard a lot of complaints, it simply didn't renew your contract, but that rarely happened. In the four years that I taught there, only one teacher left involuntarily.

I grew restless and a little bored. I didn't feel I was learning very much. I wasn't being challenged, and I was weary of feeling alone and isolated in my work. So, with ten years of high school teaching experience behind me, I decided to apply for a position as principal of a K–8 school in New England. Much to my surprise, I was offered the job.

Life in the Fast Lane

I was completely overwhelmed in my new position. Parents who needed to see me right away, students who required disciplining, a newsletter to write, a teacher who wanted to know if he could have time off to attend a conference, another teacher coming to tell me that there was no toilet paper in the girls bathroom, a copier that was always jamming, the janitor who was yelling about an upturned trash barrel in the boys bathroom, phone calls to return, a school renovation project to launch, planning parents night and my first faculty meetings—these are just a few of my vague memories from the barrage of people, problems, and needs that bombarded me daily.

And I loved it—at least, in the beginning. I felt far more challenged and engaged than I had in my previous year of teaching. But I soon began to realize that all of my time was totally consumed by day-to-day management and maintenance issues. Of course, these are many of the responsibilities of a principal, but just trying to keep all the balls in the air and not drop any of them required *all* of my attention, leaving me no time or energy to work on the things that most concerned me—what was happening in classrooms.

This school had a long-standing reputation as a "progressive" school, which was one of the reasons I'd decided to apply for the job. In other words, it was a school built on the philosophy of active, discovery-based learning. My dream was to create a school that could be a "laboratory" where I would work with others to test and develop better teaching methods and curricula. I'd figured out how to run a pretty good classroom; now, I wondered, what would it be like to work with a group of teachers to create a model school together? But I worried that the school had a problem. When I'd visited classes and talked to parents as part of the interview process, some parents complained that the kids were not being asked to do challenging enough work. As a former high school English teacher, I was surprised by the poor quality of writing demonstrated in the upper grades. The kids also appeared out of control more often than I thought was acceptable. Running and shouting in the halls was a constant problem, and many of the kids seemed to think that interrupting adults whenever they wanted something was their birthright. But what did I know, really? I was just a high school teacher.

Now, several months into the new job, I had a *real* problem. It quickly became clear to me that virtually all of the teachers in this school felt that the school in general, and their teaching in particular, was just fine the way it was. More than fine, in fact—they thought it was truly wonderful! And there were certainly *some* parents who agreed. It was a very precious little school—in both the positive and negative sense of the word. Who could I talk with to try and figure out if my instincts were right, and what was I going to do if I had some ideas for change? I was totally unprepared.

After a few months, I was finally able to make some time to visit classes and even to teach a few. I loved being back in the classroom again, and I certainly saw what I thought was some good teaching— especially in the lower grades. But I continued to believe that not enough was being asked of the older students—either intellectually or behaviorally. They seemed more indulged than challenged. So-called self-esteem mattered more than critical-thinking skills—a problem that I've since seen time and time again.

When I tried raising these issues with some of the teachers, the common response would be that I simply didn't know the culture of the school or how elementary and middle schools really worked. After all, I had just recently arrived. In an early faculty meeting I suggested that we might need to review the school's discipline policies, and my comment was met with silence and stony stares. As I tried to talk to more and more teachers, resentment against me grew, and I couldn't really blame them. I had absolutely no idea how to be a leader—a change leader— and, in fact, I was still mostly consumed by the tasks of being a day-to-day manager. I was more alone now than I had ever been as a teacher. After two years of struggle and feeling more demoralized than ever before in my career, I resigned.

These twelve years of experience as a teacher and an administrator had taught me a great deal about what was wrong with the ways educators are prepared for their profession and how their work is structured. But not knowing then what I might contribute to solving these problems of my profession, I decided to try working in nonprofit organizations— first co-founding and then heading up a rapidly growing organization called Educators for Responsibility and eventually directing a national project for the Public Agenda Foundation in New York. These projects were extremely challenging, and I learned a great deal about worlds that are very different from what I had known, but I missed being in schools. After six years of this work, I returned to graduate school for further study.

I earned my doctorate in education at Harvard, and although there is much that I could say about the experience, the short version is that the challenges of change leadership and improving instruction were not a focus in my classes, except for one. At the time, the only course offered on instruction and supervision was an elective, taught by a lecturer, Catherine Krupnick. In Catherine's course, we spent class time looking at and discussing videotapes of real teachers in their classrooms and then role-playing what we would say in a supervision conference that might help the teacher improve. It was an enormously engaging class and the only one that I took in all of my graduate years that had any practical application to the teaching and leadership issues that most concerned me. The course should have been required for my master's program.

Later, when I worked as a faculty member in a university teacher education program and supervised others' practice teaching, I required my students to bring copies of videotapes of their lessons to our seminars and found them to be a powerful tool for improving their teaching. I truly believe that viewing and discussing videos of teaching and supervision is *the single most effective strategy for improving instruction for all schools;* yet it is almost never done, for reasons that we'll explore in a moment.

Another Perspective

Randy Moore, a retired CEO of a major Hawaii real estate venture, currently serves as assistant superintendent for facilities for the State of Hawaii public school system. He was in his third year teaching middle school math in an economically disadvantaged neighborhood in Honolulu when we first met four years ago. We've continued to get together and compare notes from time to time. I recently asked Randy why a businessman would become an educator, what his first years as a teacher were like, and how he compares this new universe to the one from which he'd come. This is Randy's story:

"I've always had an interest in education and had been a part of discussions with foundation and corporate grant makers for years about what to do about public education. Back then, they'd pretty much concluded that the problem was too big—and besides, they already paid taxes, so why should they give more? More than this, though, they knew that they didn't understand the problem. But I wanted to do something. As I looked around, it seemed to me that the role of school principals was key—that they made the greatest difference—and so I set out to become a principal. But you can be a principal in Hawaii public schools only if you've been a teacher first. So I went back to school for my teaching certification.

"It took me just under two years to get my certification. I enjoyed some of the courses such as history of education because it gave me a perspective that I hadn't had before, but the courses didn't prepare me for the classroom. Now I think that our courses should have been more like those in business or law school, where you study cases.

"Teaching is by far the most challenging job I've ever had. In business, almost nothing has to get done in the next ten minutes, but in teaching you have to be there and be prepared. The definition of a nanosecond is how long it takes for kids to figure out you're not prepared. . . . Classroom management was a huge problem—it was the beginning of my fourth year before I felt I could handle this." (Later during that year, Randy was "discovered" by Hawaii State Superintendent Patricia Hamamoto and asked to come over to work in the Department of Education.)

"What kind of help did you get as a new teacher?" I asked.

"Everybody meant well," Randy replied. "But they all had their plates full. Everybody was so busy. In hindsight, I understand that the problem of getting real support for teachers is that no one in school has time. It's a systemic problem, not a case of neglect. Everybody reports to the principal, which burdens him with far more direct reports than he can effectively lead, manage, and support. He can't supervise and evaluate seventy people effectively—especially when some of the teachers are brand new."

"How are the two worlds of business and education similar and different?"

"There are many similarities. With both, you need to know where you're going and to lead and manage for individual and organizational outcomes. What's different is that most folks in education have spent their careers there and have a difficult time imagining what they've not experienced. So it's hard for many to imagine how things can be done differently, whereas in business you have to constantly innovate in order to survive. Schools districts are also very hierarchically organized."

"What about the unions?" I asked. From conversations with other business leaders, I knew that many are highly critical of the educators' unions and so was curious what Randy would have to say.

"The only reason you have a union in your shop is because of a historical failure of management that led employees to believe that the only way to redress their grievances was to unionize. If you wave your wand and the union vanishes, all the problems are still there. . . . The major problem in education is the adults, not the students. They came through the system, and they were successful. . . . It's all they know."

Lessons Learned: Teacher and Administrator Preparation

I've talked to dozens of teachers and administrators from both public and private schools about their professional preparation, as well as to students currently enrolled in teacher education programs. Their experiences were essentially the same as mine. Very few teacher preparation programs focus on developing the skills needed to be an effective teacher, and they rarely give student teachers meaningful teaching experiences with knowledgeable and effective supervisors. Certification programs for administrators focus a great deal of time and attention on subjects like history of education, education psychology, philosophy of education, school law, and research methods, but none at all on how to be a change leader—or even how to supervise teachers effectively.

Recent research by Arthur Levine confirms what I've found through my conversations and fieldwork. Dr. Levine was president of Teachers College at Columbia University from 1994 to 2005 and now serves as president of the Woodrow Wilson National Fellowship Foundation. He has conducted two highly influential studies of how teachers and education administrators are prepared for their profession by teachers' colleges and university schools of education. In his 2006 report, *Educating School Teachers,* which is based on surveys of education school alumni, principals, and faculty as well as on visits to twenty-eight programs around the country, Levine writes: "Many students seem to be graduating from teacher education programs without the skills and knowledge they need to be effective teachers. More than three out of five (62 percent) report that schools of education do not prepare their graduates to cope with the realities of today's classrooms."[2]

A major reason for this failure, Levine asserts, is education school faculty's lack of understanding of the current challenges in schools and classrooms:

> While almost nine out of ten education professors have taught in a school at some point in their careers, alumni and students complain that too often the experiences of faculty were not recent or long enough. As a result, they say, lessons are often out of date, are more theoretical than

practical, and are thin in content. The curriculum is often fractured, with a lack of continuity from one course to the next, and [there is] insufficient integration between course work and field work.[3]

Lack of adequate teacher preparation and support is considered the primary cause for the astounding public school teacher attrition rate. Studies show that nearly one in two teachers who start out in the classroom leave after just five years! The National Commission on Teaching and American's Future (NCTAF) estimates that the national cost of this teacher dropout problem is *over $7 billion dollars a year.*[4]

Dr. Levine's study of school and district administrators' preparation reveals that these leadership development programs are of even lower quality than teacher education programs. *Educating School Leaders* made news when it was released in 2005 for its conclusion that "most university-based preparation programs for administrators range in quality from inadequate to appalling." Unlike his teacher study, which at least highlighted a few exemplary teacher preparation programs in this country, Levine could not find a single example of an effective education leadership preparation program in the United States.

These programs fail to adequately prepare administrators for many of the same reasons that teacher preparation programs don't measure up, including "curricular disarray, low admission and graduation standards, weak faculty, inadequate clinical instruction, and inappropriate degrees," according to Levine. One of his most significant recommendations calls for replacing today's Ed.D. degree with the equivalent of an MBA for school administrators.[5]

In response to the growing criticisms of administrator preparation programs, Harvard and other universities are actively considering new approaches to education leadership preparation. Faculty from the Harvard Graduate School of Education have partnered with Harvard Business School and Kennedy School of Government faculty to create a new continuing executive education program for teams of school, district, and state education leaders called ExEL.[6] Faculties from the University of Virginia are engaged in a similar effort. Both projects are funded by the Wallace Foundation. The Change Leadership Group, with a grant from the Bill & Melinda Gates Foundation, has also pioneered new approaches to developing educators' skills as change leaders.[7] Veteran educators who have participated in these programs have been extremely positive about their experiences. However, they are all short-term programs that are dependent on foundation funding and serve only a handful of educators every year. It remains to be seen whether programs like these will influence the development of entirely new institutional approaches to preparing future education leaders—new approaches that completely re-envision both what educators should be taught and how.

Core Competencies
Versus Content Coverage

My view of the real problem with educator preparation programs—as well as with the state licensure requirements for teaching and administration—is that they focus on ensuring that future teachers and administrators have covered a broad range of required academic content—content that, in many cases, has little to do with the actual requirements of the job. At the beginning of the chapter, you read about my experience in the courses I was required to take as an aspiring teacher at Harvard. Here, in turn, is what Arthur Levine learned about the courses of study most aspiring school principals must complete:

> The typical course of study for the principalship has little to do with the
> job of being a principal. In fact, it appears to be a nearly random collec-
> tion of courses. The Principals Survey asked school heads, who had grad-
> uated from or were currently attending a university-based degree or

certification program, what courses they had taken. More than 80 percent of them reported the same nine courses—instructional leadership (92 percent), school law (91 percent), educational psychology (91 percent), curriculum development (90 percent), research methods (89 percent), historical and philosophical foundations of education (88 percent), teaching and learning (87 percent), child and adolescent development (85 percent), and the school principalship (84 percent). . . . These courses are, in effect, the core curriculum for the nation's principals, adding up to somewhere between 75 and 90 percent of the credits required for a master's degree. But they seem little more than a grab bag of survey courses offered in most education schools. If one removed the class on the principalship from the list, it would be a real challenge to guess the purpose of the program.[8]

What one has to do to become certified as a teacher or administrator is nearly identical to what students have to do for a high school diploma—take a disjointed collection of courses of uneven quality and then pass tests that rarely measure the skills that matter most. So just as we must facilitate the evolution of students' classes and assessments from memorization to mastery, we must do the same for those of adults. We need to identify the *competencies* that are most important to be an effective teacher or administrator and then develop ways that adults can show proficiency. Instead of having student teachers and would-be administrators memorize the parts of the car, metaphorically speaking, they have to demonstrate that they can actually drive!

Formed in 1987, the National Board for Professional Teaching Standards (NBPTS) is a voluntary teacher certification program that has pioneered such performance-based assessments of teacher effectiveness. It was set up to demonstrate how individuals who were already teachers could become even more skillful through a very different kind of advanced training. To become NBPTS-certified teachers, candidates spend a year or more developing a portfolio in which they demonstrate their ability to plan, teach, and analyze the effectiveness of their lessons. All teacher portfolios must include sample lesson plans, videotapes of at least two lessons, samples of student work, and "one 'documented ac- complishments' entry that provides evidence of your accomplishments outside of the classroom and how that work impacts student learning." Each of these portfolio elements must be accompanied by an analysis of the material and what the teacher learned from the exercise. Portfolios are then reviewed by a national panel of peers. In addition, candidates must complete six exercises online that are specific to their content area and that show how they apply understanding of their subject to specific student-learning challenges.[9]

Here is the Pennsylvania State Department of Education's summary of the research on the impact in classrooms of National Board Certified Teachers, or NBCTs (i.e., individuals who have successfully completed the National Board for Professional Teaching Standards program):[10]

- Students of NBCTs scored 7–15 percentage points higher on year-end tests than students of non-NBCTs. NBCTs were particularly effective with minority students.

- In forty-eight comparisons (four grades, four years of data, and three measures of academic performance), stu- dents of NBCTs surpassed students of non-NBCTs in al- most three-quarters of comparisons. The learning gains were equivalent (on average) to spending an extra month in school.

- Math NBCTs helped their students achieve larger testing gains in 9th and 10th grades than did their noncertified colleagues—demonstrating particular benefits among special-needs students and African American and Hispanic students.

- Students of NBCTs exhibited deep learning outcomes more frequently than students of non-NBCTs.

A New Kind of Teacher

What if this board certification process—or something similar—became the requirement for getting a license to teach in every state? (Several states are now piloting approaches to teacher licensing that are similar to the National Board's certification program, though it is unclear whether they have the same high standards for a "passing grade" as does the National Board.) And what if all the states required teachers to periodically update their portfolios to keep their licenses, instead of merely earning a few meaningless in-service (continuing education) course credits, as most states now require? In other words, to get and keep a teaching license, teachers would have to show evidence that they're competent—and that they have continued to improve—in the skills that are critical for effective teaching. If they don't have a license, they can't teach.

These new requirements would necessitate that teachers have better preparation, as well as more effective supervision. Teacher training would need to look more like the system of internships and residencies that are at the heart of how third- and fourth-year medical school students and resident physicians are trained—a system that entails much more mentoring and hands-on experience. And teachers' continuing education and supervision would be closer to the model of how performing artists or athletes are helped to advance. Teaching, like a performing art or a sport, is indeed a live performance under pressure. Teachers, too, need expert coaching and regular critiques of their performances in order to improve. Providing this kind of support for all teachers would dramatically reduce the number of educators who leave the profession in the first five years because they were ill-prepared for work in classrooms and received little or no assistance once they were on the job.

The problem with my proposal, of course, is that it appears to threaten what have been the twin pillars of the teaching profession for most of the last century—teacher autonomy (which we'll explore in a moment) and tenure. But I wonder to what extent the teachers' unions may actually be prepared to negotiate changes in working conditions and a phasing-out of the tenure system, in return for a better compensation, evaluation, and promotion system for teachers. I have found that educators today are profoundly demoralized, and union leaders know this as well. Teachers no longer believe that their profession is well-respected in this country. What I am proposing—raising the bar for both the initial training of teachers and for continuing certification, while also increasing their salaries as professionals and providing more opportunities for advancement by creating new master teacher and mentor teacher roles—would increase the status of the profession and likely result in more individuals wanting to become teachers. My proposal would also have a growing appeal to the rank and file of the teaching profession, as retiring teachers are replaced by a new generation who are less interested in tenure and want more opportunities for collaboration and intellectual challenge in their work. We'll meet some of the young adults who represent this new breed of teachers in Chapter 6.

Some of my proposals for transforming the teaching profession—and the importance of this work as a key strategy for improving all students' learning—have already been proven in other countries. Members of the McKinsey & Company consulting firm recently completed a study of the twenty-five highest-performing school systems in the world—as measured by the PISA tests—to better understand how these systems get such outstanding results. Their conclusion was quite clear: "The experiences of these top school systems suggests that three things matter: 1) getting the right people to become teachers, 2) developing them into effective instructors, and 3) ensuring that the system is able to deliver the best possible instruction for every child."[11]

I recently interviewed Andreas Schleicher, who, as you may remember from the last chapter, is head of the Indicators and Analysis Division, OECD Directorate for Education—the international organization that sponsors the PISA tests. He worked closely with the McKinsey researchers, providing them with data he'd gathered, and he talked to me about the importance of transforming the teaching profession:

"You cannot run a modern education system with the idea that someone decides what's taught and then tells teachers what to do. Take Finland, for example. [It was the highest-scoring country on the math, science, and problem-solving PISA tests.] The system there is highly selective in hiring teachers, and the best people come into the profession not because they pay well but because of attractive incentives and working environment. Finland relies on the minds of the profession to develop the system, rather than thinking of teachers as assembly-line workers, which is the model we still have in many other education systems. The quality of an education system cannot exceed the quality of its workforce."

Administrator Competencies

Thus far, unfortunately, no one has introduced a certification program for administrators similar to that offered teachers by the National Board for Professional Teaching Standards. However, as part of the project with Department of Defense education leaders that I described in Chapter 2, my colleague Lisa Lahey and I developed a draft of per-

formance standards for school leaders and recommended that principals be required to demonstrate proficiency through portfolios, as National Board Certified Teachers do. A principal's collection of work
might include

- a written School Improvement Plan (i.e., a spelled-out
  strategy for continuous improvement of teaching and
  learning), which includes an analysis of student achievement data.

- samples of agendas for faculty meetings and samples of
  communications to staff and parents, such as newsletters.

- an example of one week of the principal's schedule.

- a videotape excerpt of a faculty meeting, along with
  commentary.

- a videotape excerpt of a supervision conference with a
  teacher, along with commentary.

- a principal's written self-assessment and analysis of the
  portfolio elements.

Once again, the challenge is for education leaders and policymakers
to agree on the skills that matter most for administrators and then to develop ways to assess them. A portfolio requirement like the one above
would be a good start—both for conferring an educator MBA and for
getting a state license to be a school administrator, as opposed to merely
having to take and pass courses such as those Levine's study listed above.

The Culture of
the Education Profession

There are wonderful and effective teachers in every school across the country, and there are great schools that work to help kids with critical thinking every day. There are also schools in which faculty members work collaboratively to continuously improve their practice, and I will introduce you to some of these teachers and schools in Chapter 6. But these teachers and schools are the exception—what I call the random acts of excellence in a system that is more frequently characterized by mediocrity—through no fault of the majority of teachers and administrators who want to make a difference in students' lives. The problem is not just how teachers are trained and supervised. It also lies in the very nature of the *culture* of the education profession and the profound isolation of educators.

My colleague at Harvard, Richard Elmore, often says, "Education is a profession without a practice." He means that we have no clear standards for what is good practice in our work—no standards for what is effective teaching or leadership—unlike doctors or lawyers or accountants or architects, all of whom have clear standards of practice that are continuously reviewed. And as educators we work alone, all day, every day. Lacking both standards of practice and colleagues from whom we can learn, we must try to figure out how to be competent teachers or leaders all by ourselves.

The culture of the education profession, in my view, is influenced by the laws of both nature and nurture. *Nature:* Since the beginning of the twentieth century, the sort of person who was attracted to teaching as a profession was a kind of craftsman—someone who enjoyed honing a skill and greatly preferred working alone. This was also a person who valued security and continuity above challenge and change. *Nurture:* The ways in which educators have been trained traditionally, and in which their work is organized in schools, reinforce all of these tendencies. As noted above, educators at every level must work alone, whether they want to or not. And their work has a kind of craftsman's regularity and repetitiveness in that they often teach the same lesson two or three times a day and the same courses for years, with little or no change.

The system is held together though compliance to traditional bureaucratic authority—which is more characteristic of yesteryear's blue-collar assembly lines than of the ways in which most work is organized today. At my first teaching job, I remember having to punch in on a time clock every morning. In some districts today, principals have to get permission from the superintendent to leave the building—even for a quick errand. Authority and accountability in education—from state, to district, to school, to individual classroom—are very much top-down and one-way and, as such, create a culture of compliance. But it is a culture that, surprisingly, doesn't penetrate very deeply. Many teachers go through the motions of complying with school or district mandates, while doing as they please in their classrooms.

The implicit and unspoken contract that educators have traditionally signed onto with the system goes something like this: I'll agree to fill out your forms, attend your meetings, and appear to go along with whatever is the "Reform Du Jour"—just so long as you leave me alone to do as I please in my classroom or school. Many teachers and principals still think of themselves as independent subcontractors and see central-office administrators as just the compliance cops. The classroom or school has historically been their fiefdom. Principals—especially high school principals—often think of themselves as mayors of a village or CEOs of a small business. Even when there is a mandated curriculum, many teachers continue to teach whatever they like. Historically, some of our best educators have been noncompliers—pioneers like Deborah Meier and others who have always believed in teaching all students to use their minds well. But many others have also been among our worst—teaching things that may interest them, but that in no way prepare students with the skills they need. And then there are the teachers who still believe that their job is simply to give a decent performance: "I taught it. It's not my fault if they didn't learn it."

Most business leaders assume that there is no meaningful evaluation of teachers because of unions and the tenure system, which make it very difficult to fire teachers. But I have found no difference in the toothless teacher evaluation systems, the anemic supervision programs, and the tiny numbers of teachers fired in unionized schools and districts when I compare them to the private or charter schools where no one is tenured and to the districts where there are no unions. In other words, unions and tenure are not the only barriers to removing teachers. As a profession, we are extremely reluctant to criticize or evaluate one another. Another of Elmore's aphorisms is that "education is the 'Land of Nice'"—and he doesn't mean it as a compliment.

The reality is that, even if administrators wanted to evaluate their teachers more effectively, they have not been trained to assess teaching or to coach teachers. And it is the rare superintendent who expects his or her administrators to spend time in classrooms, helping teachers improve. Traditionally, the job of the administrator has been to make sure that there are no food fights in the cafeteria, that the buses run on time, and that parents' complaints are at least given a hearing. To really take a critical look at what's going on in classrooms would be to violate the unspoken contract, whereby teacher and principal autonomy remains the preeminent value of the profession.

However, this "agreement," which has been in place and relatively stable for much of the twentieth century, has revealed its Achilles' heel, creating a new opportunity for change. It is simply this: Teachers and administrators, working alone all day every day, cannot possibly meet the new demands for improvements that are being thrust upon them with increasing urgency from all sides. Even though current accountability systems are primitive and do not yet measure the skills that matter most, they are nevertheless beginning to have a disruptive influence on old established patterns. Teachers cannot figure out all by themselves how to get *all* students to be proficient, and administrators, working alone, do not know how to create a system where *all* their teachers improve continuously. Indeed, no one could solve these problems, working alone. The challenges are too complex. Some educators know this; they know that, in the words of noted education leader Anthony Alvarado, "isolation is the enemy of improvement." A growing number of educators are now much more open to—even hungry for—opportunities to collaborate and to learn from one another than ever before.

What happens when teams of educators are given regularly structured opportunities to observe classes together and discuss common problems of practice? Do they become more effective in their work—and, if so, in what ways? I was fortunate enough to be given an opportunity to explore these and other questions in a very exciting project in Hawaii that is still going strong today.

The Hawaii Story

It was a bright summer day in 2003 when I received an urgent call from Patricia Hamamoto, the school superintendent for the state of Hawaii. She asked me to work for a day with teams from every high school in the state. "Our high schools need reinventing," she said.

When I arrived in Hawaii, we discussed how important the "learning walk" exercise would be in our journey to understand what was going on in her schools and decided to complete a few learning walks in several high schools. After our first walk, Pat told me she was a little shocked at what she had observed. I remember one 11th grade English class we observed in which students had been placed into small groups to learn cooperation skills. The groups' task was to brainstorm all of the places in Hawaii that began with the letter "H." Later in our de-brief,

Pat and I agreed that this was an assignment more suitable for 3rd graders than for teens who would soon be graduating.

Robert Witt, who heads the Hawaii Association of Independent Schools and the Hawaiian Educational Council, invited me to speak at the annual conference for heads and board members of Hawaii independent schools and then at an Executive Education Conference for business and community leaders from the Pacific Basin. Here, too, I had an opportunity to explore with very engaged groups ideas about what kind of rigor is needed in today's world and how adults might work differently in schools.

I made several trips to Hawaii over the next year and a half to work on a wide variety of projects. In all of my talks, I referenced what I had described in an article as the "New Three R's" for reinventing our schools—*Rigor, Relevance,* and *Relationships.*[12] After one such talk, I was asked if I would be willing to work with a group of principals to help them understand how the New Three R's would be put into practice. And so I agreed to meet with a group of six principals from South Kona in a three-day workshop to better understand what rigor really looks like in classrooms and what it means to teach all students to use their minds well. Art Souza, the new area superintendent at the time, was very excited about the project and readily agreed to join the group of principals for our explorations of rigor.

That first day, we met in one of the principal's homes, and I began by engaging the group in discussions of what I considered to be some essential questions: How do you define *rigor,* in what ways might rigor today be different or the same compared to what we know about education fifty years ago, what are teachers and students doing in a class you would define as rigorous, and what evidence in classes would tell you they were more rigorous than others? The discussions were very lively, and the group was looking forward to assessing the practices shown in the videos I'd brought along for them to see.

The morning's euphoria quickly turned to disappointment after lunch when I showed a video and we went around the circle, listening to each person's assessment of the lesson. Just as in my seminars, opinions varied widely. The principals in the group were surprised at the divergence of views about the lesson. I suggested that the main reason for this difference was that they were never given a chance to really analyze and talk about teaching before. They expressed how nervous they were about the upcoming learning walks, but having found such disagreement on the assessments of several videoed lessons, they realized how important it was to practice looking at teaching together.

Over the course of the next two days, we observed and discussed a sample of classes in each of the six principals' schools. We spent as much time discussing the classes as we'd spent observing. Our pattern for the discussion was always the same: I'd go around the table and consider one class at a time, asking each person how they'd rated the class—low, medium, or high rigor—and their reasons why. Next, we'd discuss the different views and the evidence from their observations. With each discussion, everyone's observations grew sharper and ratings much more consistent. Something else happened, too. The more time we spent together, the more relaxed everyone became. We had several potluck dinners together, where there was much good-natured kidding and laughter. They were having fun discovering how much more engaging it is to work collaboratively rather than in isolation.

But would this be just another random professional development event for them, I wondered? Would anything come of it? We gathered at the end of the three days to assess the workshop and to discuss possible next steps. The room grew quiet, but eventually each person took a turn talking about what the time together had meant to them.

Middle school principal Nancy Soderberg, who was just a few years from retirement, led off: "This has been the most important professional experience of my career." Heads nodded all around the room.

Faye Ogilvie, a veteran elementary principal, added: "What was so important about this experience was to get a K–12 perspective. They're all our kids." But it was Tim Lino's speech that brought tears to our eyes. A former football coach, Tim heads one of the few Hawaiian language immersion schools in the state. It is an exciting school, but Tim was burning out, he told us. "I've been feeling lost in a bureaucratic maze. I didn't know what the real purpose of my job was, other than to fill out a bunch of forms for DOE. I didn't know why I was coming to school every day. But now I know. I have a purpose. I want to learn how to be a good coach for my teachers."

Previously, the only time this group had met was early in the morning over a hastily eaten breakfast every six weeks or so for announcements and other business. In their words, they were each working in an isolated castle. Now they wanted to work together, they said, to improve not just their individual castles but also their common kingdom. At the conclusion of our three days, they agreed that they would meet for a full morning every month on a rotating basis in one another's schools and begin each meeting doing a learning walk together. They would take turns presenting a "problem of practice" related to improving instruction—a real case study—to one another for discussion. Later that spring, they were invited by Pat Hamamoto to talk about their project at the state-wide education leadership conference. They titled their presentation "From Castles to Kingdom."

I began to realize that this effort might be a model for a different kind of leadership development—based on the idea of a leadership "community of practice." In a meeting with Robert Witt and Mitch D'Olier, a prominent Hawaii community leader, businessman, and philanthropist, we agreed to seek funding for this effort so that I might be able to come more often and perhaps include my colleagues from the Change Leadership Group. Robert and Mitch were excited about the project as a possible model for the preparation of future Hawaii school leaders. That summer we received a grant from the Harold K. L. Castle Foundation, which is committed to finding better ways to develop education leaders, and my colleagues at CLG agreed to take on this project as one of our initiatives.

Throughout the next year, we made several trips to Hawaii to meet with the South Kona group. Some of the principals videotaped their faculty meetings or invited a colleague to sit in as a way to get feedback on their leadership. It set a powerful example for their teachers—as did principals' discussions of what *rigor* really means, which they all conducted with their school faculties. Then, in the spring, we had a conference for teacher leaders from each of their schools. Our idea was to foster the development of communities of practice within each school as a way for teachers to come together to talk about what good teaching is and how they might improve. The response was enthusiastic, and groups formed in each school to talk about curricula, and to visit and even videotape one another's classes.

Art Souza now wanted to involve another group of his K–12 principals in North Kona, and there were expressions of interest from other areas of Hawaii as well. Robert and Mitch agreed to help us think about how to expand the effort. We received one grant from the Kamehameha Foundation, which sponsors a network of schools for Hawaiian native children, and a second grant from the Castle Foundation, and we were able to add three additional cohorts of K–12 principals and to recruit and train a "Hawaii Faculty," who could eventually replace the CLG faculty on the project. Two and a half years later, as I write this, all four cohorts are well established, and we have three Hawaii faculty whom we work with here at Harvard and go onsite with to do learning walks or conduct discussions about developing more effective, systemic strategies for improving teaching and learning.

Sandra Taosaka is a woman whose job title is School Renewal Specialist. She has worked with the six principals in South Kona and attended their meetings for years and so has a unique perspective on their work:

> Our meetings have changed a great deal. Before becoming a community of practice, our meetings focused primarily on operational items. We could all physically be there, but not 'be there.' Now, our meeting agendas are focused on improving our leadership practice. Our focus and commitment are quite different now. . . . People would describe teachers as sticking to the four walls of their own classroom and not wanting to share with others. The same goes for schools and principals. Not anymore in South Kona. Principals attend other school openings to hear their colleagues' opening message; principals share PowerPoint presentations they create for their openings; principals welcome others to attend their faculty meetings. Teachers notice the changed relationship among the principals, and they like what they see and how it's affected the practices at their schools. They know that when we talk about a community of practice, it's not just talk. Teachers see it in action!

For a principal's perspective on how being in a community of practice has transformed the work within their schools, I interviewed Faye Ogilvie, an elementary school principal, and this is what she told me:

> My thinking has definitely changed since we've started working together and it continues to evolve. . . . When we started these conversations, I realized that just because teachers were using research-based strategies and providing a quality learning environment, they weren't necessarily engaging students in using their minds well. By engaging teachers in conversations about rigor, we prompted them to reflect on their own practices and to make gradual changes to instruction that focused on student thinking rather than right answer responses. It seems that when we start talking about the changing needs and

demands for our children and *their* future, and when I challenge teachers to look ahead fifteen to twenty years and consider what life will be like for our elementary school students, some who at present are only 5 years old, teachers develop a different contextual understanding of purpose and responsibility. Teaching is about providing students not with a textbook curriculum but with a *thinking* curriculum that will serve them well into adulthood in a world that may be quite different from the one we live in today.

And *yes,* as a result of our work together [with other principals], I've noticed changes in how I'm leading my school. I look at education and leadership differently. I'm much more intentional and purposeful—and I realize that more than anything, as a principal, I need to develop deep capacities to engage my school staff in continuous improvement, and to do so, I must ensure that my teachers understand the context and sense the urgency to make things happen now.

I asked Art Souza, the area superintendent, how working more collaboratively has influenced both his own work and that of the principals, and he said: "We lead differently and our individual commitments to personal and professional improvement and accountability are greater than at any other time in our careers as educators."

New Questions

When I next return to Hawaii, it will be for a very different set of conversations—this time, with state legislators as well as philanthropists. There is a growing demand to extend the project all around the state. Now the questions are: How can we "scale up" the project to serve a substantially larger group, and what can we learn in this project that might lead to very different ways of preparing our future leaders in education?

There are, of course, other essential questions to be explored about this project, the most important of which is: Does this approach actually improve student learning? To address this key question, the project has hired experienced external evaluators. Indeed, the evaluation team includes individuals who have had extensive experience assessing the education initiatives of the Bill & Melinda Gates Foundation and who thus will know what to look for. (Their initial report should be posted on the Change Leadership Group's website by the summer of 2008.)[13]

If the data are positive, and early indications suggest that this is the case, then the challenge for policymakers will be whether they are willing to fund a different and more expensive system of training and professional development for teachers, as well as leaders. This is a question that will—indeed must—be considered in every state legislature and in Congress. If we want to see dramatically better results from our schools, then we are going to have to make significant additional investments in both initial and ongoing training for our educators. In most other countries, teachers have much more time in their day to work collaboratively. Japanese teachers, for example, typically spend only about half of their day teaching. Much of the rest of the time is taken up with colleagues in planning and perfecting lessons, in what is called the "lesson study" process.[14] Historically, most American communities have been very reluctant to pay teachers and administrators to meet without students, and for some good reasons. For one thing, local boards of education have rarely seen evidence of increased student learning simply from giving educators more time to talk to one another. To get and keep additional resources, the educators will have to be accountable for how they use their additional professional development time and produce demonstrable results—as their counterparts in Japan have done.

We know that isolation is the enemy of improvement in education—and in all other professions—and that working more collaboratively to improve teaching and learning is really *the only way* educators are likely to get significantly better results. We also know that educators must be accountable for how they use their time and be able to show that students are learning more—including more of the content that really matters. What we don't yet know is whether American taxpayers and our government care enough about the future to pay educators a more professional wage and to provide them with the working conditions they need to succeed: smaller classes, teachers organized into teams with shared responsibility for groups of students, more effective coaching for continuous improvement, better and more frequent local assessments of students' progress, and more time to work and learn with colleagues. We also don't yet know whether schools of education and the education profession and its unions, even with the right incentives, are willing to rise to the new challenge and give up old behaviors and beliefs. However, based on my conversations with young people coming into the profession, as well as my experience with courageous veterans with whom I have had the pleasure of working, I think there is much reason for hope.

Summing Up

In the first chapter, we learned that there are a critical set of core competencies for individual success in the New World of Work, and that they are the same skills needed for success in college, as well as for informed and active citizenship. In the second chapter, I discussed the fact that these skills aren't being taught even in our best schools. Increasingly, what's being taught instead is preparation for tests. In the third chapter, we explored the nature of these tests, discovered why they have been dumbed down, and considered what an assessment and accountability system that focused more on the Seven Survival Skills might look like. And, now, in the present chapter, we've taken a hard look at how teachers and school administrators are being prepared for their profession, how they actually work in schools, and why their training and daily experience severely limit their ability to improve teaching and learning. We have also learned about some new ways teachers and administrators might work together for continuous improvement.

Focusing teaching and learning on the new survival skills, having better tests that assess the skills that matter most, and reinventing how we prepare educators, as well as how they work together, are all necessary if we are serious about eliminating the global achievement gap. Necessary, but not sufficient. There is one more critical piece of the puzzle—one more big question: How do we motivate today's students and tomorrow's workers to want to work hard and to achieve excellence?

CHAPTER 5

Motivating
Today's Students—and
Tomorrow's Workers

WHAT DOES IT take to bring out the best in young people today, both in school and in the workplace? Although business leaders and educators rarely agree on anything, they have one unexplored concern in common: Both groups are worried about the decline of the work ethic among young Americans. Apprehension about young people's lack of work ethic was a frequent theme in many of the interviews I conducted with business leaders. It has also been the subject of several *Wall Street Journal* articles in the last year, which decried the hunger for praise and impatience for promotions that the authors of these articles claim are far more prevalent among 20-somethings today than was the case in previous generations.[1] Similarly, one of the biggest stresses of the educators I talk to is how to motivate their students to do the required work and memorize the material they need to know to pass the state tests.

Here are some of the most frequent kinds of comments I hear from middle and high school teachers:

"Kids today don't read, and they don't do homework. I cover all the content standards in class, but if they don't read the textbook, they'll inevitably do poorly on the tests."

"They don't proofread their papers. It's as though they think spell-check will catch all the errors. They just don't seem to care very much about their work."

"Young people today have no respect for authority. They talk to each other in class, as though the teacher wasn't even there. And if they get into trouble, their parents are all over me with phone calls and e-mails—and even complaints to the school board. The problem with these kids is that many of them are growing up kind of spoiled. They have everything they could ever want or need—except some adult discipline in their lives."

Echoing the concerns of many educators whom I've interviewed, Mark Maddox, human resources manager at Unilever Foods, is very worried about people coming into the workforce today. "There's a failure of work ethic in the younger employees," he said. "They don't want to work weekends, or long hours—they're disgruntled with putting in 110 percent. They don't see it like we used to see it."

Susan, the woman from the large retailing chain whom I highlighted in the first chapter, echoed Maddox's concern. "The work ethic is definitely not as strong as it was five years ago," she said. "There are much more job hopping and attendance issues—and parents even calling in excuses for their kids when they don't come to work!"

Annmarie Neal saw the problem of young people's lack of work ethic in terms of how they performed their actual tasks while on the job at

Cisco: "They have three web pages open at once and bounce back and forth, while chatting with all their friends. . . . It creates the appearance of a sloppy work ethic."

Clay Parker from BOC Edwards is worried about the competition this younger generation will face, but he sees young Americans' poor work ethic as resulting from the quality of teaching. "Most of my travels are in Asia where people are incredibly dedicated and hard-working. The poor work ethic in the U.S. is one of my biggest concerns about the future. And I think it starts in schools. My wife and I have seen that there's a tendency of some teachers to accept mediocrity, a low level of performance from students."

John Abele, recently retired chairman and co-founder of Boston Scientific Corporation, an international $6 billion company that has pioneered new approaches to less invasive medicine, told me in a recent conversation that "the work ethic issue in this country is one of the greatest concerns of corporate leaders today."

While these views represent the majority of the educators and executives whom I interviewed, I did speak with a number of individuals who disagree that there is a work ethic problem among young people today. Ellen Kumata, the managing partner at Cambria Associates, said, "The people making up the new workforce are quite different from more senior employees. They don't have less of a work ethic. They have a *different* work ethic." Colonel Rob Gordon, recently retired from the Army and currently serving as senior vice president for Civic Leadership at CityYear (a national youth service nonprofit organization), shared Kumata's view. "The work ethic issue is way over-blown," he asserted.

Some educators I've interviewed agree with Kumata and Gordon. Rob Fried, a former teacher and school principal, is a keen observer of schools and author of three books on schooling in America. In his most recent book, he describes how school is a kind of "game" for many students who are bored in classes and so give the adults only the minimum required to get a good grade, while craving opportunities to do more intellectually challenging or creative work.[2] Denis Littky, co-founder and co-director of The Big Picture Company, which sponsors a national network of very successful high schools that serve mostly at-risk students, is adamant about the importance of what he calls "interest-based learning." "These kids can do amazing things when you build the learning around what interests them," he explained. We'll see how this philosophy plays out in classrooms in the next chapter.

So, are today's students—and tomorrow's workers—less motivated or just motivated in ways that may be unique to their generation? Both my classroom experiences and my discussions with many young people and the adults who work with them have convinced me that the 20-somethings (and younger) are differently motivated today—very differently motivated. And bringing out the best in young adults—motivating them to be productive and to aspire to excellence in school and at work and in their communities—will require both an understanding of these differences as well as new kinds of relationships between the younger generation and the adults in their lives.

Growing Up Digital

To better understand how young people today are differently motivated, we need to see that they're growing up in an environment that is radically different from previous generations. In the simplest terms, they are coming of age while tethered to the Internet, as well as to a host of instant communication devices that were unimaginable twenty years ago. The Net Generation, as they are often called, is "growing up digital"—a phrase that forms the title of an influential article by John Seely Brown.[3]

One of the first (and most astute) observers of the impact of new technologies on this younger generation, Brown is perhaps best known as an interpreter of change and innovation to the corporate world, having served as Xerox's chief scientist and director of its Palo Alto Research Center for more than twenty years. He's written several books and articles on corporate strategy, but what I have found especially interesting in his writing and our conversations are his thoughts on growing up in the digital age. Brown's view is that the Internet will have as transformative an effect on how future generations learn, work, and play as the introduction of electricity had on daily life in the nineteenth century. He argues that we're just beginning to see the full effect of the World Wide Web and other technologies on our lives— and most especially on the lives of the young people who've grown up with new and radically different communication, information, and creativity tools.

In a just-released book, *Me, MySpace, and I: Parenting the Net Generation,* Larry Rosen cites some stunning data that show just how pervasive the use of these new technologies is among the Net Generation today. According to Rosen's research:

- 87 percent of teens are online, increasing from 60 percent of 12-year-olds to 82 percent of 13-year-olds and 94 percent of 16- and 17-year-olds.

- Teens are online an average of five days a week, two to three hours a day.

- 67 percent of teens and 40 percent of preteens own a cell phone, spending an average of an hour per day talking. Two-thirds of tweens and teens who own or have a cell phone send text messages daily.

- 87 percent of 8- to 17-year-olds play videogames, the vast majority of them on a daily basis.

- 75 percent of online teens use instant messaging (IM), chatting with an average of thirty-five people per week, for three hours total.

- 75 percent of adolescents spend two to three hours per day downloading or listening to music online.

- 80 percent of 12- to 17-year-olds use MySpace weekly.[4]

While there is still a digital divide between different races and ethnic groups in terms of Internet access, a recent Kaiser Family Foundation study found that it is closing rapidly. "Over the past five years there has been an increase of nearly 40 percentage points in home access among children whose parents have a high school education or less (from 29% to 68%), compared to an increase of just under 20 percentage points among those whose parents have a college or graduate degree (from 63% to 82%)."[5]

Judging from the articles in *Educating the Net Generation,* an online book edited by Diana and James Oblinger, it would seem that use of computers both accelerates and changes once young people enter college. Teens do use computers for research and other schoolwork, but their primary use of their computers is for entertainment—in effect, as a more engaging and interactive form of TV. In college, however, the computer becomes more important as a tool for learning and communication, as we see in this vignette:

> A junior at the university, Eric wakes up and peers at his PC to see how many instant messages (IMs) arrived while he slept. Several attempts to reach him are visible on the screen, along with various postings to the blog he's been following. After a quick trip to the shower, he pulls up an eclectic mix of news, weather, and sports on the home page he cus-

tomized using Yahoo. He then logs on to his campus account. A reminder pops up indicating that there will be a quiz in sociology today; another reminder lets him know that a lab report needs to be e-mailed to his chemistry professor by midnight. After a few quick IMs with friends he pulls up a wiki to review progress a teammate has made on a project they're doing for their computer science class. He downloads yesterday's chemistry lecture to his laptop; he'll review it while he sits with a group of students in the student union working on other projects. After classes are over he has to go to the library because he can't find an online resource he needs for a project. He rarely goes to the library to check out books; usually he uses Google or Wikipedia. Late that night as he's working on his term paper, he switches back and forth between the paper and the Internet-based multiplayer game he's trying to win.[6]

As many of us know if we're the parents of young adults or if we work with them, this isn't just an example of the typical routine of a "computer geek." Indeed, this stereotype is long gone. I interviewed Carie Windham, a 2005 college graduate who is now a freelance journalist, and asked her how she uses technology in her life, now that she's out of college. "Wow . . . I'm talking to you now on my laptop on Skype," she told me. "And I sleep with my laptop underneath my bed. I do that because as soon as my alarm goes off—before I brush my teeth or do anything—I'm checking CNN, people.com, my e-mail, and celebrity blogs. These are the things that get me up in the morning.

"And then, throughout my day, the Internet and that connectivity is vital. If I need directions, I go online. Same for my banking—I haven't written a check since I opened the account. If I need a word, I'm going to go to Google or dictionary.com. All my basic tasks are influenced by the web. I use iTunes all the time—and I'm hooked on watching TV online. I can watch it when I want, with or without commercials, and pause it when I want. I listen to a lot of podcasts—NPR and things like that. I also use Facebook. I look for people from high school—who's getting married, who's still talking to whom. I don't think I could live without Internet access."

Young people also use the Internet as a serious tool both for creating and for disseminating their artistic work. Carie's 18-year-old brother is a case in point. "He is in a band," Carie told me. "And it's amazing to me that instead of thinking 'we're going to go play some shows and we're going to get picked up by a record executive,' he and his friends go out to our barn and they record their own mp3s and put them up on their band's MySpace page, where people download them. He totally understands that the Internet is this great platform for getting noticed. And he promotes all his shows and sells tickets online."

Fueled in large measure by the Net Generation's use of the Internet, the growth of some of their favorite websites has been exponential. MySpace, for example, first came online in 2003. By August 2006, it had grown to 100 million users. One year later, there were over 200 million, and 230,000 new accounts were being established every day.[7] Because the vast majority of users are adolescents, Larry Rosen refers to young people growing up today as the "MySpace Generation." The growth of YouTube, which debuted on the Internet in 2005, has been even more spectacular. By January 2007, the site boasted 150 million visitors a month, a nine-fold increase from one year prior.[8] And, according to Nielsen's 2006 NetRatings Report, visitors between 12 and 17 years of age are nearly 1.5 times more likely than the average web user to go to YouTube.[9]

Researchers are just beginning to explore the impact of the use of technology on how today's young people work and learn, but certain patterns are already quite clear. Young people who have grown up using the web relate to the world and to one another in ways that are very different from those of their parents' generation.

Multitasking and Constantly Connected

In 2001, John Seely Brown decided that he would begin to hire 15-year-olds to join him and his colleagues as researchers at the Xerox lab to better understand the impact of media and technology on young people. He invited them to design their ideal work and learning spaces and studied what they created and how they worked. The first thing he observed is how young people multitask and are constantly connected. They rarely—if ever—did just one thing at a time. Moving back and forth among multiple open web pages while listening to music and talking on their cell phones or responding to friends' instant messages was clearly the common culture of young people today and the typical way they interact with the world around them.

Former Microsoft executive Linda Stone, whom I first met some years ago when I gave a talk on the Microsoft campus, sees multitasking or what she calls "continuous partial attention" as the way many of us work today, often out of necessity. But it also captures how young people in their tweens to 20s want—or even need—to relate to the world:

> Continuous partial attention describes how many of us use our attention today. . . . To pay continuous partial attention is to pay partial attention—CONTINUOUSLY. It is motivated by a desire to be a LIVE node on the network. Another way of saying this is that we want to connect and be connected. We want to effectively scan for opportunity and optimize for the best opportunities, activities, and contacts, in any given moment. To be busy, to be connected, is to be alive, to be recognized, and to matter.[10]

The connections that young people long for today are not just with the information and games that the Internet provides. They also crave a constant connection to others. Young people are growing up today with an astounding number of tools for communicating with friends and making new ones. As we've seen, they use all of them every day, often in nuanced ways. In *Educating the Net Generation,* Diana and James Oblinger effectively capture this hunger to connect through an ever-expanding variety of technologies:

> Prolific communicators, they gravitate toward activities that promote and reinforce social interaction—whether IMing old friends, teaming up in an Internet game, posting Web diaries (blogging), or forwarding joke e-mails. The Net Gen displays a striking openness to diversity, differences, and sharing; they are at ease meeting strangers on the Net. Many of their exchanges on the Internet are emotionally open, sharing very personal information about themselves. The Net Gen has developed a mechanism of inclusiveness that does not necessarily involve personally knowing someone admitted to their group. Being a friend of a friend is acceptable. They seek to interact with others, whether in their personal lives, their online presence, or in class. . . . Although technology can't change one's personality, introverts, for example, use the Internet as a tool to reach out. These social connections through e-mail might not have happened before. Extroverts can make their circle of friends even larger."[11]

Explaining the popularity of MySpace, Rosen writes, "Somehow, in a few short years, MySpace has become an American teen hangout. Not unlike Arnold's Drive-In of *Happy Days* fame, where Richie and Fonz spent their afternoons, MySpace is the ultimate mall where teens can meet and chat. . . . They post their thoughts in bulletins, comment on other people's bulletins and journals, instant message, email, blog, and, most importantly, collect friends."[12] Rosen interviewed Anastasia Goodstein, author of *Totally Wired: What Teens and Tweens Are Really Doing*

Online, who told him that young people's use of the Internet is "less about using technology to transact—find a plane ticket, look up a movie time, send an e-mail—and more about using technology to interact."[13]

Instant Gratification and the Speed of Light

Accustomed to broadband Internet speeds that allow for .005-second Google searches, young people thrive in a world of ever-changing images, constant updates, and immediate access to whatever information they may want. They take as a given instant messages to and from friends, who are also always available by cell phone. In dozens of interviews I've done with 20-somethings about the impact of new technologies on their lives, their first comments are almost always about how they've become captivated by what they, themselves, call "instant gratification." I recently conducted a focus group with students at a New England college, where one young man said: "It's made us less patient, more demanding. We don't want to have to wait for anything." Others agreed, and a young woman described how a friend of hers had become upset because she hadn't replied until the following morning to her friend's cell phone call from the night before. "There was no crisis or even anything special that she wanted to talk about—she was just upset that she couldn't get in touch with me when she wanted to. She couldn't understand that I just didn't feel like talking." And Carie Windham confessed, "When I go to my grandparents' house and have to use their dial-up Internet, I feel so disconnected from the world."

The authors of *Educating the Net Generation* provide a related insight: "Whether it is the immediacy with which a response is expected or the speed at which they are used to receiving information, the Net Gen is fast. They have fast response times, whether playing a game or responding to an IM."[14]

New Learning Styles

The desire to multitask and be constantly connected to the net and to friends as well as the hunger for immediate results influence how young people today interact with the world—whether in school or at work or at home or while traveling—and must be taken into account by both educators and employers. However, the ways in which young people are different today as learners may be the most fundamental change we need to understand as we consider how to close the global achievement gap. The use of the Internet and other digital technology has transformed both *what* young people learn today and *how* they learn.

Learning Through Multimedia and Connection to Others

Young adults who've grown up on the net are habituated to multimedia learning experiences, as opposed to merely interacting with text. According to the Oblingers, "Researchers report Net Gen students will refuse to read large amounts of text, whether it involves a long reading assignment or lengthy instructions. In a study that altered instructions from a text-based step-by-step approach to one that used a graphic layout, refusals to do the assignment dropped and post-test scores increased."[15] My interviews with students, as well as with their high school and college teachers, confirm that students are increasingly impatient with the lecture style of learning and the reliance on textbooks for information and crave more class discussions.

The Net Generation much prefers doing research on the Internet rather than in stacks of library books—in part, because of the very different experience it offers. "Prose is supplemented by song. Photographs are accompanied by video. Issues are even turned into online polls and discussions. For the Net Gen, nearly every part of life is presented in multimedia format," writes Carie Windham. "To keep our attention in the classroom, a similar approach is needed. Faculty must toss aside the dying notion that a lecture and subsequent reading assignment are enough to teach the lesson. Instead, the Net Generation responds to a variety of media, such as television, audio, animation, and text."[16]

Once they're on the Internet looking for information, Net Gen students develop a vital proficiency in what John Seely Brown calls "information navigation." According to Brown, "The real literacy of tomorrow entails the ability to be your own personal reference librarian—to know how to navigate through confusing, complex information spaces and feel comfortable doing so. 'Navigation' may well be the main form of literacy for the 21st century."[17]

And as UCLA's Jason Frand observes, today's college students want to be connected to others, as well as to different kinds of information sources, while they learn: "Students with an information-age mindset expect education to emphasize the learning process more than a canon of knowledge. They want to be part of learning communities, with hubs and spokes of learners, rejecting the broadcast paradigm of television (or the note-taker in the lecture hall.)"[18]

Learning as Discovery

The experience of learning or conducting research on the web is radically different from that of classroom learning or library research. As we're all now aware, on the Internet you type a search string, the results of which show you hundreds or thousands of potential information sources—not just text but also video, audio, and graphics. You click on links that, in turn, have other links you can follow. You may find the name of a person or book or issue that you want to learn more about, and so you conduct a new search, which leads you to a new treasure trove of information and images, with countless additional links. It is an active, dynamic, nonlinear, discovery-based process—more like traveling along a spider web than moving in a straight line from point A to point B. As John Seely Brown writes: "Most of us experienced formal learning in an authority-based, lecture-oriented school. Now, with incredible amounts of information available through the web, we find a 'new' kind of learning assuming pre-eminence—learning that's discovery based. We are constantly discovering new things as we browse through the emergent digital 'libraries.' Indeed, web surfing fuses learning and entertainment, creating 'infotainment.'"[19] Confirming Brown's observation, one young woman in the focus group I mentioned earlier confessed that she Googles topics for fun: "There's not a day that goes by that I don't Google something—anything. It's not even just when I have to Google something for school. I Google everything. If I'm bored, I'll Google something about my life."

John Beck and Mitchell Wade have studied the "gamers"—as the young people who play videogames are called. In their book *The Kids Are Alright,* they report that gamers (who, according to their research, represent 92 percent of the teenage population), "learn differently. Their game experience . . . emphasizes independent problem solving and the rapid acquisition of technical skills, as opposed to sustained attention to the subtleties of Shakespeare or calculus."[20] James Paul Gee has also studied gamers, and in *What Video Games Have to Teach Us About Learning and Literacy,* he writes that "video games make players think like scientists. Game play is built on a cycle of 'hypothesize, probe the world, get a reaction, reflect on the results, reprobe to get better results,' a cycle typical of experimental science."[21]

When PJ Blankenhorn directed the Boston Center for Adult Education, she was discussing proposals for new courses with a young staff member. "A few people have asked for a class on how to use PDAs," PJ said. "What do you think?" The staff person, a young woman in her 20s, stared at my wife in astonishment, finally saying, "Why would anyone need to take a *course* to learn that?"

John Seely Brown's observations help us to make sense of this inter-action. "My generation tends not to want to try things unless or until we already know how to use them," he writes. "If we don't know how to use some appliance or software, our instinct is to reach for a manual or take a course or call up an expert. Believe me, hand a manual or sug-gest a course to 15-year-olds and they think you're a dinosaur. They want to turn the thing on, get in there, muck around, and see what works. Today's kids get on the Web and link, lurk, and watch how other people are doing things, then try it for themselves."[22]

Learning by Creating

New developments on the web are giving young people a set of experi-ences that create a hunger for more than merely learning through dis-covery. Web 2.0—as it is often called to differentiate web use today from early Internet use, which was primarily as a source of information—provides an extraordinary number of opportunities to exercise one's passion to create. Today, anyone who has even a rudimentary under-standing of how the Internet works can fashion new web content that will be seen by all users.

Whether it's creating your own web page on MySpace or Facebook or uploading your band's music or sharing your photo album or post-ing a video you just shot with your cell phone on YouTube or con-tributing to a Wikipedia entry or writing a blog about what you think or what you've experienced or reviewing a movie, an album, a product, a service, or a restaurant, web 2.0 is a vast and ever-expanding palate for personal creativity and self-expression—especially for young people growing up today. According to Rosen's research, the most common ac-tivity of MySpace users involves posting new photographs and videos on their personal web pages. An astonishing 88 percent of MySpace users have added photo or video content to their pages.[23]

Cautions

None of what I have described above is necessarily meant to suggest that these developments in how young people today interact with the world and learn are all positive. For every upside, there is an equally important caution or concern. Let's review some of the concerns that have been raised regarding the trends noted above:

- *Multitasking and Constantly Connected.* While multitasking may be a useful skill and a pleasant diversion while performing routine tasks, the practice appears to come at a cost. According to Russell Poldrack, an associate professor of psychology at the University of California at Los Angeles, who co-authored a study that examined multitasking and brain activity: "Multitaskers may not be building the same knowledge that they would be if they were focusing. While multitasking makes them [college students] feel like they are being more efficient, research suggests that there's very little you can do that involves multitasking that you can be as good at when you're not multitasking."[24] Linda Stone agrees: "Like so many things, in small doses, continuous partial attention can be a very functional behavior. However, in large doses, it contributes to a stressful lifestyle, to operating in crisis management mode, and to a compromised ability to reflect, to make decisions, and to think creatively. In a 24/7, always-on world, continuous partial attention used as our dominant attention mode contributes to a feeling of overwhelm, over-stimulation and to a sense of being unfulfilled. We are so accessible, we're inaccessible."[25] Indeed, young people's connectedness through sites like MySpace and Facebook can sometimes be used in ways that are deeply hurtful. Cyberbullying has become a growing concern for school administrators. Adult cyberpredators are another concern. As I talked to young people who have collected hundreds of new friends electronically through Facebook or MySpace, I wondered to what extent they differentiate between an electronic friend, whom they have never met and who may pass out of their lives in a nanosecond, and an in-person friend, with whom one builds trust and shares experiences over time.

- *Instant Gratification and the Speed of Light.* You'll recall the young man I highlighted earlier in this chapter who observed that use of fast technologies has "made us less patient, more demanding. We don't want to have to wait for anything." Later during the same focus-group session, several students expressed concerns about how overreliance on cell phones and instant messaging may be eroding social skills. "People don't talk as much face-to-face," one young woman said. Another added: "You know, when you go to someone's house for dinner with their family, you have to know how to talk to them, to interact. I worry that we may be losing our ability to relate to people who are different than we are."

- *Learning Through Multimedia and Connection to Others.* The Oblingers, quoted earlier in this chapter, have noted young people's impatience with text-based learning. Tracy Mitrano, who works in the Office of Information Technologies at Cornell University, worries about the ways in which "this generation has been entertained to death." And Susan Metros, who holds a similar position at the

University of Southern California and is also a professor in visual communication, told me that college students today "are media-stimulated, but not necessarily media-literate." These researchers are concerned that young people may be avoiding book learning because they've been raised on multimedia that is more entertaining. Metros went on to point out that being a consumer of multimedia doesn't necessarily mean that one has developed the ability to really understand the media and think critically about what one is experiencing. Young peoples' preference for learning with peers may also become problematic when they need to work on something alone—such as a research paper—for long periods of time in order to get the best result.

- *Learning as Discovery.* This style of learning is much more engaging than other ways of learning, and there is a great deal of research showing that it leads to a deeper understanding of basic concepts in math and science when compared to simple rote memorization.[26] However, not everything can be learned through discovery. We don't "discover" the times tables, for example. We have to memorize them. And while we will better understand the concept of an ecosystem through observation and experimentation, we must first know something about basic processes such as photosynthesis. Similarly, some basic knowledge in geography and history, essential for informed citizenship, can be gained only through memorization. Finally, the desire to constantly "do" and interact often comes at the expense of contemplation and reflection—essential aspects of both learning and growth.

- *Learning by Creating.* Quality is also a question in these times, when anyone can throw anything up on the Internet. Flooded with an ever-expanding torrent of "creative" work coming at them from thousands of websites, how do young people learn to discern the difference between impulsive forms of self-expression versus works of art that are the product of training and discipline? This is an aspect of what Metros meant by being "media-literate." And Carie Windham worries about the impact of all of the creative shortcuts young people take when they IM each other. "I've seen some of my brother's messages to his friends, and I have absolutely no clue what he's writing— which is maybe the point anyway. But he doesn't know how to spell. When I try to tell him that's not the way the word is spelled, he just says, 'Well, it is in IM.' I was an English major, and I worry that he'll never know how to use the language correctly."

Here is a list of some popular IM terms:[27]

Teen-favored acronyms	
A/S/L	Age, sex, location
BF/GF	Boyfriend, girlfriend
BRB	Be right back
CD9	Code 9, means parents are around
GNOC	Get naked on cam (Webcam)
G2G	Got to go
IDK	I don't know
(L)MIRL	(Let's) meet in real life
LOL	Laugh out loud
MorF	Male or female
MOS	Mom over shoulder
NIFOC	Naked in front of computer
Noob	Often an insult to somebody who doesn't know much about something
NMU	Not much, you?
P911	Parent emergency
PAW	Parents are watching
PIR	Parent in room
POS	Parent over shoulder
PRON	Porn
PRW	Parents are watching
S2R	Send to receive (pictures)
TDTM	Talk dirty to me
Warez	Pirated software
W/E	Whatever

Researchers do not agree on the long-term consequences of these trends—especially about the impact of the increasing amount of time tweens and teens spend playing Internet games. John Seely Brown sees gamers as having more than just the skills most needed by corporations today. He told me that they have what he calls the "critical dispositions" that are essential for thriving in a highly competitive world of constant change. "First, the gamer disposition is incredibly bottom-line-oriented. These kids want to be measured. Second, there's a mantra among the gamers: If I ain't learning, it ain't fun. Third, they understand the power of a diverse team. Fourth, gamers thrive on change—they embrace it and they generate it. Finally, gamers marinate on the edge. They are constantly searching for better ways to play the game, even after having reached mastery level in the game."

Beck and Wade come to similar conclusions in their book *The Kids Are Alright,* but they also cite research suggesting that we ought to be concerned about the amount of violence in videogames: "The Harvard Center for Risk Analysis found that of fifty-five games awarded an E rating (where E stands for 'everyone,' the G rating of the game industry), thirty-five contained intentional acts of violence. These violent acts ranged from 1.5 percent of total game play in a hockey game to 91 percent of the time in an action game. Twenty-seven percent of the games showed people dying from some form of violence."[28] And Tracy Mitrano, who is both an academic and a parent, worries that habituation to gaming will require schools to adapt in fundamental ways, and that they may not be able to meet this new challenge: "If we don't figure out how to deliver more learning in a game format, we'll lose a lot of the boys. . . . My 11-year-old spends every minute of his free time online playing a game with someone in South Africa."

There are some early indications that Internet gaming may have even darker consequences for some. Indeed, the "web obsession" in South Korea illustrates the extent to which this gaming may be putting the

lives of an entire generation at risk. Ninety percent of Korean house-
holds have high-speed Internet access, and for many young people
there, the web is the only place to be. But a recent article reported that
up to 30 percent of South Koreans under 18 are at risk of Internet ad-
diction: "It has become a national issue here in recent years as users
started dropping dead from exhaustion after playing online games for
days on end. . . . Dr. Jerald J. Block, a psychiatrist at Oregon Health
and Science University, estimates that up to nine million Americans may
be at risk for the disorder, which he calls pathological computer use."[29]

Interactive Producers
or Isolated Consumers?

I believe that younger generations have enormous potential either to become lost in an endless web of fantasy and entertainment or to use their
skills with these new technologies to make significant contributions to
our society as learners, workers, and citizens. What is needed to tip the
balance to the positive is an older generation that better understands
what drives the younger generation and has learned how best to harness
and focus its energies.

Growing up in this era of remarkable abundance (for many, at least)
and with a vast array of new toys at their fingertips, young people want
lives that are different from the ones they see their parents living.
Whether they are hardcore gamers or just Googlers off in MySpace,
whether at school or in the workplace, young people hunger for a more
creative and interactive relationship with the world. The older they get,
the more they disdain TV in favor of the net, because it is a two-way
medium. There is much that they are willing to put up with in school
or the workplace—not all the conditions I've outlined above have to be
in place for them to be engaged. But one thing does, I believe: They
have to be interactive producers, not isolated consumers. They want to
neither passively consume information at school nor just go through

the motions at work—which is why many employers worry about their apparent lack of work ethic. They long to interact—with the net, with ideas and problems that need solving, with friends and colleagues—and even with older adults—but in new ways, as we'll see. Wherever they are, they long to learn and to create in a collaborative, collegial environment.

John Seely Brown described this fundamental difference between the Net Generation and their parents in this way: "The older generation defined itself by what they wear and own; this generation defines itself by what it creates and co-creates with others, and others build on." Louisa Brown, a recent Penn grad (no relation to John Seely Brown), put it slightly differently when she told me that "what matters most to my generation isn't money or conventional success—it's our reputation, what we're known for, what we've contributed." Carie Windham echoed this idea: "We want to find the occupation that fulfills us—we don't want to work just for money. We want to make a difference." Andrew Bruck, currently enrolled in law school at Stanford, describes his former Princeton classmates as "kids walking around with briefcases—working 24 hrs a day, but for different things. They dream of founding a start-up or working on climate change or global health or political reform." Ben McNeely, who graduated from North Carolina State in 2005 and now works as a journalist, told me: "We have a different work ethic—we're not out to secure the bottom line for the corporation. From their perspective, my job is to improve the bottom line. My job, as I see it, is to inform my community first and foremost."

If the members of this generation are to be truly engaged as students, workers, and citizens, they must be given new challenges at school and in the workplace, as well as have different kinds of relationships with the authorities in their lives. Henry David Thoreau wrote, "If you have built castles in the air, your work need not be lost; that is where they should be. Now put the foundations under them." The Net Generation needs a new kind of support transitioning from the cyber world to the real world and constructing a lasting foundation for its dreams. As Tracy Mitrano observed, "If we want to tap into what's creative and exciting with this generation, we have to find a way of translating from entertainment into work."

Producers at School

It isn't just the need to teach the Seven Survival Skills that compels us to rethink much of our instructional methods and curricula. Motivating young people to do their best in school today requires teachers to rethink what and how they teach as well. Susan Metros at the University of Southern California sees clearly what high school teachers must do differently. "We knock creativity out of kids, with our focus on memorization, teaching to the test, and making them learn things that they don't have to. Because of the web, they don't have to memorize all of what we used to memorize. . . . Also, we need to teach subjects in a broader context. For example, social studies isn't just the study of war and politics. It is also about food, music, culture. We have the ability to bring all of this into classrooms now. Finally, young people need to analyze and interpret new media; they need to produce and create, and they need to understand the ethical implications of their work and the new technologies." In other words, in order for young people to respect learning and school, we need to think more carefully about what we're asking them to learn—to ensure that schoolwork is not busywork or make-work but real, adult work that requires both analysis and creativity.

In interviews and in numerous focus groups I've conducted over the last five years, I've asked young people to share with me the advice they would give to high school educators about how to make school a more productive, engaging experience. Taken together, their responses create a clear mandate for change—and one that is consistent with what Metros told me.

Matt Kulick, a 2007 Cornell graduate who now works at Google, observed the following: "School is boring for kids today because it hasn't caught up with what kids can do outside of school. I see that young people are apathetic because of a gap between what exists in the real world—what kids can pursue outside of school—versus what they are made to do in school." Again, for Kulick, a teacher's passion can be a bridge across this divide. "I loved the impassioned teachers," he told me. "I had a history teacher who challenged me by the questions he asked. He asked college-level questions, not just ones about names and dates, and he made you feel proud when you got them right. He made us write lots of essays as well." Unfortunately, as we saw in Chapter 2, this teacher is one of the few exceptions that prove the rule.

Carie Windham talked about how much anxiety had dominated her earlier school experience. "Since middle school, I've had the fear that if I wasn't at the front of the pack, I'd end up with a horrible job—the fear that I had to be Number One or I wouldn't amount to anything. And it didn't come from my parents. Looking back on school, I was always preparing and competing for the next step. I wondered if it would ever stop. I can't think of any classroom that did anything but prepare me for tests. I did well because I knew how to take tests—but now I can't recall a thing.

"It's not about memorizing, but rather critical thinking through authentic learning," Windham continued, as she contrasted the work she was asked to do in college versus high school. "High school teachers need to have kids do real research and experiments. Instead of being receivers of knowledge, they need to be participants. Let them be a scientist, a historian. Wouldn't it be great to see more interaction and engagement? More chances to work in a team and tackle a problem for which there's no easy solution?"

Ben McNeely was similarly concerned about the negative impact of testing on teaching and learning in schools now. "Teachers aren't allowed to engage kids in learning. In North Carolina, because of pressures for more testing, teachers have to produce higher scores and students who can pass standardized tests—not learners. . . . But if you tap into kids' interests, they're very motivated."

Having an opportunity to pursue a real interest made all the difference for Stanford law student Andrew Bruck. He contrasted his high school classroom learning with his learning outside the classroom, which he found far more exciting and engaging. "I learned the most in my extracurricular activities," he said. "I learned about how organizations work by editing my school paper, and I learned more about editing and writing there than I did in my English classes. It was more exciting to have projects to work on than a curriculum I had to follow. We could use our own creativity to find things of interest to us."

The pattern seems to be still holding true for Bruck in law school, where, for the last year, his passion has been focused on founding and growing a new organization, called Building a Better Legal Profession. The organization researches data on law firms' hiring of minorities, women, and gays, as well as firms' percentage of pro bono work, and then compares and grades them on these criteria as a way to give law school graduates better choices—and to pressure firms to change. The fledgling organization has already received very positive coverage in both the *Wall Street Journal* and the *New York Times*.

Henry Rutgers, one of America's founding fathers for whom Rutgers University is named, is alleged to have advised: "Don't let your studies interfere with your education." Judging from the stories related above, some in this generation are, indeed, learning the Seven Survival Skills—but more often in spite of their high school classes than because of them.

As I suggested in the first chapter, education ministries in other countries are beginning to understand the importance of bringing thinking and creativity back into the classroom—or, in some cases, into the classroom for the first time. John Seely Brown chairs the International Advisory Board for the Ministry of Education in Singapore. He believes that the Singapore educators are on the right track toward reinventing their education system for the twenty-first century. "Their new mantra is 'teach less, learn more,'" Brown told me. "Schools need to focus more on projects and the inquiry method. They need to engage students with passion."

Rethinking Teacher and Parental Authority

When I spoke with Cornell University's Tracy Mitrano, she was concerned about the need for teachers to work with students in different ways: "We truly have to reorient the concept of who a teacher is and what a teacher does: the teacher as facilitator versus information dictator. Teachers also have to model the behaviors they're trying to teach. They need to show critical thinking and problem solving. Finally, they have to really listen to what kids do in their free time and then try very hard to figure out how to get students from where they are to where they need to be."

Ben McNeely also sees the role of the teacher as needing to be different than it has been. "In high school, kids are starting to figure out who they are, their interests, and what careers may interest them. The job of a high school teacher should be to encourage kids to explore their interests and to help them make sense of the world as they explore."

In focus groups with high school students—from wealthy suburban enclaves to struggling inner-city schools—the most frequent comment from students has to do with their longing for a different kind of relationship with their teachers. "I need a teacher I can really talk to," many have said. "And not just about school things, but things going on in my life." "I want to know that a teacher cares about me," others have said. In addition, several students in my college focus groups told me that what was most important was having a teacher "who didn't talk down to you—who was someone you could relate to."

Several of the young adults I spoke with also offered advice to parents that, overall, reflects this generation's unease with "helicopter parents" who hover and constantly fret about their children's future. Andrew Bruck said that "parents need to respect the extraordinary capabilities of students. Our generation wants to do things. They don't want to be stymied by hierarchy or authority. It's important to nurture children's creativity. There's so much pressure to succeed and to go to a brand-name school. There's no need for parents to pile on the stress."

In college focus groups, young adults have mentioned that parents need to encourage their real interests and trust them to succeed. "Parents need to support children in their dreams—even if it's wanting to be an artist," one young woman said. Another agreed, saying, "Parents shouldn't worry so much about how their children are doing in school. They should find out more about what their extracurricular interests are."

Matt Kulick was also concerned that too many parents try to manage their children's future, instead of letting them explore and discover for themselves. "A lot of my friends never had a good idea of what they liked or wanted to do," he observed, "because their parents said 'you're going to be a doctor' or . . . And it doesn't help to tell your kids to do more homework or to always ask them what grade they got or to always be worrying about whether they're 'normal.'" Parents need to find out what their kids like. . . . My parents motivated me to do well—not to get A's but to give my best effort. . . . They trusted me."

Producers in the Workplace

Schools aren't the only institutions that will have to change if we are to bring out the best in the Net Generation. In order to fully engage young people coming into the workplace for the first time now, we

need to understand how they are differently motivated and to consider
the implications for employers. Describing the different work ethic of
these young people, Ellen Kumata told me that "they don't see coming
into a company as being a career experience. They don't want to climb
the corporate ladder and make more money and please the boss. And so
you can't manage them the same way—you can't just put them into a
cubicle and expect them to perform." Tracy Mitrano agreed: "You have
to make the work more interesting and allow them to work in different
ways. They are prepared to work just as much and just as hard—but
not at a desk eight hours a day."

Susan Metros's comments echoed these themes. She has observed this
generation's differences firsthand, having supervised both young people
and older adults who work at college computer help desks. Metros advises employers to really get to know the particular skills and strengths
of young people today. "They bring a lot to the table," she thinks.
"They can connect in new ways, they collaborate, they are visual learners, and they have great spatial awareness. Why put them in a room
where all they do is staple reports? Why insist on a 9-to-5 schedule
every day? They're likely to get more work done at home. Put them in
teams with traditional workers where they can learn from each other."

The longing for more meaningful work and the desire for a different
kind of relationship with adults were recurring themes among the
young people I spoke with as they told me what advice they would give
to employers. In fact, their descriptions of the ideal workplace and su-
pervisor were strikingly similar to what they wanted from schools and
teachers. In both environments, they wanted to engage as active learners and creators, and they longed for adults to be coaches and mentors.

Andrew Bruck, who has talked to law students all over the country
as he's recruited members for his nonprofit organization, observes that
"we want to feel ownership. We have a craving for an opportunity to do
something really important. People in my generation have been in a

constant state of training. Now they're excited to go *do* something. That's why we've gotten such a phenomenal response to Building a Better Legal Profession. The problem with big law firms is that you have maybe seventy attorneys on project. The younger ones will never go into a courtroom or interview a witness. But they can contribute so much more than just document review or due diligence. The more responsibility you give people, the better they produce. . . . There are more and more recent law school grads who are willing to take a lower salary in return for an opportunity for more meaningful work."

Ben McNeely described to me the difference between his former employer and his current one. "At the paper where I worked previously, the publisher would kill stories if they portrayed an advertiser in a negative light. At the paper where I work now, I have an opportunity to contribute something in a growing community. I was brought in to cover the new bio-tech research campus under construction nearby, where the Canon towel factory used to be, and to cover health care issues as well. I have support from the editor and publisher, who both have strong journalistic ethics. I like it that the editor pushes us to dig deeper."

In addition to work that's more meaningful and creative, John Seely Brown notes that this generation "craves dignity," and he sees this need as being in conflict with trends in many workplaces. "As the corporate world moves more and more to barely reachable efficiency levels, they're stripping all dignity from jobs. They say they want creative, innovative thinkers, but then they benchmark them for speed. In the U.S., a lot of service jobs have no dignity. By contrast, in start-ups, even secretaries get stock options." What Brown has observed is that many companies do need workers who can innovate, but in many cases they have not yet created the working conditions and incentives that encourage employees to give their best. In effect, they are trying to play a new game by the old rules.

The need for dignity was a strong theme in my focus group with college students. Many of them have worked part-time in service jobs during the school year and through the summers to make money for college, and their experiences echoed Brown's observations. "I want my boss to take the time to get to know me and to treat me more like an equal," one young woman said with passion, and there was a chorus of agreement around the room. "Treat us like we're human, instead of someone who just does a job," another woman added. She went on to describe how her Dunkin Donuts boss recently told her to speed up getting the coffees for customers. "I was working as fast as I could. . . . This guy owns twenty stores and is probably a millionaire," she said. "But what does he know about serving coffee? I'd like to see him get behind the counter and see if he can serve people faster than I can."

Carie Windham describes the best boss she's ever had. "He asked me where I want to be in ten years. He talked to me about creating the experience I want to have. He understood I wouldn't be there forever. . . . Mentoring is a huge motivational tool, someone showing an interest in you and giving you feedback." Her next comment echoed Brown's observation about the importance of dignity for this generation: "We want to feel we have a creative, individual role—that we're not just working on an assembly line. We want to feel like we have ownership of an idea."

Employers Who Meet the Standard

Is it realistic to think that work can be about learning and creating and collaborating—as well as about the bottom line? Will our young people end up disillusioned or settling for less, as they grow older and pressures to earn a decent living in order to buy a house or support a family become more intense? Or might this generation exert a positive pressure on employers to change in order to attract the best talent? Indeed, that seems to be what's happening in the legal profession as a result of the work of Bruck and his colleagues, who report that law school grads around the country are making different decisions about which job offers to accept based on the data his group has publicized.

Whether it's to attract the best talent or create a better product, some companies are consciously restructuring work in ways that better meet the needs and interests of the Net Generation—often with stunning results. Google, for example, is one of the most successful and fastest-growing companies today. It is also the number-one pick of a place to work for many people in the Net Generation. In 2006, Google had nearly 1 million applications for 5,000 jobs![30] Some in the older generation might assume Google's popularity is due to the extraordinary job perks there, such as its eleven gourmet restaurants and gym facilities that include volleyball, swimming, and rock climbing—all onsite. Or the free massages, shuttles, and laundry services. Yet, as Matt Kulick pointed out: "I was blown away the first month on the job at Google, but now the work I do is the main attraction."

I asked Kulick, who is 22, to describe what he did at Google. "I'm an associate product manager here," he explained. "Being a product manager means being an entrepreneur in the company—an advocate for a product that you're working on, which is very important to the company. You're responsible for the product vision; you're responsible for coordinating with the engineering team on the project and getting buy-in and agreement on your vision of what the product will be and what features it will have. You're responsible for coordinating with Legal, setting expectations with your managers and securing the necessary resources to be successful. The position is entrepreneurial because you're not controlling the means of production and the other teams you impact resemble external stakeholders. You have to reach out and evangelize for your team's product. You're the connector for everyone, the 'go-to' guy."

Kulick told me that he ultimately chose to work at Google for several reasons: "First, they share ideals that I believe in—open source software. And their products are solving important problems for people—doing good in the world. I believe in what they're doing—these values are very important to me. I wanted to help out, to make a contribution. The second reason I came to Google is because they give me the resources I need to accomplish major things that will really make a difference in the world. The third reason is the responsibility they give you from the day you start. It is a winning combination. It makes me happy to go to work every day. . . . It's kind of like the hobby I had as a kid—taking apart computers. I feel that same kind of passion and excitement."

But what about other kinds of jobs outside of the dot com world? What about assembly-line work, for example?

Toyota has managed to earn a significantly higher profit on the cars it manufactures, while simultaneously developing a reputation for high quality. The secret of its success is something it calls the Toyota Production System. One key element of the system is the development of a lean, "just-in-time" manufacturing process. The parts needed to build a car arrive from suppliers as they are being used, rather than being stockpiled. Another is the company's emphasis on the development of every employee's ability to be a critical thinker and a problem solver. Teruyuki Minoura, who is senior managing director and chief officer of the Business Development Group & Purchasing Group, explained that "[a]n environment where people have to think brings with it wisdom, and this wisdom brings with it *kaizen* (continuous improvement). . . . Perhaps the greatest strength of the Toyota Production System is the way it develops people. . . . There can be no successful *monozukuri* (making thing) without *hito-zukuri* (making people). To keep coming up with revolutionary new production techniques, we need to develop unique ideas and knowledge by thinking about problems in terms of *genchi genbutsu* (hands-on experience). . . . This means it's necessary to think about how we can develop people who can come up with these ideas."[31]

John Seely Brown has spent a good deal of time studying Toyota, and has observed work on its assembly lines. "Every single person on the line in Toyota has a tremendous sense of dignity. Why? Because if you look carefully at the Toyota Production System, it is almost identical to what the gamers do. They are constantly experimenting, trying things out. And they are doing it in a very methodical way. They are constantly expecting to be measured. It is continuous R & D [research and development] at the personal level. They are organized around five-person teams, and every team is a problem-solving, creative group. They are constantly figuring out if they can do something better. They are what I might call a Respectful Organization. Workers there are willing to earn respect, and to deliver on it. And in return they want respect."

There are also some schools that "meet the standard" and are successfully engaging all students, harnessing their extraordinary potential to problem-solve and to collaborate and to create. We'll spend time exploring three such schools in the next chapter. But before I take you to visit them, we need to better understand both the similarities and the differences in what motivates subgroups of students and what they need to succeed.

The Overachievers and the Unengaged

The overwhelming majority of students today want learning to be active, not passive. They want to be challenged to think and to solve problems that do not have easy solutions. They want to know *why* they are being asked to learn something. They want learning to be an end in itself—rather than a means to the end of boosting test scores or a stepping stone to the next stage of life. They want more opportunities for creativity and self-expression. Finally, they want adults to relate to them on a more equal level.

Understanding these new conditions for motivating real learning and productive engagement in classrooms is essential if we want to close the global achievement gap and help *all* students master the Seven Survival Skills. But closing the other achievement gap in this country—the gap between white middle-class students' achievement and that of poor, predominantly minority students—requires a better understanding of each group and their needs. While this gap is mostly about race and class, it can also be defined as the gap between students who are, in a sense, driven to succeed—the Overachievers—versus those who have very little hope of success—those whom I call the Unengaged. As a way to make sense of these differences—as well as to understand why so many of my interviewees stressed the importance of having adults in their lives who will help them to discover what most interests them—let me introduce you to two 20-year-olds: Kate and Juan. They are real students whom I've known (but whose names I've changed.) Their struggles are similar to those faced by many students—though certainly not all—of their race and class.

Kate's Story

Since she was born, Kate has been programmed for success. Ballet classes, riding lessons, piano—she's had it all and, for the most part, enjoyed it. Having been read to every night for as long as she can remember, and with a house full of books, she began reading to herself at an early age and so naturally did very well in the good suburban public school she attended. In high school, she was a whirlwind of constant motion: Enrolled in a total of six AP classes in her sophomore and junior year, while playing two varsity sports and serving on the staff of the yearbook, she often stayed up until one or two in the morning just to get all her homework done and to study for tests. By her senior year, Kate was feeling a little burned out. The pace and pressure were almost too much. The college obsession was totally out of control, with everybody going around fretting that if they didn't get into an Ivy, then they wouldn't have much of a life. She hadn't done that well on her SATs, so she'd had to attend Saturday SAT-prep sessions, on top of everything else.

Both of her parents went to Ivy League schools and had high-powered careers—one was a doctor, the other a lawyer. More than anything, they wanted Kate to attend one of the colleges they'd attended and to have a successful career. When she didn't get into her first-choice school, they were shocked and disappointed. The mood in the house was dark for months. Eventually they got over their disappointment, however, as they saw how happy Kate was in her freshman year at a small liberal arts college in Maine. And it was a well-known and highly regarded college, after all, though a Harvard or Yale sticker would have looked much better on the back window of the station wagon.

But tensions with her parents came to a head again in her sophomore year. In addition to having worked with kids in summer-camp jobs for her last two years of high school and first year of college, Kate had begun taking an education course at college. And it was that class she looked forward to the most. Over Christmas break, she finally confessed to her parents that she was seriously thinking of being a teacher.

"You mean, go into Teach for America for two years before you choose your career?" her father asked, hopefully.

"No Dad, I mean being a teacher as a career," she replied.

"Teaching isn't a real career," her mother now chimed in. "How would you ever be able to afford the lifestyle you've grown up with—the nice house, all the vacations, the good clothes and car? And what about your friends? Practically all of them are pre-med, or planning on going to law or business school."

The "success" that Kate was carefully groomed for all her life, she discovers, has limits. At one level, she's always known that her parents wanted her to have a high-powered job. They used to joke about Kate supporting them in their old age, claiming to have spent their money on lessons and tuitions, instead of saving for retirement. But what they don't know is that she's always *dreamed* of teaching. She even used to play teacher, with her younger sister as the student. It's her passion—which became all the more real with summers spent working with kids and finding that she loved it!

How will she manage this? Kate wonders. Her mom was right about her friends. And the money part, too, probably. Maybe she wouldn't be that good a teacher, anyway. She's not the most patient person in the world, she knows. Kate wishes there had been a way to explore her interest in teaching back in high school. And, more than anything, she wishes she'd had a teacher she could have really talked to about what she was thinking. But so many of her teachers seemed just as worried about her getting into a name-brand college as her parents were. None of them knew her—not really.

Juan's Story

Juan's parents moved to the United States from El Salvador when he was very young, seeking a better life for the family. His dad got work with a landscaping company, and his mom found a job cleaning offices at night, so that she could be home with the kids during the day. They lived in a two-bedroom apartment in a rough neighborhood, with Juan and his two younger siblings sharing a bedroom. Ever since he was old enough he's had a job after school, in order to help pay the rent.

School has always been hard for Juan. He never really learned to read all that well, and none of the teachers seemed to notice. Or maybe they just didn't care. He felt invisible in high school. He always sat in the back of the room, so that he wouldn't be called on. It wasn't that he didn't study. He tried—he really did—because he knew what it would mean to his parents for him to graduate from high school. His dad was always saying, "Juan, the way to get ahead in this country is to get a good education. You have to study hard and to finish high school." And his mom would nod in agreement. But he'd come home from his afternoon job in the auto body shop, totally exhausted. And trying to find a quiet place to study in the tiny, cramped apartment was practically impossible.

And the stuff he was supposed to study—that was the worst part. The textbooks were hard to read and really boring. Why did he have to learn all that stuff—like algebra? No one ever explained how he'd ever use it in real life. He wished he could learn more about cars—that was his passion. He was always buying car magazines, with what little money he had. He was fascinated by how the manufacturers created shapes that would allow cars to go faster—and to burn less gas at the same time. How did they do that? And what would cars look like in the future—ones that ran on electricity or bio-fuels? He'd been reading in his magazines about "green" cars: They were going to have to be very different, he thought. Wow, what a puzzle. . . .

Juan had graduated from high school—just barely. His parents came to the graduation, and they were so proud, beaming and clapping wildly when he walked across the stage to take his diploma from the principal, who didn't even know his name. But now, two years later, he was still living at home and working at the auto body shop. It seemed like running that sander across the bare skin of a newly straightened quarter panel was as close as he would ever get to his dream of designing cars.

He wished he'd known back in 9th grade what he knew now—what it would take to get into a technical school or college. His parents didn't know. All they knew was that they'd come to the land of dreams, and that their dreams—such as owning a house—weren't any closer to coming true, no matter how hard they worked. He wished somebody had told him that he might someday be able to earn a living designing cars. Or that he could have learned how to use a CAD/CAM program if he'd transferred to another high school. But no one had said anything to him. No one sat him down and explained that to make it in this country—to get a good job—a high school diploma isn't enough. No one had even noticed how much difficulty he had reading. None of that ever happened. So long as he passed his classes and didn't get into trouble, he was just another number in the computer.

Why, he wondered? Was it his dark skin? Or were the teachers just too busy to notice—overwhelmed with the huge numbers of kids in their classrooms needing some kind of help, just like Juan? And now what? What would he do with the rest of his life? He was taking a night school course, but . . . there were so many more he'd have to take just to pass the entrance test to get into a community college. It seemed like an impossible mountain to climb.

What Did They Need?

There are, of course, many students of color who are very successful, just as there are white students who struggle. My intention in sharing these vignettes is not to reinforce stereotypes but, rather, to explore some of the significant differences, as well as important similarities, in what Kate and Juan—and many students like them—needed in high school to become happy, productive adults.

Kate suffered from too much of the wrong kind of adult authority. She was overmanaged for success—success being narrowly defined as getting into a college her parents and teachers considered to be top-notch and having a high-paying job. Juan, on the other hand, did not have enough of the right kind of authority. He needed an adult advocate in his life—a mentor who could help him see the possibilities the world might offer him and coach him in the skills and the courses that he would need in order to take advantage of those possibilities. Both needed opportunities in high school to explore their real interests. Both needed adults in their lives who would ask, "What most interests you? What are you excited about learning or doing?"

Michael Jung, senior consultant at McKinsey & Company, believes that "there are only three reasons why people work or learn. There's *push*, which is a need, threat, or risk, but this is now a less plausible or credible motivating force [in the industrialized countries] than it has been, even for the disadvantaged. There's *transfer of habits*—habits shaped by social norms and traditional routines. But this, too, is becoming weaker now, because of the erosion of traditional authority and social values. That leaves only *pull*—interest, desire, passion." I understand Jung to be talking about three kinds of human motivation. Physiological need is one—the need for food and shelter and so on. But he suggests that with high rates of employment and government safety nets, this is less of a motivational force in many young people's lives than it once was. The desire to adhere to social norms is another human motivation that is weaker than it used to be, because traditional sources of authority, religion and family, have less influence on young people today. Jung believes that it is the third motivational force—interest, desire, and passion—that increasing numbers of young people are seeking and responding to in school and at the workplace.

Colonel Rob Gordon understands that nurturing passion is *the* job of adults who work with young people today. "At City Year, our charge is to help people find their passion and to mentor them," he said. "And when they do, they work very hard at it. They're passionate about a lot of things, and when you give them opportunities to pursue their passions, they step up to the plate."

This is not to suggest that adults should make things easier for the younger generation. Rather, the point is that young people who have discovered their passion are far more likely to have the will and discipline to learn and do the difficult things that school and work often require. John Abele, you'll recall, is the retired chairman and co-founder of Boston Scientific. He currently serves as chairman of the nonprofit national after-school program FIRST, founded by inventor/entrepreneur Dean Kamen, who has sought a new way to inspire adolescents' interests in science, math, and engineering—through robotics competitions. Abele told me that he worries most about "this generation's loss of opportunity to struggle. . . . So in the robotic competitions, we build in frustrations. And to win, [the kids] have to master many skills, besides just the ability to build a robot that can compete. They learn teamwork, fundraising, project management, strategy. . . . But having an adult mentor makes the critical difference—the difference between productive and unproductive struggle."

Both FIRST and City Year have learned that the way to bring out the best in young people is to give them the right mix of challenge and support, combined with thoughtful adult mentoring.[32] In the next chapter, we'll spend some time in schools and with teachers who work to motivate students in similar ways—schools that teach the Seven Survival Skills by engaging students' passions to learn and to create.

CHAPTER 6

Closing the Gap:
Schools That Work

High Tech High

High Tech High (HTH) is a school development organization that runs a growing network of K–12 public charter schools[1] currently serving about 3,000 students in the San Diego area—in effect, a "mini" school district. These schools have gained international recognition for their highly innovative education practices—and for their results. Since graduating its first class in 2003, 100 percent of High Tech High students have been accepted to college—80 percent to four-year colleges, including Johns Hopkins University, MIT, Stanford, Howard, University of Southern California, University of California at Berkeley, NYU, and Northwestern. More than half of HTH grads are first-generation college students, including some who are the first in their family to complete high school. Last year, HTH had more students accepted to Stanford than any other nonlegacy high school—a high school where none of the parents of students applying are alums of the university. All this is accomplished on the $6,200-per-student operating budget that the state provides charter schools.

The national average of college graduates who get a technical degree from college is 15 percent. High Tech High's is 27 percent, the result of the very different approach the school takes to teaching math, science, and engineering, as we will see. But High Tech High does not track students by ability or offer any Advanced Placement courses in its academic program. Although the California accountability system (called the Academic Performance Index) reports the HTH schools' test scores as among the highest in the state, the schools steadfastly refuse to teach to these tests, in the belief that doing so would dilute their curriculum. Test-prep simply has no place at High Tech High. Nor do textbook-driven, stand-alone courses such as 9th grade English, world history, chemistry, and so on that have defined the high school experience for a century. Instead, all academic content (with the exception of 11th and 12th grade math and science) is taught through interdisciplinary projects—and even the science and math classes are organized around project-based learning, rather than based on textbooks. To pass from one grade to the next, students have to show samples of their work, collected in digital portfolios, to a panel of teachers, students, and other adults from outside the school. They must also complete a ten-week internship in 11th grade, and a senior project, in order to graduate.[2]

A Different Kind of "Business" School

To make sense of High Tech High and the innovative methods used by its teachers, you have to get to know HTH founder and CEO Larry Rosenstock. I asked Larry about the formative experiences that have shaped his educational philosophy. "It's very personal for me," he explained. "In the 1970s, I was a single dad, working my way through law school as a carpenter. After I finished school, I got a job teaching carpentry to working-class kids in the Boston Public Schools—which were, at the time, being desegregated by court order. Three days in, I realized that these kids, who had been slotted into the vocational education programs, were every bit as bright as the middle-class kids I'd gone to law school with."

Teaching inner-city kids in Boston's toughest neighborhoods, Rosenstock began to understand how the practice of separating out vocational students from a college-prep curriculum was damaging to these students. But he also knew that a traditional high school program wouldn't work for them, either. As staff attorney for Harvard's Center for Law and Education, he helped draft provisions of the 1990 Perkins Vocational Education and Applied Technology Act, which called for vocational and technical education to be linked with rigorous academic content. To put some of his ideas into practice, Larry sought the principalship of the Rindge School for Technical Arts in Cambridge, Massachusetts. He was eventually named head of the traditional Cambridge Latin School as well. But when the school board rejected his plan to eliminate academic tracking and merge the two programs, he resigned. He believed passionately that it was profoundly unfair to track students according to perceived academic ability.

For the next two years, 1996 and 1997, Larry directed the federally funded Urban High School Project, researching what types of practices lead to a highly effective urban high school. "It was sobering. No one could give us the name of a great high school," he explained.[3] As part of this project, Larry and his colleagues developed three design principles for high school: personalization, real-world connections, and a common intellectual mission.

Larry had also figured out that the foundation of a good high school is excellent teaching—but not the usual kind. "There's a great deal of misapprehension about what academic rigor is all about," he observed. "First, it's not about more content. Advanced Placement courses are a mile wide and an inch deep—which is why we don't offer them at HTH. AP Biology, for example, requires you to memorize the definitions of 3,000 words. . . . Rigor is about discerning among the avalanche of content that's coming at us all the time—and increasingly so in the Age of Google. Second, it's not just about more complex content. It's about deepening the quality of analysis."

"One of the two best teachers I ever had taught a class on employment discrimination in law school. This being the '70s, we had students who were right wingers and leftists; we had people who believed in feminism and the black power movement. We'd read a case and he'd ask, 'What's your position?' And everyone would throw their fists high into the air and take a position. Then he'd very adroitly say, 'What if the facts had been like this?' And we'd put our fists up three-quarters of the way. 'And what if they'd been like this?' he'd say, and the hands would be up only halfway. He'd modify the facts pattern a little bit again, and we'd have our hands up only one-quarter of the way. By the end of that class, you weren't so sure what you thought. You'd spend the next two days, before the class met again, thinking and thinking until you could come back into some kind of homeostasis about your belief system. . . . Rigor is being in the company of a thoughtful, passionate, reflective adult who invites you into an adult conversation which is composed of the rigorous pursuit of inquiry."

Rigor also results from hands-on learning and having to *show* what you know, Larry believes. "Before law school, I had a dual major in filmmaking and psychology at Brandeis," he told me. "The other outstanding teacher in my life was a man from Great Britain who taught the Introduction to Filmmaking class. The first thing he did was to put the cameras on the table and tell us to come back in two days with a two-minute film on burnt toast. He started to walk out, and we said, 'Wait, wait! We don't know how to use the cameras.' But he wouldn't tell us anything else. It was a gift."

By the late 1990s Larry had developed some very thoughtful ideas about what a good high school should look like, but he had nowhere to go to implement them. He didn't want to take on the same kinds of problems he'd encountered as a principal in Cambridge, where he'd tangled with too many middle-class parents and school-board members who wanted honors classes for some students but not others. He was not hopeful about what could be done in any public school system at the time. So in 1997 he took a job as president of the Price Charitable Fund in San Diego, a foundation that funded innovative inner-city social-service and education projects.

During this time, business and civic leaders in San Diego were wrestling with a couple of very challenging problems. They were attempting to transition from a regional economy heavily dependent on military spending to a biotech and telecommunications economy, but there weren't enough highly qualified workers, and the number of people from India and South Korea who were allowed in on work visas was very limited. They were also very concerned about the "digital divide"—the small numbers of women and minority students who entered the fields of math, science, and engineering.

Meanwhile, under the auspices of the Economic Development Corporation and the Business Roundtable, a nonpartisan organization of area CEOs that provides leadership on a range of public policy issues related to business development, a group of about forty business, community, and education leaders began to meet to develop a plan for a new charter high school. According to Gary Jacobs, the managing director of a national real estate development firm, they had a very clear idea of the skills that mattered most and knew that public schools in the area weren't delivering what was needed. Jacobs became chair of the planning group in 1998, and he has served as chair of High Tech High's board since the founding of the nonprofit organization in 1999. He described for me the origins of the school:

"The original concept for High Tech High grew out of the concerns of business leaders and university partners who saw that kids were leaving high school very good at memorizing facts and taking tests and doing well on them, but you ask them to apply what they know or you ask them to talk about or present their work, and they weren't able to do that. So we wanted to look at presentation skills, group work skills, problem-solving skills, and so on. . . . We were also concerned about the low numbers of local students becoming engineers, which is really about the poor quality of the math and science education that they'd received. High Tech High was designed to create an environment where students are excited about math and science and want to continue their studies in this area."

In December 1998, Gary and his father Irwin Jacobs, founder and CEO of the wireless technology firm Qualcomm, met with Larry Rosenstock and sketched out the idea of starting a technology-focused public charter school that might become a model for other schools. (The impetus for many who start charter schools is to create new models for public education.) Larry agreed to build, start, and run the school; Qualcomm agreed to support the project with $100,000 a year for five years. High Tech High opened the doors to its temporary classrooms for the first class of 200 9th and 10th graders in September 2000. Students were—and still are—chosen by a lottery system that ensures a student population that is demographically representative of the area. (In the current school year, about 55 percent of High Tech High's students represent minority populations, and 22 percent of all students qualify for a free or reduced-rate school lunch, a widely used indicator of poverty. The percentage of special-education students—those who have physical or learning disabilities such as ADHD, dyslexia, and so on—is about 12 percent, which is the state average.)

Today, the main High Tech High campus comprises a village of six schools situated on the grounds of a former naval training facility in San Diego. Realizing that the development of the skills Jacobs described couldn't wait until kids were in 9th grade, Rosenstock and his crew founded High Tech Middle School in 2003. A year later a high school with a focus on international studies, High Tech High International, opened its doors. And 2005 saw the founding of High Tech High Media Arts and High Tech Middle Media Arts and the Explorer Elementary Schools. In 2007, High Tech High began to spread to outlying areas, with the founding of High Tech High Chula Vista and High Tech High North County. Each of the schools has about 100 students in a class. While some of the schools have a different theme, they all share the same design principles of personalization, real-world connections, and a common intellectual mission that Rosenstock had conceptualized a decade ago. They also have a common set of goals:

- Serve a student body that mirrors the ethnic and socio-economic diversity of the local community.

- Integrate technical and academic education to prepare students for post-secondary education in both high tech and liberal arts fields.

- Increase the number of educationally disadvantaged students in math and engineering who succeed in high school and post-secondary education.

- Graduate students who will be thoughtful, engaged citizens.[4]

I asked Rosenstock to translate these for me—to talk about what he's trying to accomplish at HTH.

"What we're trying to do is create future leaders—civic, nonprofit, and profit—who have a sense of who they are, have a passion with purpose, and have a set of skills. We want them to be able to think, to work in groups, and to work independently. We want them to have a set of intellectual behaviors—Deborah Meier (a nationally prominent educator and winner of a MacArthur "Genius" Fellowship) calls them 'habits of mind': to think about *significance*—why is it important; *perspective*—what is the point of view; *evidence*—how do you know; *connection*—how does it apply; *supposition*—what if it were different.[5] These 'habits of mind' are really habits of question-asking. There's something about being perplexed that is at the core of inquiry; problem posing is more important than problem solving. What is interesting is that when lawyers come to visit the school and see a student's work, they say, 'That looks like legal analysis'; when engineers come in, they say, 'That's an example of critical path' (a way of analyzing essential elements of a project and possible bottlenecks); and scientists say, 'That's the scientific method.'"

"Other habits are important, too, like persistence. Students have to learn what you do when you hit a wall. And, of course, clarity and precision in communication skills are important: *inquiry*—where do you get your information; *voice*—descriptive, persuasive; and *audience*—who are you talking to, what are you trying to convince them of. The ability to empathize with others and understand another perspective is also critical. And because our curriculum is project-based, we agree with Einstein's idea that imagination is more important than knowledge—making things, innovating, creating, and building. It creates elasticity in thinking . . . and the ability to take responsible risks."

It all sounds great—in theory, anyway. Larry claims to be teaching the concepts underlying the Seven Survival Skills, without calling them that. Read through his list of desired outcomes above, and they are all there: critical thinking and problem solving, collaboration across networks and leading by influence, agility and adaptability, initiative and entrepreneurialism, effective oral and written communication, accessing and analyzing information, curiosity and imagination. But when Larry explained all of this to me, I wondered if it really worked. What and how are students learning at HTH? Are they truly engaged in their work—or just going through the motions, as students are at most high schools? And if they're truly engaged, in what ways are they differently motivated to learn?

Teaching and Learning

I arrive at the entrance to High Tech High—which has not been easy to find because it looks nothing like a conventional American high school. No football field, no yellow buses pulling up in front. (Most students take public transportation or carpool.) Reflecting its former life as a military facility, the exterior is a somewhat plain, rectangular box. Students are streaming into school all around me—many with the ubiquitous iPod earbuds and telltale white cords snaking to their backpacks, others in lively conversations with peers or a teacher who walks beside them. There isn't much evidence of the reluctant, drag-ass, sleepy slouching that I see at the entrances to most high schools in the morning.

Inside the front entrance of the building, as 8:30 approaches—a far more adult and civilized hour for the start of school than the 7 A.M. start time dictated by most districts' bus schedules—the flow of students is reduced to a trickle as the masses disburse to rooms throughout. The babble of boisterous conversations becomes a quieter, more purposeful buzz. No bells, no burly assistant principal standing at the door, yelling, "You're late! Get to class!" The two pleasant, casually dressed young administrative assistants who sit behind the blond-wood counter in the entranceway to the school barely look up at the last few stragglers. A quick nod to a wall clock or a quiet word suffices to hasten them along on their way.

In the atrium center of the building, which is the commons area, light streams down though long slits of skylights that line the tall ceiling—its exposed beams, ducts, and wiring a sharp juxtaposition to the student work that hangs down from above. Sculptures, three-dimensional physics projects, art, and posters crowd the air space every-where you look. All around this central space are clusters of cubicles and classrooms—all with glass doors and walls. The inside of the build-ing looks more like a high-tech adult workspace than a school. Outside the classrooms are scattered odd collections of couches and ottomans. Neither new nor tattered, they are soon filled with students engaged in all sorts of conversations—all the while clutching notebooks or laptops or papers they've written. I listen as two young men discuss an editorial one of them has printed off the Internet about China's economic inter-est in Darfur. "I think China refuses to speak out against the genocide because they need Sudan's oil," one says heatedly. "But they've blocked U.S.-sponsored UN Security Council sanctions before when it wasn't about oil," the other counters. "So maybe it's just politics."

I walk into the classroom next to the couch where the guys are talk-ing. Students are in small groups or working alone on laptops, as the teacher quietly consults with a student in one corner. After a few minutes, she looks up and addresses the room: "Remember, you need to finish the second draft of your resumés before we go to our Darfur discus-sion." Returning her attention to the student beside her, I hear the teacher quietly reminding her: "Now look at your verb agreement here: Is this sentence construction the right way to describe your internship last summer?"

Behind her, the white board lists a series of questions, under the heading "Things We Want to Know about Darfur":

How do we know who supports the rebels?

Are oil and tobacco motivations in Darfur?

Why was there minimal intervention in Kosovo versus Bosnia?

How does the genocide in Darfur compare to other genocides?

On another wall of the room are two typed posters, neatly framed in green construction paper, that describe "Camp Darfur"—evidently an evening program for parents and students where "tents similar to those used in the refugee camps" will each have an exhibit on a different genocide that has taken place in the past 100 years. It seems that students have to show adults what they know here, rather than just pass tests.

Back out in the open-plan hallway, I strike up a conversation with one of the school's art teachers. I ask him what it's like to teach here, compared to where he taught before.

"I taught up there," he says, gesturing to the affluent suburban neighborhoods in the hills behind San Diego. "I taught art, Advanced Placement Art History, and stuff to these really bright kids, but they were just going through the motions. All they cared about was the grade. And they wanted it to be easy. I even had one mom say to me, 'I wanted my son to take art because it wouldn't be hard, and now you've ruined his GPA—you've made the course too hard!' It's very different here. The kids are bright here, too, but they are really engaged in their learning. Plus I get to work with other teachers on great projects."

He points to a shelf containing an odd assortment of devices—each a unique combination of part Rube Goldberg machine, part sculpture.

One is a clear plastic cube with wheels inside and cranks on the outside; another is a brightly painted box with a series of round holes with one or two strings stretched across and a device for tightening them. "Kids did these as part of a unit of study the physics teacher, engineering teacher, and I worked on together. Each one of these devices illustrates a physical law. My job was to introduce art aesthetics into the criteria for their project. The engineering teacher worked with them on functional designs. When they completed these, they had to take a physics exam. It was a great project—for us and for them," he says, beaming with pride.

As I walk back into the main gathering area, I'm almost hit by a flying ping-pong ball, launched from a large wooden catapult that is surrounded by a cluster of students. Ambush of a school visitor by disaffected students? No, a standard physics class. As the students set up the next launch, they carefully measure the distance of pull to determine how much force is required to put the ball into a bucket ten feet away. The teacher stands to one side, observing and taking notes, while the students work to make sense of their experiments.

In another class, I listen as the teacher asks students to write a review of their discussion of the role of advertising in the creation of new consumer desires and then to comment on the impact of advertising on their own lives. As the students write, I talk to the teacher about the class. The discussion of advertising and our consumer culture is part of a unit of study on global warming that he, a social studies teacher, plans and teaches collaboratively with a biology teacher and an English teacher. Already they have studied the concept of dominion in Christianity. Is the Bible advocating dominion over nature or dominion for nature—as caretakers? Is religion part of the problem or part of the solution or both? These were some of the questions the unit asked students to consider.

"My job is to question, to prod and provoke them to think and to come to their own conclusions—not to give them the answers," he tells me. "But I keep reminding them, 'It's getting very hot in here.'"

I ask about the quality of student writing. "See for yourself," he offers, pointing to a sprawl of papers on his desk in the corner. "These are some papers from another class I teach."

I pick out a student paper at random. It is a neatly word-processed document about ten pages long (much longer than your typical two- to three-page high school paper). The assignment was to describe and critique the arguments presented by the mock-trial lawyers for the prosecution and defense, as well as the witness testimony for each side, in a student-led trial of Harry Truman—accused of war crimes for dropping the atomic bomb on Japan. In clear English, this student reviews and comments on each classmate's testimony—in terms of both argument and historical accuracy. The student wonders whether the constructed testimony of the classmate who represented General MacArthur, then in command of the Pacific Theatre, was credible. "He'd built his reputation on being a warrior," the student wrote, "and he was known to believe that a land invasion of Japan would, of course, be successful. So it does not seem likely to me that he would have supported use of the atomic bomb, as was said in the testimony. He knew that he could succeed and that Japan could not be occupied without the support of the emperor." Rigorous analysis, with evidence weighed and points of view carefully considered—I don't remember the last time I read a high school paper like this.

I go to use the bathroom (I can often learn a lot about a school from the condition of the student bathrooms; the nature and extent of the graffiti on the walls and trash on the floors, for example, are good indicators of how students feel about their school)—and I am amazed at what I see as I walk into this one. The room is ablaze with colorful student murals on every wall. Not a speck of trash on the floor and no graffiti. Covering one entire wall is a map of the world in 2100: Land masses are pictured as drastically reduced from their present size, with water covering most of our existing continents.

A Teacher's Perspective

To better understand how teaching in this school is different from that in a conventional high school, I have an extended conversation with Colleen Warwick, who was an 11th and 12th grade humanities teacher at the time of my visit and now directs the High Tech High in Chula Vista:

"I started out teaching in a public high school in Michigan. All we were doing was teaching to the test. I wasn't able to teach what I loved—which is big fat novels. I wasn't even able to teach writing. I quit and went to graduate school—I got a master's in English literature and then a Ph.D. in nineteenth-century literature, and I taught college courses. I eventually came to San Diego to be with my fiancé, who is in the Navy.

"I got a job teaching in a public high school north of San Diego and was very unhappy. Students didn't engage with a topic; they were just given an assignment—like 'Write a paper about John Adams.' But they didn't learn about John Adams, they didn't ask questions about John Adams. They didn't really think about John Adams at all. There were a lot of bright young energetic teachers on the faculty, but curriculum was totally tied to the textbooks, rather than to what teachers could bring into the classroom that the textbook might enhance. Teaching writing was very test-oriented, very much removed from anything that a student might be interested in writing about. There was no cohesion in the curriculum, either—only random assignments, no attempt to build a skill set. Students weren't engaged at all—even when we had conversations about college and career options. I heard about High Tech High and came to visit. Ben Daley [the principal] invited me to a day-long interview process where you teach a lesson, get interviewed by students, and plan a project with other candidates.

"Teaching is different here because my focus is on individual students. I know what Reed's personality is, I know what Ian's personality is, and I know how they learn and what they need. We listen to them when we're planning a project. If a student says, 'I'm interested in learning about surfing,' we try to find a way to accommodate that in the project. I'm more of a facilitator to them than the instructor sitting up in front of the class giving a lecture every day. It's also different because I'm teaching things I'm interested in—often things that are new to me. We just did a project on forensics, for example. I didn't know I was interested in that until we started the project."

"How are you getting students ready for college?" I ask.

"I talk to them about the skills they'll need: analytical thinking and writing, most of all—they do it naturally, but they need to learn how to hone it. Narrative writing and reflecting on their experiences are important, too. It is how they learn who they are in the world and how they influence things around them so that, as citizens, they are more aware. It's fascinating to hear them say, 'Oh, that doesn't have to be that way. I never thought of it like that.'"

"What about the standardized tests?"

"All students take the required California high school exit exam and STAR tests—the state accountability tests. But we don't prepare them for these. We just teach our classes. We don't do test-prep, and we don't have AP classes. But all students can elect an honors option. In my class that means reading longer novels and writing longer papers. I start by asking each student, 'What's going to challenge you more?'"

"How do you get students 'work-ready?'"

"Team-building and working together are things that they do on a daily basis with each other when they're working in a project-based environment. I think that those, along with the analytical thinking and writing skills, are what they most need. We also talk to the mentors in their internships about specific skills they may need for an individual placement, but for the most part, they can learn to write a computer program or other technical skills in the workplace. Learning to work with other people who are different, though, is what they have to do on a daily basis here and in whatever job they'll have. We have to teach them those skills. It's fascinating to see how they begin to internalize the language we've used with them when there's a dispute, like 'What I hear you saying is . . .'"

Warwick went on: "Whatever they end up doing—whether in or out of college—they're going to be prepared: They can hold an adult conversation, they know about current events, they know what their civic duties and responsibilities are, they know what their rights are, and they can articulate their thoughts, beliefs, and feelings."

"What do you see as your biggest challenge in starting Chula Vista next year?"

"Making students feel loved and honored. Making sure teachers *feel* the culture of the school. I love the culture in our school. I have never in my life enjoyed going to a faculty meeting. But I enjoy going to our meetings. I have a good time, and I actually learn."

Meet the Principal

Ben Daley came to High Tech High to teach physics when the school opened. He has served as director for the past three years and has now assumed the position of chief academic officer for the organization. (HTH designated *CAO* as the term for the person who oversees all aspects of the academic program in the schools.) I talked with Ben to better understand some of the challenges of maintaining high academic standards in an innovative program.

"What defines a 'good' teacher here, and how do you help teachers improve?" I ask.

"We judge teachers by the quality of their students' work. If the student work is good, then the teaching is good." (All teachers at High Tech High are on one-year contracts.)

"How do you determine the quality of student work—how do you know if 'good' is good enough?"

"We make student work public, and then we consider it carefully. We have many different ways of getting kids to put their work out there, such as inviting people from the outside to look at it with us— parents who view the students' digital portfolios and presentations, of course, but also engineers for an engineering project, architects for an architecture project, and not just at the end, but also along the way, so that the feedback is much more meaningful. . . . We use different kinds of protocols to have conversations about the quality of the work, but we're beginning to understand that even more important than rubrics is finding great examples of student work, calling them out for the kids and saying, 'This is a fantastic example of what we're talking about,' and then getting the kids to describe the qualities. Once they name it, they can do it. You also give examples—anonymously from other classes—of what you do not want, of work that is deficient. This helps build the culture where everyone wants to do really excellent work."

"What is your greatest challenge in hiring new teachers?"

"What we're finding among our applicant pool is that there are young teachers who 'get it'—and many people who are experienced often don't 'get it.' So we're hiring lots of young people—many of whom haven't had a lot of experience. This led us to start our own teacher credential program and to become much more intentional and systematic in our development of teachers—having young teachers work in a cohort and be teamed with a teacher from one of the schools in the village who has been here a number of years.

"We also have an hour together in school every day before students get here, when we'll do things like look at samples of student work and talk about what's good and what could be better. Every teacher works in a team with one other teacher and, together, they are responsible for fifty students. They meet twice a week to plan and to talk about their kids and their work."

I was impressed by HTH's thoughtfulness in helping all teachers continue to improve. I was also impressed by how this effort has evolved into establishing a new graduate school of education. In the fall of 2007, HTH transitioned its teacher credential program into a full-fledged graduate school of education—offering a Master's of Education degree with a concentration in either school leadership or teacher leadership. It is the first new graduate school of education to be established in California in decades. Unlike conventional master's programs in education, where students spend 80 percent of their time taking courses and 20 percent in classes with students, HTH master's students spend 80 percent of their time working with mentor teachers in classrooms.

Two Students' Experiences

Gabriel Del Valle and Ruth Garcia were seniors at High Tech High when I interviewed them late in the fall of 2007. Ruth came to HTH as a 9th grader because she and her family did not want her to go to her area high school. "It's really big, and there are a lot of problems there," she tells me. So they took a chance on HTH. Gabriel came to High Tech High from High Tech Middle School, where he started as a 7th grader. His mother didn't want him to go to his area high school because it was teaching English as a second language—basic English for recent immigrants.

"What do you like most about High Tech High?" I ask.

"I like that it's a small school; I know my teachers, and they know me. Whenever I have a question, I can talk to a teacher. I get a lot of guidance about applying to colleges. I also really like the projects we do," Ruth explains. Gabriel agrees: "The teachers really care; they want to help you graduate and go to college. They're also engaging you in classes—not just lecturing."

"What do you like least? What could be improved?" My question is met with quizzical expressions and silence. "Nothing, really. I enjoy school," Gabriel finally answers, and Ruth adds, "I feel the same way."

"What are your plans for next year?"

"I'm planning on going to college," Ruth replies confidently. "University of San Diego is my first choice. I want to study political science or international relations. I've been interested in these subjects ever since freshman year, when we did a model UN project. Each student was assigned a country and had to research a problem the country was facing—and possible solutions. Then we had a delegates meeting where we presented and discussed the issues. My country was Sierra Leone, and I researched the problem of trafficking."

"I'm going to college as well," Gabriel tells me. "I'm leaning toward a major in mechanical engineering. But I might switch to theology—or maybe study both."

All students at High Tech High complete a ten-week internship with a local company or nonprofit organization in their junior year as a mandatory part of the academic program. I ask Gabriel and Ruth about their internships.

"I worked at General Atomics—an engineering firm," Gabriel explains. "I was assigned to the nuclear reactor division. I wrote a manual on how to retrieve information from a legacy VAX computer and transfer the data to a desktop. I learned a lot about problem-solving. But I also learned that I don't want to work at a computer all day. Engineering has a lot of difference facets; I want to do more construction. I'm more of a hands-on person. I like to take a thing apart and put it back together and see how it works."

Gabriel goes on: "For my senior project, three of us are designing and building a shelving system for a nonprofit organization called Auntie

Helen, which does laundry for people who have AIDS and other ill-nesses. We have to use different engineering skills—figure out the shelving system that would work best for their needs, take careful meas-urements, sketch the project, do up a 3-D design, and now construc-tion. It's almost finished. Beyond the engineering, the project taught us how to take initiative. We had to go find the organization, first, and then ask them what they needed. . . . I also keep learning more about how to get along better with the other people on my team. You have different opinions, and you have to work it out."

"I interned at the Port of San Diego," Ruth tells me. "Another stu-dent and I were in the Environmental Service Department. We designed two animated games for kids that are now posted on the Environmen-tal Service Department website called Project Orca. The first game is about the different kinds of birds that people can find in San Diego and the birds' habitat. The second game is about the different equipment that scientists can use to test for certain things in the water."

Since hands-on, project-based learning in teams and public exhibi-tions of student work are at the heart of the High Tech High curricu-lum, I ask these two students to describe other memorable projects and what they learned.

Ruth describes hers first. "Last year, we did a maritime project. We had to re-create a voyage that had taken place in history, working with other kids on a team. I chose Charles Darwin's *Beagle* voyage. We had to create an accurate blueprint of the ship, using AutoCAD. When we started, I had no idea how to use the program. Each one of us had to do a different view of the ship. We also built a sextant together. And then, using our research, we had to pretend to be a person on the ship and write a log book from their perspective. I was Darwin. We presented our work at the Maritime Museum of San Diego, where it was exhib-ited for three months. It was really challenging to create a museum ex-hibition. I created something, I learned something, and I got to share what I learned with the community. We also learned to work together. And then we got to take a three-day sailing trip where we used the sextants we'd built."

Gabriel reflects on a project from his junior year: "I worked on a project for biology where every student helped to write a book about the different animal species that live in San Diego Bay. The book was published and is for sale at the natural history museum. I researched the snowy plover—its habitat, the biology of the bird, its population growth and decline, and the ways it is endangered. I'd never contributed to writing a book before. It's hard to make the writing sound interesting, instead of like a usual research paper. I also got an understanding of how important the environment is. I didn't understand before how important just one creature could be. The plover eats the larvae of bar flies—if they become extinct, our beach will be infested with flies."

"What are some of the most important skills you've learned here?" I ask them.

"I've learned how to state my position in a debate, and make an argument in a paper—write an effective essay," Gabriel replies. "It was hard for me initially because I had very different points of view than my friends. I've also learned critical thinking and problem solving. You get halfway through a project, you reach a roadblock, and you have to solve it. I've learned how to work with people who are very different from me. If my partner on a project isn't doing what he's supposed to do, the teacher tells me to figure it out—just like it is in a job."

"How to present your work and how to communicate," explains Ruth. "We have to present every project to adults. I've learned to speak confidently—I used to be shy. I've also learned how to make my work look professional. I've learned a lot of technology. We didn't use computers in middle school. Projects make us figure things out—we're always thinking, planning, organizing, working in a team."

"I'm a lot more confident now," she continues. "I know I can take a college course [Ruth leaves school three mornings a week to take a college French class] and have a career. . . . Neither of my parents went to college. I make them proud. We rent a really small house. Some day, I'd like to buy them one of their own."

School Choice

The High Tech High family of schools is a truly extraordinary example of what it takes to teach *all* students the Seven Survival Skills: a laser-like focus on the results that matter most and a willingness to rethink teaching, learning, assessment, and even the school buildings in order to get these results. Equally exciting, High Tech High schools are figuring out how to replicate themselves though the systematic seeding of new schools. They're also rethinking how to best prepare new teachers for a different kind of instruction.

But these schools are by no means the only models of a different kind of high school. For nearly two decades, courageous educators around the country have been quietly but persistently engaged in a kind of educational "research and development" to redesign the American high school experience. Beginning in 2001, this work was greatly accelerated with substantial grants from the Bill & Melinda Gates Foundation and other philanthropies that have supported a wide range of nonprofit organizations that are starting new high schools or breaking up large, comprehensive (and dysfunctional) high schools into small autonomous academies.[6] The federal Department of Education, too, has been giving grants to school districts for the past seven years to transform their large high schools into smaller "learning communities." Today, there are several thousand restructured high schools or new smaller high schools and charter schools around the country. New York City alone has over 200 new small high schools and hopes to have twice that number in the next five years, according to Adam Tucker, senior program officer at the Bill & Melinda Gates Foundation. But they're not just in the large cities. Restructured high schools and new charter schools can now be found in a growing number of suburbs and in rural areas as well.

I've spent time observing and talking to teachers and students in at least 50 of these new or restructured small high schools all over the country during the past decade—both in my capacity as senior advisor to the Bill & Melinda Gates Foundation and as an independent researcher. What stands out for me as I think back on all of the schools I've visited is how different they are from one another. When it comes to high schools, one size most definitely does not fit all. Even among the High Tech High schools, I see variation in the school's themes. Some are more focused on science and engineering, while others focus on the media arts or cross-cultural learning experiences.

Different kids do best in different kinds of environments. For example, some students need more structure than others. Some thrive best in themed schools like HTH where they can explore particular interests, while others prefer more opportunities to explore a range of interests. Indeed, having a choice of schools is critically important. It is also important psychologically, as parents and students who are able to choose their school have a deeper level of commitment to the school. They have chosen to be a part of a community.[7]

To explore just how diverse some of the most successful schools that teach the Seven Survival Skills can be, I'm going to take you on very brief tours of two additional schools.

The Met

"One Student at a Time"

The Met network of schools is a project of the Big Picture Company, a school development organization directed by Dennis Littky and Elliot

Washor. They co-founded Big Picture in 1995 in the hopes of creating a new model for high schools. The Big Picture Company's mission is

> [t]o catalyze vital changes in American education by generating and sustaining innovative, personalized schools that work in tandem with the real world of their greater community. We design break-through public schools, research and replicate new designs for education, train educators to serve as leaders in their schools and communities, and actively engage the public as participants and decision makers in the education of our youth.

Our philosophy is grounded in educating "one student at a time." We promote and create personalized education programs that are unique for each student.

> We believe that true learning takes place when each student is an active participant in his or her education, when his or her course of study is personalized by teachers, parents and mentors who know him or her well, and when school-based learning is blended with outside experiences that heighten the student's interest. In a country obsessed by "test-score accountability," we promote "one student at a time accountability."[8]

Littky and Washor had first worked together in a rural New Hampshire high school where Dennis was principal in the 1980s. In 1993, Stanley Goldstein, founder of the CVS Corporation, asked Littky and Washor to come to Rhode Island and think about how to improve education in the state—especially the high schools for minority and economically disadvantaged students who were dropping out of the Providence schools at high rates. Later that same year, Theodore Sizer, chairman of the Coalition of Essential Schools at Brown University in

Providence, invited Littky and Washor to be the first senior fellows at the newly formed Annenberg Institute for School Reform.

During this time, Rhode Island was beginning to rethink its vocational and technical programs. In 1993, the Rhode Island Department of Education (RIDE), headed by Peter McWalters, its visionary leader, began the research for the development of a new career and technical school in South Providence. The resulting report called for the development of a new model for a high school that "should aim at educating a cross-section of students with varying interests and abilities, integrate business and technical training with life skills and academics, and focus on fostering good citizenship among its students."[9]

Following successful voter approval of a $29 million bond issue for a new school, RIDE contracted with the newly formed Big Picture Company in 1995 to develop the design and implementation plan for what was to be called "the Metropolitan Regional Career and Technical Center" (the Met). The school was required by the state to draw 75 percent of its students from Providence—where the dropout rate exceeded 50 percent, and more than 75 percent of the children qualified for a free or reduced-rate school lunch. The remaining 25 percent of the students would come from other areas in Rhode Island. The overall project was a public/private partnership of RIDE, the RI Department of Employment and Training's Human Resources Investment Council, the Annenberg Institute, the CVS Corporation (then the Melville Corporation), and the Big Picture Company. The original Met School opened its doors to the first class of fifty students in September 1996.

The new school model was so successful that, within a few years, requests for help began to come in from communities all over the country that wanted to establish their own Met Schools. With support from the Bill & Melinda Gates Foundation and other philanthropies, the Met network now consists of more than fifty alternative district and charter schools all over the country, which have been developed in partnership with Big Picture. The schools and their students thrive in some of the most educationally challenged and violent urban environments in America—including Camden, New Jersey; Detroit, Michigan; and Oakland, California. Operating in these exceptionally difficult circumstances, the Met has gained a national reputation for graduating nearly 100 percent of its students, with 95 percent of its graduates accepted into a two- or four-year college.

Currently, the Met School District in Rhode Island enrolls 800 high school students in seven small schools—four on the main campus in South Providence, one downtown, one in the west end of Providence, and one in Newport. The main South Providence campus consists of four buildings—Equity, Justice, Liberty, and Unity—plus a state-of-the-art media center, all grouped around a grassy field, where students have their physical education classes and play a variety of intramural games. A basketball court and gym facility are also on campus and are open to the community. Each building, which is considered a separate school, houses 120 students who are organized into eight advisory groups. The advisory group is the 'instructional unit" of the school: A teacher stays with his or her advisory group for all four years of the students' experience and is responsible for developing an Individual Learning Plan for each student, which is reviewed four times a year by the student, his or her family, and the teacher. The student's internships and individual projects are at the heart of the Individual Learning Plan. Throughout their four years at the Met, all students spend two full days a week off-campus, learning through year-long internships in a wide variety of nonprofits and businesses in the community.

As Elliot Washor explained to me, "Instead of having students take classes and maybe eventually figuring out what their interests are, we start with helping every student to find their interest and then build a learning plan around it." It is what co-founder Dennis Littky calls "interest-based learning." The Met curriculum uses students' interests as the driving motivation for developing the skills they'll need for college, careers, and citizenship. Students score decently on the required state math and reading tests, but a lot of the other academic subject content, Littky and Washor argue, can be acquired later in college—so long as students have the skills and the will to succeed. Think of it as a kind of educational triage in that the teachers put motivation to learn and mastery of the most important learning and communication skills first, ahead of subject content.

The Met's Five Learning Goals represent specific intellectual and interpersonal skills in which students must demonstrate mastery through their projects and internships. Again, we see a great deal of overlap with the Seven Survival Skills.[10]

1. *Communication: "How do I take in and express ideas?"* This goal is to be a great communicator: to understand your audience, to write, to read, to speak and listen well, to use technology and artistic expression to communicate, and to be exposed to another language.

2. *Empirical Reasoning: "How do I prove it?"* This goal is to think like a scientist: to use empirical evidence and a logical process to make decisions and to evaluate hypotheses. It does not reflect specific science content material, but instead can incorporate ideas from physics to sociology to art theory.

3. *Personal Qualities: "What do I bring to this process?"* This goal is to be the best you can be: to demonstrate respect, responsibility, organization, leadership, and to reflect on your abilities and strive for improvement.

234 The Global Achievement Gap

4. *Quantitative Reasoning: "How do I measure, compare, or represent it?"* This goal is to think like a mathematician: to understand numbers, to analyze uncertainty, to comprehend the properties of shapes, and to study how things change over time.

5. *Social Reasoning: "What are other people's perspectives on this?"* This goal is to think like an historian or anthropologist: to see diverse perspectives, to understand social issues, to explore ethics, and to look at issues historically.

Teaching and Learning

I've come for another visit to the main campus of the Met in Providence at the beginning of the school year as students are doing research on the internship they will choose to focus on. The school day begins with a "pick-me-up," in which all of the students and teachers in a building gather in the central meeting area of their school. As I walk in, an adult is making announcements, while the group of about 100 students and adults stand or sit in chairs in a large semicircle around the room. "So, there are job openings at the new Whole Foods Market that just opened up, and don't forget to sign up for the talent show during Friday's pick-me-up."

A few quiet whispers and rustlings of backpacks can be heard around the room. Chris Hempel, the principal of Unity, reminds the group: "Hey, guys, you need to show a little respect to each other by listening." The room immediately settles down.

Four young men in the 10th grade stand up in front of the group. Each takes a turn reading his written apology to the whole group. Apparently, several had been drinking in the parking lot after school the previous Friday; others had known but had not told anyone. All seem genuinely remorseful as they apologize to the community. They talk about how they will come up with a plan for regaining the community's trust, as well as a plan to create an alcohol abuse awareness program for younger students. "But don't judge the other kids in our advisory," one says. "It was our fault. We let them down."

Hempel talks briefly about the fact that these students will have certain privileges taken away from them and will bring plans to the community for rebuilding trust, as well as their plans for community service. He goes on to describe a time a few years ago when a group of students called a building-wide meeting and asked all adults to leave. They'd found out that someone had brought drugs onto campus and called the meeting to tell their fellow students: "'No drugs here—not in *my* school!' This is your community," Hempel reminds them.

Francesca, a young woman in her senior year, gets up to talk and show slides about her summer project in the Dominican Republic— helping to build a school and working in a summer camp for kids. She talks about how much it means to her to work with kids because she wants to be a teacher; she also talks about meeting some of her extended family. Francesca speaks comfortably, clearly, and loudly enough so that all can hear. All of the students sit quietly, their attention focused on Francesca, and a fifteen-minute question-and-answer session follows her discussion. She ends with a plea for students to explore and take advantage of all the opportunities to travel for free through the summer program, which is encouraged by the school as another way for students to explore their interests and better understand the skills they'll need as adults.

The Advisory Group meetings are next. I join one group with twelve or so 11th graders who are gathering around a long rectangular table in the small seminar room, which is decorated with a variety of posters. The Advisory Expectations are listed on a poster nearby:

- be responsible

- respect each other

- participate

Another poster describes the Culture of Critique:

- Kind

- Specific

- Helpful

- Process Steps

And yet another lists Elements of Literacy, which refer to the ways in which students can relate to what they read:

- Text to World

- Text to Self

- Text to Text

Once students are seated around the table, the teacher begins: "We don't have a lot of time for our meeting this morning: Pick-me-up ran late, and we have PE in twenty minutes. Anything anyone wants to share?" (This is in sharp contrast to most public schools where the focus is on jumping into a lesson on required content, leaving little or no time to build the kinds of relationships with students that motivate them to want to learn.)

"I have an interview on Tuesday with people from animal control," a young woman reports. She's referring to the city agency where she hopes to do her internship this year.

Another young woman speaks, "Akeda said her first word yesterday."

"What was it?" the first girl asks.

"Ma-ma."

"So how did you feel about our conference yesterday?" the teacher asks. "Did you feel you got a good sense of how to do a research paper? If not, then we need to reteach it. On the card I just handed out, I'd like you to write one thing that worked about the conference, and one thing that could be improved, and then we'll talk for a few minutes."

"I was falling asleep because T [the name of the male teacher who co-taught the lesson on how to write a research paper] was doing so much talking in the beginning. I think you should have engaged us more," says a male student in a quiet voice.

"We want to create a small committee to involve you more in the planning," replies the teacher calmly—seeming not the least bit surprised by, or defensive about, the student's comments.

"I don't understand why T read so much stuff out loud that we'd just read to ourselves," another student says.

"I liked the packet of materials you prepared for us," offers another.

And yet another student comments, "It was cool to explore the library."

"Okay, we'll talk about this some more, but we have to change for gym now," the teacher concludes. "Before we head out, let's first go over who I'm meeting with today. Alfonse, we're going to go over your essay. . . . Does anyone need to meet with me to plan their next steps for doing more research or contacting the internship you've chosen?

Write down on the card I just passed out your next step with your internship. And everybody knows: October 1st is the deadline, right?"

During a visit four years ago, I observed a student working at her internship—which was in a hospital lab down the street from the school. I talked to her mentor, who was impressed by how thoughtful and mature the young woman was. The student's understanding of the test procedures used in the lab was what most impressed me as she gave me a tour of the facilities.

Today, I want to learn more about what it's like to teach in the school, and so I talk briefly with Elizabeth, the teacher, as she hurries toward the gym, where she takes PE *with* her students. "What's most rewarding about teaching here?"

"The relationships with the kids. I've been with them since 9th grade—and this is the beginning of our third year together. The trust is there now so that I can offer more of myself, and they can bring in more of themselves—who they really are."

"What's hardest?"

"Juggling so many things—all the different projects, internships, and an individual plan for each student. . . . My job is to harness their potential and make sure they're moving ahead."

Back in the main assembly area, I meet up with Hempel and we talk briefly. He has been principal of Unity for four years; prior to that, he taught in the school for four years.

"What's the hardest thing about working in this school?"

"It's the relentless intimacy—it's the roller coaster ride of a lifetime. You take it all very personally. In traditional academic settings, your self-worth is your knowledge of academic content; here it's your genuineness as a person—what you know versus who you are."

"How do you develop your teachers' skills?"

"We pair veteran and new teachers, and the grade-level teachers are also paired and meet regularly. We have one-hour weekly staff meetings before school, plus one full day a month for professional development. . . . It's very different from when I started teaching at Hope High School in downtown Providence. There, I was thrown into a classroom and left alone, and all the teachers' meetings were grieved by the union" [meaning that the union filed grievances whenever an administrator asked teachers to stay a few minutes after school for a meeting that wasn't explicitly negotiated in the contract].

One Student's Perspective:
A Conversation with Christina

When I last visited the Met, I spent about two hours conducting a focus group with a representative group of 11th and 12th graders. They all spoke powerfully about their experiences at the Met and what the school had meant to them, but I was especially moved by the story of one senior whom I will call Christina.

"How did you decide to come to the Met?"

"In middle school, I skipped classes and got into drugs. I had a messed-up life and no future. I heard about the Met from my best friend: 'No grades, no tests, you don't do much, and kids travel a lot and go to college' is what she told me."

"I came into the school and I didn't know what I was doing here; I felt like I didn't have a future; I didn't know what I was doing with my life. Before, I had hated school because teachers thought I'd never go far. But I had a secret that I didn't tell anybody until I finally told my advisor in 9th grade. I told him that I had dyslexia. I kept that a secret for the longest time. I took this test in 4th grade, and my teacher told me, 'This is not normal—you don't read, you're always making up excuses.' Before I went into middle school, this counselor did me in for some reason—he didn't write that I was dyslexic in my student record. They put me in special-education classes because of my behavior—they had no clue what was wrong. Building the trust with my advisor when

I got here and telling him my secret was really hard, but he found me help and I started tutoring with a new program."

"Now I'm at the 8th grade level with reading and writing, and I know what I want to do with my life. I want to study political science and early childhood development because my future vision—and I never thought I'd have one—is to build a school for dyslexic kids. I'm Dominican and bilingual, so for my senior project I'm going to El Salvador to teach 15- to 18-year-old girls about HIV and STDs and work in a health center. . . . I've learned to like reading and writing. I've learned self-confidence and responsibility."

Francis W. Parker Charter Essential School
"Less Is More" and "Student as Worker, Teacher as Coach"

Theodore R. Sizer is an icon in American education—widely known and respected for his well-researched, scathing criticisms of our nation's high schools. He was the youngest dean to serve at the Harvard Graduate School of Education, and he went on to the prestigious Phillips Andover Academy, where he served as headmaster for almost ten years. He left Andover to lead a five-year study of the American high school, which resulted in the publication of three books, including *Horace's Compromise,* the first in his famous trilogy.

Formed in 1984, the Coalition of Essential Schools (CES) was an outgrowth of Sizer's studies, which were among the first to document many of the problems we still see in most of our high schools today. The CES began as a group of eleven high schools committed to reinventing themselves around nine (now ten) Common Principles that were designed to counteract many of the problems that Sizer's research had documented. In other words, each of these principles refers to a specific lack in existing high schools or to a problem that his research had uncovered:[11]

1. Learning to use one's mind well

2. Less is more, depth over coverage

3. The same intellectual goals apply to all students (i.e., no tracking)

4. Personalization

5. Student as worker, teacher as coach

6. Demonstration of mastery

7. A tone of decency and trust throughout the school

8. Commitment to the entire school (i.e., teacher's first commitment is to the students and the school, not [to] his or her academic discipline)

9. Resources dedicated to teaching and learning (i.e., additional costs to implement these reforms, if any, should be no more than 10 percent above [those pertaining to] the regular high school, and the money goes to the classroom, rather than to [the] administration or expensive sports programs)

10. Democracy and equity (i.e., a commitment to non-discriminatory and inclusive practices and to honoring diversity)

Today, the CES is a national organization that supports the development of Coalition schools around the country and internationally though its publications, conferences, and teacher training and curriculum development programs. Francis W. Parker Charter Essential School, a regional public charter school of choice located in the outer suburbs of Boston and enrolling 365 students in grades 7–12, is one of the royal jewels in its crown. It is the only Coalition school founded by Ted Sizer and his wife Nancy, who is also an educator. They formed the school in 1995, with help from a group of concerned parents who wanted their children to have an education that was based explicitly on the Ten Common Principles.

"When I first came to the school as an arts and humanities teacher twelve years ago, people sending their kids to the school were pioneers who were drawn to our educational philosophy. Now we have a very different group of parents and students," explained Teri Schrader, Parker's principal for the past seven years. "Today, we have a track record of success and so draw a lot of parents who simply want a better education for their children."

Francis Parker's track record is impressive, indeed. It has consistently ranked among the top-ten schools in the state's MCAS tests—while absolutely refusing to teach to the tests. Since graduating its first class in 2000, 100 percent of its students have been accepted to college, and 95 percent of Parker graduates have gone on to college—with 96 percent of those students attending four-year colleges. The college graduation rate is 85 percent. These numbers compare well to the ones associated with the most elite private schools—as does the list of colleges Parker grads have attended, which include some of the most highly selective in the country: Amherst, Brown, Cornell, Dartmouth, Middlebury, the University of Chicago, and Wesleyan—to name just a few.[12] However, Parker does not offer any AP or honors classes, nor does it rank its students, nor do students receive any letter grades. More than 20 percent of Parker's students are classified as "special-needs" kids—that is, students who have a variety of learning disabilities—a proportion higher than that in surrounding public schools because of Parker's reputation for being able to give every student more individual attention than most large public schools do.

Curriculum and Assessment

Francis Parker is divided into three Divisions: Division I (grades 7 and 8), Division II (grades 9 and 10), and Division III (grades 11 and 12). In Divisions I and II, all classes are two hours in length, are interdisciplinary, and are taught by teams of two teachers in what the school calls its two "Domains": Arts and Humanities; and Math, Science, and Technology. All students must also take Spanish and Wellness. Learning in both of the interdisciplinary Domains is organized around the exploration of an "Essential Question." This year's Essential Question is "What Is Cause and What Is Effect?"

Students pass from one Division to the next by demonstrating proficiency in what are called "Gateway Exhibitions," in which students have to show mastery through a range of collected work in their portfolios, which must meet specific school-wide standards. The portfolios are judged by a panel of teachers. Performance "standards of excellence" are clearly defined in Reading, Writing, Listening, Oral Presentation, Research, Artistic Expression, Scientific Investigation, Mathematical Problem Solving and Communication, Systems Thinking, Technology, Wellness, and Spanish. Exemplars of outstanding student work provide all students with a clear picture of what "excellence" looks like in these areas. Narrative reports describing each student's work during the semester and his or her strengths and weaknesses are sent home twice a year to document student progress, in lieu of a conventional report card. The school's comprehensive summary of these reports is sent to colleges, along with the student's transcript.[13]

Students can apply to do their Exhibitions in the middle of the year and at the end of the year, but they are not promoted to the next Division until they have met the performance standards for their work. There is also a Gateway Exhibition for Spanish, roughly at the end of 9th and 11th grade, in which students must speak the language to a defined level of proficiency. Because the school believes that, before they graduate, students should have some experience going into depth in an academic discipline, it offers a limited choice of discipline-based courses that students can take in Division III. For example, the Spring 2007–08 Online Course Catalogue highlights four math classes, three science classes, and fourteen English and social students classes from which students can choose—reflecting the school's explicit bias toward the humanities. In addition to taking four courses, all 12th graders complete a year-long Senior Project, which must be presented and defended to a juried panel that consists of the student's advisor, the student's outside project mentor, an 11th grader, another teacher, and an adult from outside the school (often a parent or interested community member). You might think of this as a "Merit Badge" approach to learning and to exhibiting the ability to be curious, take initiative, think critically, and communicate effectively what you have learned.

"Habits of Learning" in Action

The skills that students are expected to master—"the habits that the Parker community expects its students to develop and exhibit in their academic work and in daily life"[14]—are clearly defined by the school. Once again, note the overlap between this list and our Seven Survival Skills:

> *Inquiry.* In both school work and daily life, you show intellectual curiosity and wonder about the world. You ask thoughtful questions, and seek out their answers.

> *Expression.* In both school life and daily life, you communicate honestly what you know or want to know, and what you believe or feel.

Critical Thinking. In both school life and daily life, you analyze, synthesize, and draw conclusions from information. You generate solutions to problems using both creative and rational thought. You keep an open mind and appreciate different points of view. You seek out excellence.

Collaboration. In both school life and daily life, you contribute to the overall effort of a group. You work well with diverse individuals and in a variety of situations, using effective communication skills (consulting, listening, speaking).

Organization. In both school life and daily life, you sift through ideas and data, arranging them wisely and making sense of them. You come to school prepared with what you will need. You set reasonable goals, then plan and manage your time so as to meet them. You persevere in the face of obstacles.

Attentiveness. In both school life and daily life, you focus on the task at hand, observing and taking in the information you need to do it well.

Involvement. Both in school and in the larger community, you take the initiative to participate in the process of learning. You contribute your questions, ideas, and actions in group discussions, activities, and projects.

Reflection. In both school life and daily life, you review and think about your actions and the work you produce, with the purpose of learning more about yourself and the work.[15]

The first time I visited Francis Parker was about ten years ago, when it was a start-up school housed in a windowless former Army Intelligence building in what was once Fort Devens, a military installation about forty miles outside of Boston. Seven years ago, it moved down the street to a building that was the elementary school for the base. Parker does not have the kind of corporate support that High Tech High enjoys; nor does it have access to state money for facilities, as the Met does in Providence. Like most charter schools around the country, which are not given money for facilities, Parker must make do and so is shoehorned into this building that it now finally owns. The building also houses the Theodore R. Sizer Teachers Center, which provides tours and workshops for visiting educators and technical assistance to other schools exploring membership in the Coalition, as well as the New Teachers' Collaborative, a year-long credentialing program, designed to graduate teachers who have successful experience teaching in a Coalition school.

On this snowy December day, the school has a two-hour delayed start, due to icy roads. In most high schools, this would mean that classes are reduced to thirty minutes or so, and that there is even less teaching and learning than normal. But not here. I walk into a Division II Math, Science, Technology class. Sixteen students are working in pairs at rectangular tables. They have two worksheets that contain perhaps twenty examples of four different ways to represent a mathematical relationship: words, equations, table of values, and graphs. But the examples are all out of order. Their task is to match up the correct equation, table of values, word description, and graph that all represent the same numerical relationship. In addition, each partner was given only one of the two worksheets, so the pairs must work together to puzzle out all the answers. They are all focused and conferring with their partners frequently.

I talk quietly to one of the two teachers in the room as she observes the students.

"I want them to be fluent in the different ways of representing a mathematical relationship. I see math as an important way for students to model the world around them and to understand trends. This is a part of a larger Math, Science, Technology unit on the relationship between form and function. Later, we will study anatomy and physiology, looking at form and function in our body's organs, as well as data from the human body."

I visit a Spanish class, where students are listening to a video, in Spanish, of U.S. State Department officials and their critics who offer opposing points of view on the cocaine eradication program in Columbia. Students have a worksheet in front of them, with questions like (1) How has the fumigation program affected the cocaine market? Evidence? (2) How does the fumigation program affect the Columbian people? Evidence?

A Division II Arts and Humanities class is my next stop. The AH program alternates between a national and a global focus every other year. This year, the focus is national and the year-long topic is "Understanding American Identity Through Conflict and Compromise." According to the Curriculum Overview I was given at the school, "This year in AH, we will try to uncover America by asking the questions *who are we?* and *how did we become what we are?* We will explore these questions by focusing on three areas of American history in which a crisis, or series of crises, provoked a lasting change in our national character." The students are studying three periods: Colonial and Pre-Revolutionary America, the Civil War, and America in the 1960s.

The class I observe is divided in half, with each teacher working with ten students.

"Today, we're going to do a close reading of chapter 17 in *The Red Badge of Courage*," the teacher begins. "I know you haven't read that far yet, but we want to look closely at this chapter because the literary critics say it is a turning point in the book. We're going to read the chapter together and see if we agree, and if so, then explore why it is a turning point. We're also going to practice looking carefully at imagery. I've prepared a worksheet that will help us focus on imagery as we read together."

She passes out a sheet that is divided into four blank boxes, each labeled for a different kind of imagery: Animal, Nature/Atmosphere, Religious/Authority, and Machine. At the bottom of the sheet there is a list of questions: "What moods or sensations are evoked by these types of images? What *themes* do they suggest? Are there any contradictions presented through these sets of imagery? How do we make sense of these? How can we reconcile this Henry [the protagonist] with the one we saw earlier, particularity in chapter 15?"

Contrast in your mind, for a moment, the kind of challenges students were given and the discussions they were having in these three classes with what we saw in the classrooms we visited in Chapter 2. Parker's classes were more like college seminars I've observed than what we see even in our "best" high school Advanced Placement classes. And this wasn't just a good day or a show for visitors. In fact, it was my third visit to the school, and each time I've come, the teaching and learning seem stronger than what I'd seen in the previous visit, as the program and its teachers have matured.

Teachers' Viewpoints

After I had observed a number of classes, I talk with Deborah Merriam, the school's academic dean, and four teachers who volunteered to spend a few minutes answering questions. (Because the school is a showcase for many hundreds of visitors who come every year wanting to see a new education model in action, teachers consider it part of their job to be available to visitors.) I ask Merriam how the school helps teachers to grow. "We have an instructional rubric for new teachers," she replies. "Beyond that, most of the classes are team-taught, and the teacher teams have a two-hour common planning period every day.

Plus we have an early release every Wednesday, which gives teachers two and a half hours a week for full faculty meetings where we often look at student work together or have a common professional development program or meet by division. And once a month, all teachers meet in small Critical Friends Groups, where they look at student work from one another's classes and talk about what kind of teaching produces the best work."

A teacher tells me, "Everything we do here is public. Other teachers are always in and out of my room, even if I'm not co-teaching a lesson, and we're expected to bring our students' work to meetings for discussion."

I ask the teachers what's most satisfying about working at Parker and hear a range of replies:

"Teaching the things that matter in a kid's life—real skills versus information."

"The way we work with one another . . . flexibility in what and how we teach . . . shared responsibility as a team."

"It's a humane place. There's time to get to know the kids—and there's support [from parents and school leaders] to push the kids, to get them to do their best work. . . . [And there's] the respect we give students and the respect that they give back to us."

"What's most challenging?" I want to know.

"Some teachers find the freedom and flexibility challenging," an experienced division head responds. "They're used to just following a textbook. And when I see a teacher falling short, it bothers me. You can't just close your door, go about your work, and pretend you didn't see it, as you do in most schools."

"The conversations can be hard," a colleague adds. "Whether it's a kid with a substance abuse problem or a teacher whose professional development you question."

"Getting all students—even those with real learning disabilities—to perform at the level we expect," chimes in another.

Students' Perspectives

I talk to three seniors—Kelsey, Rachael, and Arielle—about their Senior Projects and what they've valued most about the school.

Kelsey, who is doing a digital photographic portfolio for her Senior Project and plans to take a pre-veterinarian course of studies in college, tells me: "I've grown as a learner by being able to choose my own path. I used to be horrible at test taking, and doing projects here has given me a chance to show my best. Now I'm even able to do pretty well on tests. . . . I also like the sense of family here."

Rachael is designing a menu for living in a weightless environment as her senior project—having first researched the effects of space on the body and human nutritional needs. "I like it that you can question anything here. My cousin goes to a high school nearby, and she has no idea why she's told to do a certain assignment, and she could never ask. Here, no one minds if you ask a question like that." Rachael has been accepted Early Decision into George Washington University, where she plans to study geography.

Arielle is researching the history of animation, as well as taking an online course in 3-D computer animation, and she will produce a three- to five-minute video for her Senior Project. She had a long list of what she most values about the school, including "The sense of community—the fact that we can call our teachers by their first names makes them a part of the community, too. We also have a much better sense of why we're working on something here. We're doing a lot of real-world tasks—like the mock trial we just did. I also love it that every semester is different. I get to try new things, and I'm never bored." Arielle will pursue her interest in art at college.

When I ask about some of the skills they've learned, all three agree that they had become much more confident and competent as writers—especially when working on research papers. They've become much better presenters as well. "I was really shy when I first came here," Kelsey explains. "Now I don't think anything about getting up and giving a presentation—we do it all the time." Finally, they've learned to manage their time effectively, they tell me.

"Ways the school could be improved?" I ask.

Kelsey and Rachael agree that they wish the student body were a little more diverse (the school's student body is mostly white and middle class—mirroring the demographics of the surrounding towns from which it draws), and Arielle would like to have had some textbooks as reference. "It's hard keeping all the handouts organized in my binder," she explains.

Of course, the best way to assess a school's effectiveness is to find out how its graduates do in college and beyond. So I interview a student who was in the first class to go all the way through Parker from 7th grade to graduation. Kaitlin LeMoine graduated in 2001 and went on to receive her B.A. with Honors from Brown University in 2005. She currently works at the Prospect Hill Academy Charter School in Cambridge, Massachusetts, where she has a range of teaching and administrative responsibilities.

I ask Kaitlin how Parker had prepared her for Brown.

"In so many ways!" she exclaims. "Parker really honed my writing and presentation skills. I learned to express ideas and to think critically. I learned how to do long-term projects and to manage my time—which is what college is all about. I learned to revise my work and to give others feedback on their work—things that other Brown freshman struggled with."

"I also learned how to make good connections with faculty—how to find people, ask questions, advocate for myself, and take ownership for my own education. And I learned leadership skills. Because Parker is so small, there were lots of ways to take initiative and have an impact. So I was used to that and just kept on at Brown."

"In what ways did Parker prepare you *least* well?" I wonder.

"Test taking," Kaitlin laughs. "Except for SATs, I hadn't taken any timed tests when I got to Brown. But Parker had taught me how to ask for help, and so it didn't take me long to connect with another student who was good at taking tests and get some pointers."

"We've learned from our interviews with our first graduates," noted Academic Dean Deborah Merriam when I visited the school. "They told us we didn't teach them how to take tests, and so we have more tests now." I am struck by the fact that while the school refuses to prepare students for the state MCAS test, they have listened to their graduates who said they needed to be taught test-taking skills and so have adjusted their program accordingly.

———

From these three school models, we can see how the "basics" and the Seven Survival Skills can be taught together—indeed, are being assessed effectively and taught to a wide range of students in different kinds of schools all over the country today. We can also observe how much better prepared the graduates of these schools truly are for college and careers, and how they will likely use their skills as citizens—young adults who have developed the "habits of mind" of being informed, involved, and effective advocates for what they believe. These schools, and others like them around the country, are graduating students who know how to think critically, collaborate, adapt, take initiative, communicate, and access and analyze information. They're also curious, imaginative, and motivated to work hard and to succeed. In short, they are ready for work, learning, and life in the twenty-first century. Contrast these results with what we saw in our "good" conventional schools.

All three of the schools we visited in this chapter are small "schools of choice"—and two of the three are charter schools. So, are small schools, charter schools, and school choice the "silver bullets" that so many seek in education—the structural changes that will improve all our schools? Unfortunately, the answers are not so simple. For every successful small high school or charter school, I can show you nine others that are getting results no different from the traditional comprehensive high school next door.

Perhaps the most important lesson I learned from a closer study of these three schools is this: While highly successful schools may look very different from one another and may or may not be charter schools, they have in common certain core principles of teaching and learning that are in sharp contrast to the schools we visited in Chapter 2 and even to other small schools. These practices, plus the very different ways in which they define the expectations and support the work of their teachers, are essential components of their success. We'll explore some of the shared principles and beliefs of these three schools, as well as some final questions, in the Conclusion.

Conclusion
A Few Answers—and More Questions

IN THE OFTEN ideologically driven debates about education, it is easy to lose sight of what matters most—which is what happens between students and teachers in real classrooms every day. I've taken you into a large number of classrooms in this book so that you can better understand what our children actually experience in public schools—both good and bad—as a way to keep the discussion grounded. National and state policy issues such as school accountability and educator certification requirements, and districts' curricula and professional development, evaluation, and tenure policies for teachers—all of these must be considered in terms of whether they support or impede effective teaching and learning.

Some effective teaching and learning practices are nearly universal, transcending the requirements of a particular time and place. Nearly 2,500 years ago, Socrates was considered a very effective teacher, and he would be today as well. Yet it is rare to find examples of the Socratic teaching method in K–12 schools today because of their narrow focus on memorization of content. Nevertheless, teaching through the use of questions, as Socrates did, is still considered state-of-the-art and is widely practiced in graduate schools of law and business. When done well, it develops students' abilities to ask good questions, play with ideas, reason, weigh evidence, and communicate clearly—skills that the elites of many societies have needed.

We must also consider teaching and learning in light of the needs of an era—of a particular time in history. In the 1800s, the kind of teaching and learning that took place for a small percentage of students in one-room schoolhouses was considered effective enough for an agrarian era, when most people worked with their hands and had minimal needs for book learning. As we transitioned to a more urban, industrial era at the turn of the twentieth century, however, effective teaching and learning consisted of "batch-processing" large numbers of students in assembly-line schools to teach the Three R's—and so to assimilate rural workers and immigrants into the new requirements of work and citizenship. For the most part, these are still the schools we have today.

Except for the recent increased emphasis on preparing students for standardized tests, the teaching in our schools has hardly changed at all. Meanwhile, the needs of our society have changed dramatically. It is no longer enough to teach most kids the Three R's and have them memorize the parts of speech, all the state capitols, and the dates and generals of famous battles. And we can no longer tolerate large numbers of kids dropping out of school or graduating with only minimal skills. The days of well-paid unskilled or semiskilled work are over in this country, due to the forces of global competition. As we know, any job that can be routinized is being either automated or offshored. Increasingly, the only decent jobs that remain in this country will go to those who know how to continuously improve products or services or create entirely new ones—the knowledge workers of the twenty-first century.

In a very short period of time, our world has changed in three significant ways, and methods of teaching and learning must adapt to these changes:

- *All students need new skills to thrive in a global knowledge economy.* In order to get good jobs and to be active and informed citizens in our democracy, today's students—and tomorrow's workers—need to learn how to think critically and solve problems, work in teams and lead by influence, be agile and adaptable, take initiative and be entrepreneurial, communicate clearly and concisely, access and analyze information effectively, and be curious and imaginative. All of today's students will need to master the skills that Socrates taught—not just the elites.

- *In the age of the Internet, using new information to solve new problems matters more than recalling old information.* Being an independent, lifelong learner and knowing how to access and analyze information, which is growing exponentially and is constantly changing, is far more important than rote learning of specific academic content. Students today must be prepared to apply what they've learned to new situations and challenges, rather than merely recite what they've memorized.

- *Today's youth are* differently *motivated when we compare them to previous generations.* Having grown up tethered to the net, young people today are curious multitaskers who hunger for immediate gratification and connectedness. They are creative and want to make a difference. They need and value mentoring and coaching from older adults—but only when those adults are respectful of their abilities and their dreams and can relate authentically, rather than from a position of power.

What Makes for Good Classrooms and Schools Today?

While the schools I highlighted in the last chapter and the students whom they serve differ from one another in many ways, they nevertheless have certain characteristics in common. Educators in all three schools have worked hard to create models of teaching and learning that are responsive to the changes I outlined above. What happens in these schools is strikingly different from what we see in most schools today—and from what you may have experienced as a student:

1. *Learning and Assessment Focus.* In all three schools, the main purpose of teaching is the development of students' core competencies for lifelong learning. Memorization is downplayed in favor of weighing evidence, reasoning, and analysis. Research, writing, and effective oral communication matter far more than performance on multiple-choice tests (though the experience of all three schools suggests that students will do quite well on the required tests when they've been taught critical-thinking skills). These competencies are clearly articulated and are calibrated to real-world expectations. Students are expected to regularly and publicly demonstrate mastery of these core competencies through their oral and written work. Promotion to the next grade and graduation happen only when students can show that they have reached the expected level of proficiency in all of their work.

2. *Student Motivation.* Students are motivated to learn in all three schools through a combination of three distinct interrelated incentives. First, the adults in their lives—both in and out of school—have close relationships to students. Students in all three schools are not only well known by their teachers but are in advisory groups with a teacher who meets with them several times a week and becomes a kind of extended family. Students also work on projects with mentors outside of school. Second, oppor-

tunities for students to explore their questions and interests are a driving force for learning. Third, learning is
hands-on and more personalized in these schools, with
the result that students perform real-world tasks and
produce public products that reflect who they are—
what they believe and care about. You can hear each
student's distinct voice in every discussion, project, internship, and paper.

3. *School Accountability and Teacher Development.* The three
schools hold themselves collectively accountable for quality student work and student success in college and beyond. Rather than measuring themselves by the results of
a standardized test, all three schools look to measures
of what students can achieve in the real world as the ultimate assessment of their school's effectiveness. They seek
regular feedback from outsiders about the quality of students' work and performance in internships, and they
keep track of how many of their students go on to some
kind of postsecondary education and how well they do
there. Most important, they use this information to refine
their academic programs.

Teachers are motivated to improve continuously in all three schools
through a combination of structures and incentives. First, because the
schools are small (no more than 100 students in a graduating class),
they have a relationship with their students that spans several years. The
people involved in the schools are able to be more invested in, informed
about, and accountable for every student's success. They share this accountability for every student's success with colleagues who work together on a team. The work of the teachers in all three schools is also

publicly visible. Not only are they in and out of one another's classrooms regularly, and frequently team-teaching, but they also analyze the quality of work that students are producing in different classes. As we know, high-quality student work is a distinguishing characteristic of effective teaching.

Significantly, these schools are also pioneering new ways of organizing the work of teachers. Teachers work longer hours in these schools, even though their salaries are equivalent to what public school teachers make in the surrounding districts. In addition, the teachers in all three schools work on a one-year contract—with no tenure. However, I observed that they have a much higher rate of job satisfaction when I compared them to teachers in conventional public schools. This is due to the respect they are given, as well as to the distinctive nature of the tasks they must perform. Their daily work is far more intellectually challenging than that of most educators. Indeed, the teachers at these three schools are expected to use most of the Seven Survival Skills themselves as they create new units of study and assess student work together. Remember what Andreas Schleicher told me in Chapter 4 about how Finland got the best test results of any country because it "relies on the minds of the profession to develop the system"? That's what these schools do.

Equally important, rather than working in isolation or doing only occasional team-teaching, teachers in all three schools are organized into teams that have explicit responsibility for the success of a group of students. Teachers also have significantly more planning and professional-development time built into their schedules than do most public school teachers. As a consequence of these different working conditions, teacher turnover is very low, and all three schools are swamped with applicants for the few positions that do open up.

In addition, two of the three schools—High Tech High and Francis Parker—are developing new ways to train prospective teachers that are very different from what is being done in most schools of education at the university level. Indeed, teacher preparation in these schools resembles the medical model of clinical supervision and extended hands-on internships. Although the three schools were founded by educational visionaries, they are now being successfully managed by a new generation of leaders, and they are replicating themselves or helping others to create similar schools. These are not just the success stories of a few charismatic leaders. Finally, the per-student operating budgets at the three schools are not very different from those at nearby public schools. These school models are replicable—meaning that there is no reason why we can't create many more of these schools, if we choose to do so.

Questions That Parents, Teachers, and Community Leaders Have Asked Me

While working on this book for the past two years, I've had a number of opportunities to present some of the key ideas described here to a variety of audiences. These exchanges have provided me with important feedback and questions—questions you may be considering as you come to the end of the book. I certainly don't pretend to know all of the answers, but perhaps these exchanges will offer you a chance to have some of your remaining questions addressed:

Q. You don't explore academic subjects and content in much detail. Why?

A. I believe some content *should* indeed be memorized, and I think core academic subject knowledge as well as what the author and literary critic E. D. Hirsch calls "cultural literacy" are important. Do I think all students should memorize their times tables? Have a basic knowledge of geography and the timelines of U.S. and world history? Be exposed to Shakespeare? Speak a second language? Absolutely.

Beyond an easy list such as this one, however, things begin to get a little more difficult, as well as more specific to a time and place. For example, E. D. Hirsch does not include knowledge of Sunni and Shiite cultures and the long history of their conflict in his list of what's critical for cultural literacy; yet without this understanding, you simply cannot comprehend what is happening in the Middle East today. Similarly, it's relatively easy for all of us to agree that the works of Shakespeare should be on the list of high school classics, but what about a more contemporary book like *Reading Lolita in Tehran* by Iranian author and professor Azar Nafisi, or world-literature giants like the South African novelist J. M. Coetzee, who was awarded the Nobel Prize in 2003, or a young author like Edwidge Danticat, the Haitian-born American writer who chronicles the immigrant experience so powerfully?

Trying to establish what constitutes or defines core academic knowledge has a number of pitfalls. First there is the sheer quantity of content, and the fact that it continues to grow exponentially. In science, what is considered "true" must be constantly updated—such as the recent change in the definition of a planet. Content in the humanities continues to expand as well. How do you decide, for example, which of the above authors all students should be exposed to—especially when scholars in the field do not, themselves, agree on who belongs on a "must-read" list and who does not? Some of our communities also have trouble deciding what's most important. Whether we teach evolution or creationism has been one of the most controversial education issues of the last few years in several states, and it illustrates the ways in which communities can become bitterly divided about what should and should not be taught.

I don't have an easy solution to these dilemmas, but I think that the professional educators' associations—such as the National Council of Teachers of Mathematics, the National Science Teachers Association, and the National Council for the Social Studies—must define what it means to be literate in their disciplines. As I discussed in the chapter on testing, academics and educators' associations have in the past been unwilling to make tough decisions about both essential academic content and core competencies. They need to describe what it means to think like mathematicians, scientists, or historians, and set down the foundational content knowledge that is required for lifelong learning in these disciplines. These descriptions of important content knowledge would, of course, have to be updated regularly.

Finally, it should be obvious that there is no way to teach the competencies of critical thinking, problem solving, effective communication, and accessing and analyzing information, and so on without also teaching academic content. Subject-content material is what you think and write about, and problem solving is initially best understood and practiced as a part of the study of math, science, and social studies. But in today's world, academic content must be the means by which we teach core competencies—rather than through merely memorizing (and often forgetting) academic content for its own sake. Students can always look up when the Battle of Gettysburg took place, or who General Sherman was, but they can't just Google the causes of the Civil War and make sense of what comes up on the screen. To understand such an issue, you have to know how to think critically, and you need a broader conceptual understanding of American history, economics, and more. As we've seen, these skills and this kind of knowledge are rarely taught or tested in high schools today.

Q. Why do you focus on the problems in our high schools? Aren't there similar problems in our elementary schools—and even in our colleges?

A. I agree that we need to rethink what students should be taught and how today's students learn best at every education level. At the elementary school level, however, we at least agree on the skills that all students must learn: basic reading, writing, and computational skills. And, for the most part, these are the skills most frequently tested in these grades, though the teaching of them leaves much to be desired, as we learned from the elementary classroom study I cited in Chapter 2. Similarly, there is at least a general agreement about the problem-solving, communication, critical-thinking, and analytic-reasoning skills that colleges *should* be teaching, though many are beginning to question whether colleges are doing a good enough job. This is one reason why the Collegiate Learning Assessment, mentioned in Chapter 3, is currently being used in over 250 colleges and universities to assess the extent to which students are learning these skills in college.

However, there is a profound disconnect between what students are taught and tested on in most high schools today and how they are expected to learn, versus what the world will demand of them as adults and what motivates them to do their best. Much of the high school curriculum and many of the methods of teaching are nearly a century old and hopelessly obsolete. And the states' accountability tests don't even begin to assess any of the skills that matter in today's world. Of the three main education areas—elementary, secondary, and college—I believe the greatest gap between what is taught and tested versus what all students need to succeed and to contribute to their communities exists in our secondary schools.

Q. You talk a lot about the importance of all students being "college-ready," and you use this as an indicator of success in your assessment of high schools. Do you think all students should go to college?
A. I do not believe that all students need to go to college to have a rewarding and successful life. Some kids choose not to go to college and instead enter a trade, preferring to work with their hands. But I think all students should have the *choice* of whether to go to college. That choice should not

be made by adults in schools, which is what happens today when students get tracked into a low-level math or English class or are not told at an early age that they can go to college or are not guided through the application process.

Another point I make about young people being "college-ready" is that the skills students need to succeed in college are the same skills they will need to succeed in today's workplace. Remember the survey of employers that revealed that the single most important skill they will look for in the next few years when they hire a high school graduate is the ability to think critically? And the interviews and surveys of business leaders who say poor communication skills is the number-one problem with their new employees? Critical-thinking and communication skills are the same abilities that college teachers say are important for success in postsecondary education. They are also essential skills that an individual needs to be an informed and active citizen in our democracy.

I, too, worry about the lack of respect for "blue-collar" professions in which people work mainly with their hands or at tasks requiring physical exertion. One of the students in my college focus groups noted the following: "Everything is more competitive and materialistic today—college isn't just for rich kids anymore. You have to go because it's not okay to be a factory worker anymore." Others around the table agreed. Over the last few years, some people have told me stories about their children who have chosen to drop out of college and pursue a trade, such as carpentry or working as a skipper on a boat. While they support their children's explorations, they've expressed the hope that this is a phase their kids will grow out of— and that they will eventually return to college and get a "real" job.

John W. Gardner had something to say about this bias. He was secretary of health, education, and welfare under President Lyndon Johnson and went on to found Common Cause, the first public interest group in the United States. In his well-known book, *Excellence,* he wrote: "We must learn to honor excellence in every socially accepted human activity, however humble the activity, and to scorn shoddiness, however exalted the activity. An excellent plumber is infinitely more admirable than an incompetent philosopher. The society that scorns excellence in plumbing because plumbing is a humble activity and tolerates shoddiness in philosophy because it is an exalted activity will have neither good plumbing nor good philosophy. Neither its pipes nor its theories will hold water."[1] Being a plumber or a carpenter or an electrician or an auto mechanic and the like are all worthwhile professions, are well-paid today, and increasingly require postsecondary education and the same skills of problem solving, teamwork, and so on that are required in "white-collar" jobs.

This brings up another question I am often asked:

Q. *Aren't the skills you're describing needed only for certain kinds of jobs?*

A. Not at all. What became very clear to me in researching this book is that the most successful businesses want to hire as many employees as they can with these skills because they see harnessing talent as the key to staying competitive. The human resources director from Unilever talked about wanting problem solvers on the assembly line, and this is also the key to success in the Toyota Production System. To stay ahead of the global competition, the best companies are working to improve their product continuously, and they need their front-line workers to help them determine how to do this.

Recently, I came across another example of this approach to continuous improvement in the service business. The Ritz-Carlton chain of hotels has gained international recognition for its outstanding service. An article from *Expert Magazine* explains one of the secrets of its success: Every employee—from the housekeeper, to the doorman, to the desk clerk—can use his or her discretion and spend up to $2,000 to solve a guest's problems, without prior management approval. In other words, every Ritz-Carlton employee is empowered to take initiative as a problem solver and to work together with others toward every guest's satisfaction.[2]

Q. You talk about the Seven Survival Skills as critical for success today, but won't they become obsolete in ten years? Won't young people need an entirely different set of skills by then?

A. The Seven Survival Skills can best be understood as the essential tools and intellectual foundation a young person needs to excel in a time of rapid social, technological, and economic change—the kind of change that is occurring now and will continue to accelerate in nearly every country around the world. These core competencies will enable young people to adapt and to acquire new knowledge and new technical skills as needed—and, therefore, to deal more effectively with a future that no one can predict.

Q. What do you have to say about moral education—about the teaching of values?

A. I wrote about the importance of a values-based education in an earlier book, *Making the Grade,* where I told the stories of several schools that had lost sight of the importance of instilling values in students and were rethinking how best to encourage the citizenship behaviors that are essential in our democracy—such as tolerance and respect for others. In my first book, *How Schools Change,* I chronicle the story of how one school—Brimmer and May—successfully re-engaged parents and teachers in a shared conversation about the student behaviors that they wanted to encourage. I continue to believe that teaching students to struggle and to persevere, to respect others, to be aware of their actions, and to appreciate people who are different from themselves—aspects of what Daniel Goleman calls emotional intelligence, or EQ—are essential for a more civil discourse in our society, as well as for individual success and happiness. A decent IQ and mastery of the Seven Survival Skills won't get you very far without a well-developed EQ.

I also think there's a strong relationship between the mastery of some of the Seven Survival Skills and the development of emotional intelligence. Students who have learned to collaborate, to think critically, and to be more confident about their own ideas also tend to make better moral judgments. One of my favorite definitions of the aim of education comes from Swiss psychologist Jean Piaget, who wrote that the ultimate purpose of education is to overcome egocentrism in both the intellectual and emotional domains. Overcoming egocentrism intellectually means learning to reason and to weigh evidence, rather than being ruled by uninformed opinion or prejudice or pressures to conform. Emotionally, overcoming egocentrism means the development of what Piaget called reciprocity (or what we might call empathy).[3]

The importance of having a strong moral foundation is one of the many reasons why parents are a vital part of all children's education. Educators cannot do it all, and the job is much more difficult if teachers are not working in tandem with parents and community members. I believe that parents and educators must work together to make clear their shared expectations for all students—moral as well as intellectual.

A New Dialogue for Our Children's Future

We are not going to transform education by simply replacing one administration with another or even by passing new laws. Instituting better assessments is the one most important change we could make tomorrow that would have the greatest impact, but before we can consider a host of other policy recommendations, we first must have a long-overdue dialogue—a discussion that might well start with a simple admission and a question: *I thought I knew what students needed to learn and what a good school looks like—because I was a student once and I went to school, and it worked for me. But times have changed. And maybe students today do need something different. I wonder what it is?*

If all students are to acquire the new skills for success in the twenty-first century, the change I describe must be *systemic,* and it must start in individual living rooms and classrooms, in school PTA and faculty meetings and district central offices. I believe it begins with a change of mind and heart—a change that comes about through adults learning together. *Above all else, what I have come to understand in this work is that powerful questions are what drive real learning and that such learning is a precondition for lasting change.* Following are some of the essential questions that we all need to explore together in every school and every community, in every state house and department of education, in Congress, and in our national educational organizations:

- In light of the fundamental changes that have taken place in our society in the last twenty-five years, what does it mean to be an educated adult in the twenty-first century? What do we think all high school graduates need to know and be able to do to be well-prepared for college, careers, and citizenship? And since we can't teach everything, what is most important?

- How might our definition of *academic rigor* need to change in the age of the information explosion?

- What are the best ways to know whether students have mastered the skills that matter most? How do we create a better assessment and accountability system that gives us the information we need to ensure that all students are learning essential skills?

- What do we need to do in our schools to motivate students to be curious and imaginative, and to enjoy learning for its own sake? How do we ensure that every student has an adult advocate in his or her school who knows the student well?

- How do we both support our educators and hold them more accountable for results? What changes are needed in how educators are trained, how they work together in schools, and how they are supervised and evaluated in order to enable them to continuously improve?

- What do good schools look like—schools where all students are mastering the skills that matter most? How are they different from the schools we have, and what can we learn from them?

If you are persuaded by the ideas and stories in this book, then I suggest that you have new work to do. Your work is to sponsor thoughtful, reflective discussions about what our children need to know and be able to do in the twenty-first century and how best to motivate them to learn. Whether it is with friends around the dining table, in a reading group, or in a church or synagogue discussion group, or at your PTA or faculty meeting, or in conversations with administrators and school boards, members of your state legislature, or members of Congress—your work is to initiate and sustain a different kind of conversation.

The questions outlined above or the topics of each chapter of this book may be useful as an outline for your discussions. You may also find it helpful for your group to view an important new documentary film, produced by Robert Compton, titled *Two Million Minutes,* which chronicles the school experiences of six adolescents—two each in the United States, China, and India.[4] However you choose to start the conversation, it will succeed only if it is a reflective discussion that is driven by the important questions rather than the easy answers—by inquiry rather than ideology. It needs to be a dialogue that demands both respect for different views and a critical intellect that enables you to ask: How do you know that? What's your evidence? Your new work, I suggest, is to start practicing the Seven Survival Skills yourself as you collaborate with others to create the schools our children urgently need for the twenty-first century.

In the early stages of my research for this book, Clay Parker told me that the most important workplace skills today are asking the right questions and engaging others in vital conversations. I was skeptical then. It was difficult for me to believe that these skills, which I have long valued as a teacher in classrooms, might be just as important to business leaders in boardrooms. Having been on this journey of discovery for several years now, I know that he was right. But these skills are not only what young people need to be successful on the job. They are also what we all need in order to be contributing citizens in a vibrant democracy—and to confront the challenges and make the changes that we must for a better future for our children.

Borrowing from the ancient wisdom of Rabbi Hillel: If not you, then who? If not now, then when?

Afterword to the Paperback Edition

SINCE THE HARDBACK publication of this book, I have traveled all over the United States speaking to a wide variety of audiences—state school superintendents, educators and parents from both public and independent schools, and community, philanthropic, business, and military leaders. I have also had opportunities to speak with leadership groups in the Middle and Far East. From Bahrain to Taiwan, from Wall Street to West Point, the response has been remarkably consistent. Almost without exception, diverse audiences have affirmed the importance of the Seven Survival Skills and shared my concern that the majority of students are leaving high school without the skills that matter most—even in those districts that score well on Advanced Placement exams and state tests.

It comes as no surprise, then, that the most frequent question I'm asked is: "What can we do about the problem?" Fortunately, because of some important work that has been done over the last several years, there are exciting new answers to this question. In this brief Afterword, I outline essential steps to overcome the "global achievement gap." I begin by considering what communities can do to create a higher level of accountability for schools and districts—beyond standardized test scores—and I tell the story of how the Virginia Beach City Public Schools set about transforming teaching and learning in their district. I then describe what many educators are doing to improve teaching and enhance learning in their classes in schools throughout the United States and elsewhere. Taken together, many of these initiatives and examples point to what we—educators, parents, business and community leaders—need to be

advocating for with our state and national legislators as essential elements of an Accountability 2.0 system for education in the twenty-first
century.

Creating Accountability for What Matters Most: All Students Graduating College-, Career-, and Citizenship-Ready

The first critical step in creating a community-wide focus on the skills
that matter most for students' success is to engage in a very different
kind of strategic planning. Typically, districts create new strategic plans
every few years in a process that is usually led by school boards with very
little community involvement. All too often, these efforts result in the
production of overly long written documents with lists of five-year goals
(such as improving test scores by a certain percentage), which rarely result in any real change in classrooms. Once in a great while, though, a
superintendent sees a strategic planning effort as an opportunity for
community engagement and adult learning—and as a way to create a
road map for significant improvements. One such leader with whom I
have worked is Jim Merrill, currently in his fourth year as superintendent of the Virginia Beach City Public Schools in Virginia.

   The third-largest school district in the state, Virginia Beach enrolls
70,000 students and has a diverse minority population that is 45 percent of the total enrollment.[1] When Jim was selected for the superintendent's position in 2006, the district enjoyed a reputation as highly
successful, with all of its schools having made "adequate yearly
progress" on state tests and meeting additional accreditation standards.
However, Jim was concerned that Virginia's tests (like those of most
other states) assessed only basic skills with a minimum level of proficiency required to "pass" and, hence, that success on these tests was not
a reliable measure of students' career- and college-readiness. In his sec-

ond year on the job, Jim and his senior administrators met with me for a day-long retreat and decided to work on a very different kind of strategic planning process—one that would involve the entire community in a conversation about how the world has changed and what were the most important student outcomes that the school district should now be accountable for.

With strong school-board leadership and support, Virginia Beach staff set out to collect the kinds of data that they thought should inform a more meaningful strategic planning process. First, they conducted focus groups with local employers and college teachers about the skills students needed to succeed. Second, they administered the College and Work Readiness Assessment (discussed in Chapter 3) to a sample population of their 12th graders and learned that—despite having scored well on state tests—the top 50 percent of these seniors who took the test were in the lowest quartile of college freshmen taking the same test. Third, they took a hard look at the state-mandated formula for computing the district's high school graduation rate and concluded that it resulted in inaccurate—and overly optimistic—reporting of the percentage of students who successfully completed high school in the district—as is the case in most states.[2] Although it turned out that the district's 82 percent graduation rate was more than 10 percent higher than the national average, Jim declared that this was unacceptable. Finally, they subscribed to the National Student Clearinghouse, which gave them data on their students' enrollment and persistence in postsecondary-degree programs.[3] To better understand these quantitative data, the district conducted subsequent focus groups with recent Virginia Beach graduates about some of the ways they felt most and least well prepared by the schools for their futures.

The culmination of this effort was a community-wide meeting to talk about these and other district data and to consider what were the most important outcomes for Virginia Beach graduates in a changing world. Nearly 1,000 people—educators, parents, community members— gathered in the Virginia Beach Convention Center on a warm summer evening in 2008 for discussion at tables seating ten. After an hour of presentations, which included looking at various data as well as at videos of the focus groups that had been conducted, and then engaging in extended conversation at each table, individuals were asked to consider a long list of possible learning priorities for the district and to select the ones they considered most important. These "votes" were then quickly tabulated electronically. To the surprise of many, there was a virtual consensus on the outcomes that should be the highest priority for the district in coming years: The skills of critical thinking and problem solving were at the top of nearly everyone's list.

Jim, his staff, and the school board then took this information and created a very different kind of strategic plan. Instead of the long laundry list of mashed-together goals, priorities, and initiatives that, all too often, is the result of most districts' strategic planning efforts, the Virginia Beach strategic plan, called *Compass to 2015: A Strategic Plan for Student Success*, has been streamlined down to one strategic goal, four outcomes for students, and five strategic objectives, with a few key strategies and measures identified for each—and it fits on the front and back of one page! The plan is quoted below, minus the key strategies and measures. (You can download the complete document at this link to the Virginia Beach website: http://www.vbschools.com/compass/StrategicPlan.pdf.)

Our Strategic Goal

Recognizing that the long range goal of the VBCPS [Virginia Beach City Public Schools] is the successful preparation and graduation of every student, the near term goal is that by 2015, 95 percent or more of VBCPS students will graduate having mastered the skills that they need to succeed as 21st century learners, workers and citizens.

Our Outcomes for Student Success

Our primary focus is on teaching and assessing those skills our students need to thrive as 21st century learners, workers and citizens. All VBCPS students will be:

- Academically proficient;
- Effective communicators and collaborators;
- Globally aware, independent, responsible learners and citizens; and
- Critical and creative thinkers, innovators and problem solvers.

Our Strategic Objectives

1) All teachers will engage every student in meaningful, authentic and rigorous work through the use of innovative instructional practices and supportive technologies that will motivate students to be self-directed and inquisitive learners.

2) VBCPS will develop and implement a balanced assessment system that accurately reflects student demonstration and mastery of VBCPS outcomes for student success.

3) Each school will improve achievement for all students while closing achievement gaps for identified student groups, with particular focus on African American males.

4) VBCPS will create opportunities for parents, community and business leaders to fulfill their essential roles as actively engaged partners in supporting student achievement and outcomes for student success.

5) VBCPS will be accountable for developing essential leader, teacher and staff competencies and optimizing all resources to achieve the school division's strategic goal and outcomes for student success.

The district leaders' next step was to begin working on creating accountability for teaching and assessing the four essential student outcomes that had been identified. They decided to start by defining what *critical thinking* means and, more important, what it looks like in the classroom. District central-office and building administrators conducted "learning walks"—using the same process I describe in Chapter 2—to help everyone be more clear about what critical thinking looks like when it's happening. The results of their efforts are summarized on their website,[4] which I have excerpted here:

> Last school year, we concentrated on looking for critical thinking skills, attempting to see how these skills were manifested in student engagement, questioning and work products. This school year, the leadership learning walks will still be looking for the hallmarks of critical thinking, but we will ask principals to specifically point out their areas of focus as the result of the *Compass to 2015* strategic plan. The goal is to support schools as they work on the needs inherent in their schools. All learning walks are followed by a conversation with the school leadership.
>
> In the meantime, we anticipate that stakeholders may ask us: How do we know when we have encountered critical thinking in classrooms? Below is a list of attributes identified collectively by the principals of Virginia Beach City Public Schools:

- Students successfully grapple with higher-order questions asked by teacher.
- Students articulate meaningful response to "so what" (what if, why).
- Students generate higher-level questions.
- Students engage in authentic learning activities and/or create authentic work.

- Students defend positions with justification based on factual evidence and data.
- Students analyze and solve new problems by generating a variety of ideas and solutions.
- Students recognize and pose problems inherent in a given situation.
- Students adapt learned knowledge to more complex/ambiguous situations.
- Students use and explain the right method of thinking (reasoning, decision making, problem solving, making judgments).
- Students evaluate and communicate their own thinking.
- Students make connections and predictions using prior knowledge.
- Students select, create, use and communicate effectiveness of a variety of tools, such as graphic organizers or grid paper.

Education is no longer just about teaching Johnny (or Juan) to read. It's about teaching him to think critically about what he reads, interpret what he reads, and relate what he reads to his own life. If we are asking students for critical examination and reflection, we must be willing to do the same. These learning walks are our common journey to better understand the needs of the children, to improve how we teach and to more clearly define what we expect of our students and ourselves.

"It's the hardest work I've ever undertaken in my career," Jim told me recently. "We're trying to effect change at scale, and we have to 'play on two playing fields' at once. We're still being judged by the criteria for 'Adequate Yearly Progress' and state accountability standards, while we are holding ourselves to a much higher standard. We have to succeed at both. It's hard but it's the right work to be doing."

Assessments of Students' Mastery
of Core Competencies

Recently, there has been much discussion about creating systems that reward teachers who improve standardized test scores and making these scores a part of all teachers' evaluations. While I strongly advocate strengthening evaluation systems for educators and phasing out tenure at every level, the risk of so-called pay-for-performance plans is that they will cause individual teachers—working in secret because they are competing against their colleagues—to figure out gimmicks for improving their students' test scores but not necessarily their learning. As we've seen, test-score improvements don't tell us very much about what students know and are able to do. If you go back and look at the Virginia Beach leaders' list of evidence of critical thinking in the classroom, you will notice something interesting: The words *teacher* and *test* do not appear. As Jim explained, "When we began doing learning walks to look for evidence of critical thinking, we initially just focused on what the teachers were doing. We soon discovered, though, that the only real evidence of critical thinking happening in the classroom was in *what the students were doing*."

The most effective way to assess the quality of instruction in a classroom—and to ensure that students have the skills they need for careers, college, and citizenship—is to systematically look at student work and to regularly require students to "show what they know." As you may recall from Chapter 6, when I asked Ben Daley at High Tech High how he assessed the effectiveness of a teacher, he answered simply: "We judge teachers by the quality of their students' work." You may also remember that all three of the schools I profile in Chapter 6 require students to show mastery of core competencies through culminating projects and portfolios of their work. Students are required to "perform" in order to show what they can do with what they know—

much in the same way that student performances in athletics or the performing arts are the only true test of competence in those areas.

There is growing interest in the idea of having all 12th graders perform senior projects as a way to assess critical thinking and communication skills. Beginning with the graduating class of 2008, all seniors in Rhode Island public schools are now required to complete a "performance-based" assessment in order to graduate. According to the Rhode Island Department of Education website, this new graduation requirement "was developed in response to concerns from colleges and employers that high school graduates—even those who performed well in courses and on tests—were not always well prepared for college and work. To succeed after high school, students must think creatively, solve problems, work in groups, speak in public, and apply what they have learned in real-world situations. The mission of the diploma system is to ensure that all students can compete in academic and employment settings, and can contribute to society." These performances can include an exhibition of student work (such as a project or internship) or a graduation portfolio. According to the Department of Education, "Each assessment is designed around the student's own interests or passions."[5] (The exact requirements are determined by individual high schools.)

Of course, individual schools—including many that are members of the Coalition of Essential Schools—have required senior projects for years. One well-documented example that I recently came across is the senior-project requirement of Quest High School, a public high school of choice in Humble, Texas. All students spent the entire second semester of their senior year working in teams to complete a three-part project, which includes a twenty-page argument-based paper, a community service project, and a culminating public presentation of the team's work and research to a panel of judges, parents, teachers, students, and community members. The Coalition offers an excellent thirty-minute video that follows the members of one team as they work on their project components during the semester. The video also includes a seven-page table of rubrics used to assess the different elements of each student's project.[6] (Similar senior projects are required in Virginia Beach's themed academies and advanced academic programs.)

While new 12th-grade project and portfolio graduation requirements represent an important innovation, they would be far more effective if they were incorporated into all courses at every grade level and became "graduation requirements" for transitioning from elementary to middle school and then again from middle to high school. Mission Hill School, founded by world-renowned educator Deborah Meier, is an excellent example of a K–8 public school in Boston that requires all students to complete an extensive portfolio and exhibitions of mastery as a requirement for completion of 8th grade. Students begin working on their portfolio and exhibition requirements in 6th grade.[7]

Another excellent example of an international program that requires students to demonstrate mastery (and one that I regret not having explored more fully while doing the research for this book) is the International Baccalaureate Program. Developed initially as a way to standardize course and curricula requirements across a variety of schools around the world, the IB Program has evolved to become a coherent K–12 approach to teaching and assessing many of the Seven Survival Skills. High school students enrolled in IB must take at least six IB courses that culminate in rigorous exams on which students must demonstrate that they can apply what they have learned. But, perhaps even more important, they must also complete the following additional requirements:[8]

Theory of Knowledge

One of the most important elements of the DP (Diploma Program) is the theory of knowledge course, which challenges students to question the bases of knowledge—to reflect critically on how they know what they believe to be facts or the truth. It consists almost entirely of exploring questions about different sources of knowledge (perception, language, emotion, reason) and different kinds of knowledge (scientific, artistic, mathematical, historical), such as:

- Do we construct reality or do we recognize it?
- Does knowledge always require some kind of rational basis? Is there any kind of knowledge that can be attained solely through emotion?
- Is scientific knowledge progressive; has it always grown? Can we reach a point where everything important in a scientific sense is known?

Creativity, Action, Service (CAS)

Another important element of the DP is creativity, action, service (CAS). To fulfill this requirement, students must take part in artistic activities (creative); sports, expeditions or local or international projects (action); and community or social service projects (service). Participation in CAS raises students' awareness of community needs and gives them an opportunity to apply what they have learned in the classroom to address these needs. It also gives them confidence in their ability to bring about change. The projects must have tangible results and offer real benefits to others. Reflection on their experience is also an important part of student involvement in CAS.

The Extended Essay

An extended essay, of at most 4,000 words, offers students an opportunity to conduct an in-depth study of a topic of special interest. The experience and skills gained in carrying out independent research and producing a structured, substantial piece of writing provide excellent preparation for independent study at the university level.

Because of these additional requirements, I consider the IB Program to be a far better standard of rigor than Advanced Placement courses, which cover too much content and require far too much factual recall on the final exams, rather than requiring students to show what they can do with what they know. In contrast to the IB Diploma Program, for which all students must write an extended research paper, students routinely take an entire AP curriculum and never write a research paper because teachers say there is simply no time for such extended independent work when so much required content must be covered. I recently conducted a focus group with some 12th-grade students who had taken courses in both programs. When I asked about the differences between them, one student replied, "AP courses teach you *what* to think. IB teaches you *how* to think." The other students at the table nodded in agreement.

There is something else I would like to see explored by schools and districts: In addition to regular exhibitions of mastery and extended independent work, all students could be required to maintain digital portfolios that would follow them from year to year. Digital portfolios offer excellent opportunities for students to have a real audience for their work and for documenting their progress over time. And, as my colleague Evangeline Stefanakis's research has shown, digital portfolios offer students who normally do not perform well on timed, standardized tests an important alternative way of demonstrating proficiency.[9]

Although individual students and their teacher would have access to all of the students' work produced during the course of a school year, students might also "publish" a few products each year—research papers, reports, presentations, and so on—that could be viewed by parents and their teachers in future years. Imagine a teacher being able to start a school year by perusing the work that students had done the previous year. Imagine, also, that such portfolios of work, which would be the property of individual students and their families, could follow the student to another school or district—or even be shared as a part of the college admissions process.

As you may recall, all three of the schools that I profile in Chapter 6 require students to maintain digital portfolios, and you can browse through some excellent examples on the High Tech High website. Recently, I learned that digital portfolios are widely used by many schools in several Canadian provinces, and the software for maintaining them is available for free.[10] A number of educational institutions are working collaboratively in Canada to continue developing the software and to research its impact in classrooms. The technologies for developing and maintaining high-quality student digital portfolios—free software, inexpensive digital cameras, and "cloud" file storage—have recently become readily available and are very reasonably priced. For this reason, I believe that digital portfolios have the potential to become another one of those "disruptive technologies" in education that Clayton Christensen writes about in his provocative book, *Disrupting Class*.[11]

Working Collaboratively—and Transparently

The work individual teachers may do to improve students' standardized test scores is usually done alone in the secrecy of a classroom, and the results are often not known for many months. By contrast, students' demonstrations of mastery through culminating projects, the IB Program, and digital portfolios lend themselves to a far greater degree of teacher collaboration—and the results are immediately and publicly evident. In schools with robust programs that require students to do final exhibitions and maintain digital portfolios, teams of teachers routinely assess the quality of student work together, and parents and community members are invited to attend special student exhibition nights. In addition, outsiders (college teachers, employers, and community members) are often asked to "audit" the quality of randomly chosen portfolios. And the IB program requires that teams of teachers from other schools grade a school's final exams and papers. In fact, schools cannot even be accepted into the IB Program without rigorous peer re-view, which includes visits from an inspection team.

All of these opportunities contribute to creating a different kind of "face-to-face" accountability, where teachers' work is more transparent and therefore subject to greater scrutiny. Their work—and that of their students—is regularly on display. If the students are consistently pro-ducing projects and portfolios that are of lesser quality, it is much harder to hide.

In addition to phasing in student portfolios, districts should encour-age teachers to develop portfolios of their own work. Here's the ideal: You are looking at an excellent example of a student's paper or project in his or her portfolio, and you want to know more about the teacher's "work"—the project or unit design—that lies behind this student work. So you follow a link embedded in the student's portfolio that takes you to the teacher's portfolio. Here you might find the following:

- The outline of the unit of study or project design, which includes goals and outcomes, assignments, re-sources, and so on

- A video clip showing how the teacher introduced the project or unit of study

- Video clips of class and small-group discussions

- The rubrics used to assess students' work, with a range of sample papers or projects produced by students (all capable of being downloaded for discussion by teams of teachers)

- Finally, a videotaped discussion of students' experiences in doing the work—what they found most engaging, ways in which they were motivated, what they learned, and so on

As we learned in Chapter 4, the National Board for Professional Teaching Standards offers voluntary advanced certification for teachers—and peer-reviewed portfolios prepared by candidate teachers that include sample lesson plans and video clips of teaching are essential elements of their certification process. Moreover, the National Board is now working on a similar certification process for principals.[12] In that same chapter, I outlined the kinds of things I think should be included in a principal's portfolio.

What student, teacher, and leader portfolios all have in common is the concept of performance standards and performance-based assessment. There is a great deal of talk about adopting national content standards, but I would like to see much more attention paid to the idea of performance standards. You may know the parts of speech (a content standard), but the real question is, can you write an effective essay?—which is the performance standard that matters most in the real world. You can quickly do an Internet search for the definition of *gerund* (something I always struggled to remember when I taught grammar), but no amount of time spent online will likely teach you how to write better essays. The Council of Chief State School Officers has recently received a great deal of attention for its advocacy of national content standards. Much less well known, and potentially far more important, is the work it has been doing in the development of performance standards—beginning with writing.[13]

In fact, the United States lags quite far behind in the development of performance-based assessments for accountability purposes. Linda

Darling-Hammond has researched how the best education systems around the world regularly use performance-based assessments in most courses and even as a part of national exams.[14] And now Cisco, Intel, and Microsoft have formed an alliance to develop online assessments of twenty-first-century skills.[15] This test will be piloted as part of the Programme for International Student Assessment (PISA) tests in 2012.

Sponsoring Research and Development

The calls to overhaul our education system often ignore an essential precondition: You cannot create new products and services without research and development. Schools, districts, and states have no "education R & D" budget. How, then, are they supposed to create the new models of teaching, learning, and school organization? Expecting compliance to top-down mandates is simply not an effective strategy for creating the kinds of change I've been describing. And while the U.S. Department of Education has recently announced a series of "innovation grants," it's not clear exactly what kind of innovations the Department hopes to incentivize beyond better ways to improve scores on bad tests.

One cannot expect an entire school district to transform itself from a model of schooling that is nearly a hundred years old—and all too familiar to virtually every adult—to a new model of twenty-first-century learning that seems far too abstract and ethereal to many. We need to create more models and laboratories—existence proofs—of twenty-first-century schools all over the country. Throughout the past decade, the charter school movement has spawned a great deal of R & D in secondary school redesign (done with significant support from the Bill & Melinda Gates Foundation and others). All of the models I describe in Chapter 6 grew out of intentional efforts to create very different kinds of high schools. But schools do not have to be charters to be innovative.

New Tech High is a national network of high schools that is growing rapidly around the country, and most of these new schools are not charters. Rather, New Tech High is often invited to start a new school in a district in order to demonstrate what a different model of education can accomplish. In fact, with the visionary leadership of Governor Mitch Daniels and strong support from the KnowledgeWorks Foundation and the Center of Excellence in Leadership and Learning (CELL), Indiana is now working toward establishing at least one High Tech High in every single school district in the state.[16]

I would like to see every large school district—or associations of smaller districts—establish laboratory schools similar to New Tech High and the three I've described in this book. In effect, they would be district-sponsored "charter-like" schools—similar to the Pilot Schools established by the Boston Public Schools and Teacher's Union in 1994 that now serve about 10 percent of the BPS enrollment.[17] Parents and teachers would choose to apply to the schools, which could have a lottery to ensure that the student composition is the same as in other schools, and these schools would have the same resources per student as other schools in the district. But they'd also have a distinct mission: to develop new models of teaching, learning, and assessment—the practices that I've described here—that would, over time, spread to the other schools in the district. Establishing such schools could have the added advantages of incentivizing the "edupreneurs" who might otherwise leave teaching and of offering competition to area charter schools.

Beyond "R & D": Creating a Culture of Innovation

A question I am asked by many educators is: "How can I teach the Seven Survival Skills to students when I haven't learned them?"—an important question that leads me to ask several others. For example: How are these skills best developed by and for adults, and to what extent is a culture of innovation an essential precondition for this new kind of adult and student learning? What do some of the most innovative companies in different sectors do to develop adults' capacities to be innovators, and what might educators learn from them? These questions lie at the very heart of the challenge to create the new innovation economy that many are now calling for, and I plan to devote my next book to exploring this topic.

In the meantime, I continue to have great admiration for the educators who—in spite of being pressured to just teach to the tests—struggle to teach their students the skills that matter most. And I continue to have great appreciation for the many parents and business, military, and community leaders who tirelessly advocate for the total transformation of our obsolete education system. Because of all that I have seen and heard in the two years since completing this book, I have an even greater sense of urgency—as well as hope—about this work we do together.

Notes

Quote on page vi is from Alice Calaprice, ed., *The Expanded Quotable Einstein* (Princeton, NJ: Princeton University Press, 2000).

PREFACE

1. Public Agenda Foundation, "Reality Check 2006," available online at http://publicagenda.org/research/pdfs/rc0603.pdf (accessed January 15, 2008).

2. See my article, "Rigor on Trial," in *Education Week,* January 11, 2006.

INTRODUCTION

1. From the report "Education at a Glance 2003," Organisation for Economic Co-operation and Development (OECD), available online at http://www.oecd .org/document/52/0,2340,en_2649_33723_13634484_1_1_1_1,00.html (accessed January 15, 2008).

2. These data are in a report prepared by David Conley for the Bill & Melinda Gates Foundation, "Toward a More Comprehensive Conception of College Readiness," available online at http://www.gatesfoundation.org/UnitedStates /Education/ResearchAndEvaluati/Research/HSImprovement.htm (accessed March 20, 2008).

3. From the Alliance for Excellent Education September 2007 Issue Brief, "High School Teaching for the Twenty-First Century: Preparing Students for College," available online at http://www.al14ed.org/files/HSTeach21st.pdf (accessed January 15, 2008).

4. Ibid.

5. From the executive summary of "America's Perfect Storm," Educational Testing Service (Princeton, 2007), available online at http://www.ets.org/Media/ Education_Topics/pdf/AmericasPerfectStorm.pdf (accessed January 21, 2008).

6. From the report "Education at a Glance 2004," Organisation for Economic Co-operation and Development (OECD), available online at http://www .oecd.org/document/7/0,2340,en_2649_34515_712135_1_1_1_1,00.html (accessed January 15, 2008).

7. From the report "Are They Really Ready to Work?" sponsored by The Conference Board, Corporate Voices for Working Families, the Partnership for 21st Century Skills, and the Society for Human Resource Management; available online at http://21stcenturyskills.org/documents/key_findings_joint.pdf (accessed January 15, 2008).

8. U.S. Census report, "Voting and Registration in the Election of November 2004," available online at http://www.census.gov/prod/2006pubs/p20-556.pdf (accessed January 15, 2008).

9. See, for example, Thomas Friedman, *The World Is Flat: Moving from the Information Age to the Conceptual Age* (New York: Farrar, Straus and Giroux, 2005); and Daniel Pink, *A Whole New Mind: Why Right-Brainers Will Rule the Future* (New York: Riverhead Books, 2005).

CHAPTER 1

1. See "Education at a Glance 2003," Organisation for Economic Co-operation and Development (OECD), available online at http://www.oecd.org/document/52/0,2340,en_2649_33723_13634484_1_1_1_1,00.html (accessed January 15, 2008); and Alliance for Excellent Education September 2007 Issue Brief, "High School Teaching for the Twenty-First Century: Preparing Students for College," available online at http://www.a114ed.org/files/HSTeach21st.pdf (accessed January 15, 2008).

2. These data were provided by the National Assessments of Educational Progress (NAEP), a series of assessments and resulting "Report Cards" on education, sponsored by the National Center for Education Statistics, a division of the U.S. Department of Education; available online at http://nces.ed.gov/index.asp (accessed July 8, 2007).

3. Robert Pianta et al., "Opportunities to Learn in America's Elementary Classrooms," *Science*, vol. 315 (March 30, 2007), pp. 1795–1796.

4. "Are They Ready for Work?" available online at http://www.21stcentury skills.org/documents/FINAL_REPORT_PDF09–29–06.pdf (accessed July 8, 2007).

5. "At I.B.M., a Smarter Way to Outsource," *New York Times*, July 5, 2007, available online at http://www.nytimes.com/2007/07/05/bune/05Outsource .html?_r=1&oref=slogin (accessed July 8, 2007).

6. Quoted from the Partnership for 21st Century Skills, "Core Subjects and 21st Century Themes," available online at w.21stcentyskills.org/index.php?optio com_conent&task=view&id=256&Itid=124 (accessed July 9, 2007).

7. "Are They Ready for Work?" available online at http://www.21stcentury skills.org/documents/FINAL_REPORT_PDF09–29–06.pdf (accessed July 8, 2007).

8. Daniel Pink, *A Whole New Mind: Moving from the Information Age to the Conceptual Age* (New York: Riverhead Books, 2005), pp. 32–33.

9. Ibid., pp. 2–3.

CHAPTER 2

1. These data are in a report prepared by David Conley for the Bill & Melinda Gates Foundation, "Toward a More Comprehensive Conception of College Readiness," available online at http://www.gatesfoundation.org/UnitedStates

/Education/ResearchAndEvaluation/Research/HSImprovement.htm (accessed March 20, 2008).

2. The data on DoDEA schools come from an *Education World* online article dated September 26, 2002, "Department of Defense Schools, Their Secret Weapon of Success," which is available online at http://www.education-world .com/a_issues/issues349.shtml (accessed August 9, 2007). The article summarizes a research study titled "March Toward Excellence: School Success and Minority Student Achievement in Department of Defense Schools. A Report to the National Education Goals Panel. Lessons from the States," by Claire Smrekar et al. (Washington, DC: National Education Goals Panel, 2001), available online at http://eric.ed.gov/ERICDocs/data/ericdocs2sql/content_storage_01/0000019b /80/19/7e/81.pdf (accessed August 9, 2007).

3. National Education Goals Panel press release (no date given), available online at http://govinfo.library.unt.edu/negp/issues/publication/othpress/re1100101 .pdf (accessed August 9, 2007).

4. The Department of Defense Education Activity and its subordinate organizations do not endorse the contents of this book or its findings. All opinions, findings, conclusions, and recommendations expressed in this book are those of the author and do not necessarily reflect the views, positions, or policies of the DoDEA or its subordinate organizations.

5. Robert Pianta et al., "Opportunities to Learn in America's Elementary Classrooms," *Science,* vol. 315 (March 30, 2007), pp. 1795–1796.

6. Ibid.

7. "Choices, Changes, and Challenges: Curriculum and Instruction in the NCLB Era," Center on Education Policy (Washington, DC: CEP, July 2007), available online at http://www.cep-dc.org/document/docWindow.cfm?fuse action=document.viewDocument&documentid=212&documentFormatId=3557 (accessed August 15, 2007).

8. Jennifer Booher-Jennings, "Rationing Education in an Era of Accountability," *Phi Delta Kappan,* vol. 87, no. 10 (June 2007).

9. Derek Neal and Diane Whitmore Schanzenbach, "Left Behind by Design: Proficiency Counts and Test-Based Accountability," unpublished but available online at http://www.aei.org/docLib/20070716_NealSchanzenbachPaper.pdf (accessed August 15, 2007).

10. See, for example, Bruce Fuller, Joseph Wright, Kathryn Gesicki, and Erin Kang, "Gauging Growth: How to Judge No Child Left Behind?" *Educational Researcher,* vol. 36, no. 5 (June/July 2007), pp. 268–278.

11. This summary is from a report prepared for the New Commission on the Skills of the American Workforce titled "International Education Tests: An Overview, 2005," by Betsy Brown Ruzzi (Washington, DC: NCEE, 2005).

12. "Problem Solving for Tomorrow's World: First Measures of Cross-Curricular Competencies from PISA 2003," Programme for International Student Assessment (Paris: OECD, 2004).

13. M. Lemke et al., "International Outcomes of Learning in Mathematics Literacy and Problem Solving: PISA 2003 Results from the U.S. Perspective," Washington, DC: U.S. Department of Education, National Center for Education Statistics (2004), available online at http://nces.ed.gov/surveys/pisa/PISA2003 Highlights.asp?Quest=2 (accessed August 16, 2007.

14. Ibid.

15. Thomas Friedman, "Worried About India's and China's Booms? So Are They," *New York Times,* March 24, 2006.

16. Yong Zhao, "A Pause Before Plunging Through the China Looking Glass: Why the U.S. Race to Reform and Catch Up Can Wait," *Education Week,* May 10, 2006.

17. From the Ministry of Education website, available online at http://www .moe.gov.sg/corpora/mission_statement.htm (accessed August 21, 2007).

18. Quoted in Rhea R. Borja, "Singapore's Digital Path," *Education Week,* "Technology Counts," May 6, 2004, p. 30.

CHAPTER 3

1. These questions came from the Texas Education Agency website, http://www .tea.state.tx.us/student.assessment/resources/release/taks/2006/gr10taks.pdf (accessed September 3, 2007), and they are used with permission.

2. Ibid.

3. Ibid.

4. Quoted from "The Fordham Report: How Well Are States Educating Our Neediest Children?" available online at http://www.edexcellence.net/foundation /publication/publication.cfm?id=363&pubsubid=1443#1443 (accessed September 14, 2007). The assessment of a state's education accountability system inevitably involves a high degree of subjectivity. The entire topic is both complex and politically charged. The best resource I have found for sorting out the many tests and assessments of their worth is available online at http://www.center forpubliceducation.org/site/c.kjJXJ5MPIwE/b.1501925/k.C980/The_nature_of_ assessment_A_guide_to_standardized_testing.htm (accessed August 30, 2007).

5. These questions came from the Massachusetts Department of Education website: http://www.doe.mass.edu/mca007/release/g10ela.pdf (accessed September 3, 2007).

6. In the public domain.

7. From the Massachusetts Department of Education website, available online at http://www.doe.mass.edu/mcas/2007/release/g10math.pdf.

8. From the Massachusetts Department of Education, available online at http://www.doe.mass.edu/mcas/2007/release/g9_10hss.pdf.

9. As quoted from the MSN Encarta online dictionary, available online at http://encarta.msn.com/dictionary_/mystical.html (accessed September 15, 2007).

10. Massachusetts Department of Education, "2007 MCAS Report (DISTRICT) for Grade 10," available online at http://profiles.doe.mass.edu/mcas.aspx (accessed January 26, 2008).

11. "Diplomas Count: Ready for What?" *Education Week,* June 12, 2007, available online at http://www.edweek.org/ew/toc/2/06/12/index.html (accessed January 26, 2008).

12. "State Report Shows Many Students Are Not Ready for College," *Boston Globe*, February 28, 2008, available online at http://www.boston.com/news /local/massachusetts/articles/2008/02/28/state_report_shows_many_students_are _not_ready_for_college/ (accessed March 20, 2008).

13. For readers wanting a more in-depth overview and critique of the law, I suggest reviewing the Alliance for Excellent Education's June 2007 policy brief: "In Need of Improvement: NCLB and High Schools," available online at http://www.all4ed.org/publications/NCLB_HighSchools.pdf (accessed September 15, 2007). I also recommend Professor Linda Darling Hammond's most thoughtful critique, "Evaluating 'No Child Left Behind,' "*The Nation,* May 21, 2007, available online at http://www.thenation.com/doc/20070521/darling-ham mond (accessed September 15, 2007). For individuals who want to get involved in advocacy for better tests, the national organization Fair Test is an excellent resource (www.fairtest.org).

14. From the report "Are They Really Ready to Work?" sponsored by The Conference Board, Corporate Voices for Working Families, the Partnership for 21st Century Skills, and the Society for Human Resource Management, available online at http://21stcenturyskills.org/documents/key_findings_joint.pdf (accessed January 15, 2008).

15. This study was conducted as a part of the process of developing the math curriculum for High Tech High School; it is available online at http://www .hightechhigh.org/resource-center/Curriculum/Curric-HTH%20Math.pdf (accessed September 19, 2007).

16. "Assessing Scientific, Reading and Mathematical Literacy: A Framework for PISA 2006," Programme for International Student Assessment, available online at http://www.oecd.org/document/2/0,3343,en_32252351_32236191 _39718850_1_1_1_1,00.html (accessed January 26, 2008).

17. PISA 2006 Results, Executive Summary, available online at http:// www.oecd.org/dataoecd/15/13/39725224.pdf (accessed January 26, 2008).

18. "Assessing Scientific, Reading and Mathematical Literacy: A Framework for PISA 2006."

19. PISA 2006 Results, Executive Summary.

20. Andreas Schleicher, "Losing Our Edge: Are American Students Unprepared for the Global Economy?" National Press Club, December 4, 2007, available online at http://www.all4ed.org/events/losingedge (accessed January 26, 2008).

21. Ibid.

22. This material came from the Massachusetts Department of Education website: http://www.doe.mass.edu/mcas/student/2006/question.asp?GradeID =10&SubjectCode=ela&QuestionTypeName=Writing%20PromQuestio64# (accessed September 15, 2007).

23. This material came from the Massachusetts Department of Education website: http://www.doe.mass.edu/mcas/student/2006/answer.asp?QuestionID =4564&AnswerID=18576 (accessed September 15, 2007).

24. As reported by FairTest, a national nonprofit research and advocacy group that opposes most forms of standardized testing; available online at http://fairtest .org/optinit.htm (accessed January 30, 2008).

25. "Sarah Lawrence College Drops SAT Requirement, Saying a New Writing Test Misses the Point," *New York Times,* November 13, 2003, available online at http://query.nytimes.com/gst/fullpage.html?res=9F0CE5D81738F930A25752C 1A9659C8B63 (accessed January 27, 2008).

26. "Many Colleges Ignore SAT Writing Test," *Boston Globe,* September 20, 2007, available online at http://www.boston.com/news/local/articles/2007 /09/20/many_colleges_ignore_sat_writing_test/ (accessed January 27, 2008).

27. An in-depth discussion of what students should know about U.S. history in order to be active and informed citizens is a widely debated topic that lies beyond the scope of the present volume. Readers interested in exploring this topic may want to look at tests given to students in U.S. History and Civics as a part of the National Assessment of Educational Progress; these are available online at http://nationsreportcard.gov/ (accessed September 15, 2007).

28. "New Tests Ask: What Does It Mean to Be an American?" *New York Times,* September 28, 2007, available online at http://www.nytimes.com/2007/09 /28/washington/28citizen.html?_r=2&adxnnl=1&oref=slogin&adxnnlx=119115 7743–0Zj06H9PgJCGwwXJSkZw2Q&oref=slogin (accessed September 30, 2007).

29. "Rising to The Challenge: Are High School Graduates Prepared for College and Work?" *Achieve* (2005), available online at http://www.achieve.org /files/pollreport.pdf (accessed September 30, 2007).

30. David Conley, "Towards a More Comprehensive Conception of College Readiness" (p. 12), a study funded by the Bill & Melinda Gates Foundation and published by the Education Policy Improvement Center, Eugene, OR; available online at http://www.gatesfoundation.org/nr/downloads/ed/researchevaluation /CollegeReadinessPaper.pdf (accessed September 16, 2007).

31. Ibid., pp. 13–14.

32. This information was obtained from the College Board website: see http://apcentral.collegeboard.com/apc/public/repository06_prog_summary_rpt .pdf and http://www.collegeboard.com/student/testing/ap/abohtml (both accessed September 19, 2007).

33. Mary Beth Marklein, "Advanced Placement: A Detour for College Fast Track?" *USA Today,* March 20, 2006, available online at http://www.usatoday .com/news/education/2006-03-20-ap-main_x.htm (accessed September 19, 2007).

34. This was a Rand Corporation study, the results of which were communicated to me during a personal conversation with Kathy Kawaguchi, the director of Curriculum and Instruction for the state.

35. See the Alliance for Excellent Education 2006 report "Who's Counted, Who's Counting? Understanding High School Graduation Rates," available online at http://www.a114ed.org/publications/WhosCounting/WhosCounting.pdf (accessed September 18, 2007).

36. These data were obtained from "The Silent Epidemic: Perspectives of High School Dropouts," available online at http://www.gatesfoundation.org/nr/downloads/ed/TheSilentEpidemic3-06FINAL.pdf (accessed September 18, 2007).

37. Ibid.

38. For more information about the Collegiate Learning Assessment, you can go to the website of the Council for Aid to Education, which sponsors the CLA: www.cae.org (accessed September 23, 2007).

39. I received this assessment originally from the dean of faculty at one of the participating schools. It is now available on the Council's website: http://www.cae.org/content/pro_collegework.htm (accessed September 23, 2007).

40. The reader can learn more about the National Assessment of Educational Progress here: http://nationsreportcard.gov/ Accessed September 23, 2007.

41. Information on the PISA problem-solving assessment can be found here: http://www.oecd.org/pages/0,3417,en_32252351_32236113_1_1_1_1_1,00.html (accessed September 23, 2007).

42. More information on the "ISkills" Test can be found here: http://www.ets.org/portal/site/ets/menuitem.435c0b5cc7bd0ae7015d9510c3921509/?vgnextoid=b8a246f1674f4010VgnVCM10000022f95190RCRD (accessed September 23, 2007).

43. Information about Sternberg's research can be found here: http://pace.tufts.edu/ (accessed September 23, 2007).

44. For more information on the Consortium, please consult their website: http://performanceassessment.org/index.html (accessed September 23, 2007).

45. Chris Gallagher, *Reclaiming Assessment* (Portsmouth, NH: Heinemann, 2007).

46. Sonia Steptoe, "How Nebraska Leaves No Child Behind," *Time*, May 30, 2007, available online at http://www.time.com/time/nation/article/0,8599,1626423,00.html (accessed September 23, 2007).

47. Partnership for 21st Century Skills, "Beyond the Three R's: Voter Attitudes Towards 21st Century Skills," available online at http://21stcenturyskills.org/documents/p21_pollreport_2pg.pdf (accessed February 17, 2008).

CHAPTER 4

1. This is an exercise that my colleagues and I at the Change Leadership Group developed. You can learn more about it in Chapter 2 of our book, *Change Leadership: A Practical Guide to Transforming Our Schools* (San Francisco: Jossey-Bass, 2006). You can also actually view the video and assess it yourself at the CLG website: http://www.gse.harvard.edu/clg/news1a.html#video (accessed October 1, 2007).

2. These findings and the quotes that follow are from the Executive Summary of Levine's *Educating School Teachers* (Washington, DC: The Education Schools Project, 2006), available online at http://www.edschools.org/pdf/Educating _Teachers_Exec_Summ.pdf (accessed October 8, 2007).

3. Ibid. Levine's study also includes "Nine Criteria for Judging Program Quality" as well as descriptions of what he considers to be four model teacher preparation programs, which many readers may find useful.

4. See "The High Cost of Teacher Turnover" (Washington, DC: NCTAF, 2007), available online at http://nctaf.org.zeus.silvertech.net/resources/research _and_reports/nctaf_research_reports/documents/CTTPolicyBrief-FI NAL_000.pdf (accessed October 10, 2007).

5. Again, see the Executive Summary of Levine's *Educating School Leaders* (Washington, DC: The Education Schools Project, 2006), available online at http://edschools.org/pdf/ESFina1313.pdf (accessed October 9, 2007).

6. Readers can learn more about this program online at http://isites .harvard.edu/icb/icb.do?keyword=k15649&pageid=icb.page8022 (accessed October 10, 2007).

7. For more information about the Change Leadership Group, please visit our website: http://www.gse.harvard.edu/clg (accessed October 10, 2007).

8. Levine, *Educating School Leaders*, pp. 27–28. See also The Education Schools Project website, available online at http://www.edschools.org/pdf /Final313.pdf (accessed January 29, 2008).

9. Readers wanting more information about the National Board and its certification process should consult its website: http://www.nbpts.org/ (accessed October 9, 2007).

10. These data were adapted from the Pennsylvania Department of Education website: http://www.teaching.state.pa.us/teaching/cwp/view.asp?A=7&Q=124484 (accessed October 10, 2007).

11. From the Executive Summary of "How The World's Best-Performing School Systems Come Out on Top," McKinsey & Company, September 2007, available online at http://www.mckinsey.com/clientservice/socialsector/resources /pdf/Worlds_School_Systems_Final.pdf (accessed January 30, 2008).

12. See my article "Secondary School Change: Meeting the Challenge with the '3 R's' of Reinvention" in *Education Week*, Commentary, November 27, 2002.

13. For the CLG website address, see Note 7 above.

14. For a description of the "lesson study" process, see James Steigler and James Hiebert, *The Teaching Gap* (New York: Free Press, 1999).

CHAPTER 5

1. See "New Grads Are Impatient for Promotions," *Wall Street Journal*, June 20, 2007, available online at http://online.wsj.com/article/SB11822956273 4041231.html (accessed November 14, 2007); and "The Most-Praised Generation Goes to Work," *Wall Street Journal*, April 20, 2007, available online at http:// online.wsj.com/article/SB1177028945776259.ht (accessed November 14, 2007).

2. Robert L. Fried, *The Game of School* (San Francisco: Jossey-Bass, 2005).

3. John Seely Brown, "Growing Up Digital," first published in *Change* magazine (March/April 2000) and currently available on Brown's website: http://www.johnseelybrown.com/Growing_up_digital.pdf (accessed November 13, 2007).

4. Adapted from Larry D. Rosen, *Me, MySpace, and I: Parenting the Net Generation* (New York: Palgrave Macmillan, 2007), p. 7.

5. "Generation M: Media in the Lives of 8–18-Year-Olds," Henry J. Kaiser Foundation (March 2005), vailable online at hp://www.kff.org/entmedia/upload/Executive-Summary-Generation-M-Media-in-the-Lives-of-8-18-Year-olds.pdf (accessed November 13, 2007).

6. Diana Oblinger and James Oblinger, "Is It Age or IT? First Steps Toward Understanding the Net Generation," in *Educating the Net Generation,* edited by Diana and James Oblinger and published online by Educause; available online at http://www.educause.edu/content.asp?PAGE_ID=5989&bhcp=1 (accessed November 13, 2007).

7. As reported by Wikipedia, available online at http://en.wikipedia.org/wiki/MySpace (accessed November 17, 2007).

8. As reported on NPR's *MarketWatch* on March 21, 2007; available online at http://www.marketwatch.com/news/story/even-slowing-growth-youtube-remains/story.aspx?guid=%7B98FB4A03–0B53–4CFB-BA2D–716D2B59CAAB%7D&siteid=myyahoo&dist=myyahoo (accessed November 17, 2007).

9. Nielson/NetRatings available online at http://www.nielsen-netratings.com/pr/pr_060721_2.pdf (accessed February 9, 2008).

10. This quote was taken from Linda Stone's website at www.lindastone.net (accessed November 13, 2007). I am also indebted to Linda for an extended in-person interview that was most helpful.

11. Oblinger and Oblinger, "Is It Age or IT?"

12. Rosen, *Me, MySpace, and I,* p. 14.

13. Quoted in ibid., p. 36.

14. Oblinger and Oblinger, "Is It Age or IT?"

15. Ibid.

16. Carie Windham, "The Student's Perspective," in *Educating the Net Generation,* edited by Diana and James Oblinger and published online by Educause; available online at http://www.educause.edu/content.asp?PAGE_ID=5989&bhcp=1 (accessed November 13, 2007).

17. Brown, "Growing Up Digital."

18. Quoted in "The Information-Age Mindset," *Educause* magazine (September–October 2000), available online at http://www.educause.edu/er/erm00/articles005/erm0051.pdf (accessed February 9, 2008).

19. Brown, "Growing Up Digital."

20. As quoted from John Beck and Mitchell Wade, *The Kids Are Alright: How the Gamer Generation Is Changing the Workplace* (Cambridge, MA: Harvard Business School Press, 2006), p. 177.

21. Quoted from James Paul Gee, *What Video Games Have to Teach Us About Learning and Literacy*, 2nd ed. (New York: Palgrave Macmillan, 2007), Conclusion, p. 2.

22. Brown, "Growing Up Digital."

23. Rosen, *Me, MySpace, and I,* p. 78.

24. Lori Aratani, "Teens Can Multitask, But What Are Costs?" *Washington Post,* February 26, 2007; available online at http://www.washinonpost.com /wp-dyn/content/article/2007/02/25/AR2007022501600.html (accessed November 13, 2007).

25. Quoted from Linda Stone's website, www.lindastone.net.

26. The best summary of this research can be found in *How People Learn: Brain, Mind, Experience, and School,* by the Committee on Developments in the Science of Learning (Washington, DC: National Academy Press, 2000).

27. "Cracking the Code of Teens' IM Slang," *CNET News,* November 14, 2006, available online at http://www.news.com/Cracking-the-code-of-teens-IM -slang/2009-1025_3-6135457.html (accessed November 18, 2007).

28. Beck and Wade, *The Kids Are Alright,* p. 53.

29. Quoted in "In Korea, a Boot Camp Cure for Web Obsession," *New York Times,* November 18, 2007, available online at http://www.nytimes.com /2007/11/18/technology/18rehab.html?_r=1&ref=todayspaper&oref=slogin (accessed November 18, 2007).

30. "Google Receives 1,000,000 Applications a Year," *Search Engine Journal,* January 24, 2007, available online at http://www.searchenginejournal.com/google -receives-1000000-job-applications-a-year/4308/ (accessed November 23, 2007).

31. Quoted from a speech given at the 2003 Automotive Parts System Solution Fair in Tokyo, June 18, 2003, available online at http://www.toyotageorgetown .com/tps.asp (accessed November 23, 2007).

32. Readers can learn more about FIRST at www.usfirst.org, and about City Year at http://cityyear.org/.

CHAPTER 6

1. A charter school is a public school that operates with a measure of autonomy from a school district. Charter schools were first established in 1992 as a way of providing educators with opportunities to explore different approaches to education and parents with greater opportunities for school choice. Currently, there are about 4,000 charter schools in forty states and the District of Columbia. For more information, go to this website: http://www.uscharterschools.org/pub/uscs_docs /index.htm (accessed February 2, 2008).

2. This information and the profile of Larry Rosenstock and the founding of High Tech High are based on information from the High Tech High website at www.hightechhigh.org; on interviews with Larry Rosenstock and Gary Jacobs; and on Victoria Murphy's article about Rosenstock in *Forbes* (October 11, 2004), "Where Everyone Can Overachieve," available online at http://www.forbes .com/forbes/2004/10/080.html (accessed December 11, 2007).

3. As quoted in Murphy, "Where Everyone Can Overachieve."

4. From the High Tech High website: http://www.hightechhigh.org/about/ (accessed December 13, 2007).

5. For a fuller description of the five Habits of Mind and their evolution, see Deborah Meier's book, *The Power of Their Ideas* (Boston: Beacon Press, 1996).

6. Information about the Bill & Melinda Gates Foundation's work in education can be found here: http://www.gatesfoundation.org/UnitedStates/Education/ (accessed December 14, 2007).

7. I explore some of the promises and perils of school choice in more detail in my book *Making the Grade* (New York: RoutledgeFalmer, 2002). See also the writing of Paul T. Hill, who has done some of the most thoughtful and balanced research on school choice.

8. From the Big Picture website at http://bigpicture.org/index.htm (accessed February 3, 2008).

9. This quote and the description of the Met's history are based on material from the Big Picture website at http://bigpicture.org/aboutus/history.htm (accessed February 3, 2008).

10. From the Big Picture website: http://bigpicture.org/aboutus/learning goals.htm (accessed December 14, 2007).

11. This history of the Coalition of Essential Schools and the list of its ten Common Principles are based on material from the CES's website: http://www .essentialschools.org/pub/ces_docs/about/il/10cps/10cps.html (accessed December 18, 2007).

12. These data are quoted from "School Profile," a document that Parker sends to colleges with students' transcripts.

13. This description, too, is based on "School Profile," as well as on information from the school's website at www.parker.org and on interviews with Teri Schrader and Deb Merriam, the school's academic dean.

14. As quoted from the school's website: http://www.parker.org/Curriculum Assessment/curriculum.htm (accessed December 18, 2007).

15. This material and other information about Parker's academic program can be found on their website: http://www.pker.org/CurriculumAssessment/curriculum .htm (accessed February 3, 2008).

CONCLUSION

1. From the revised paperback edition of John W. Gardner's *Excellence: Can We Be Equal and Excellent Too?* (New York: W. W. Norton & Company, 1995).

2. From Bill Lampton, "'My Pleasure'—The Ritz-Carlton Hotel, Part II," *Expert Magazine* (December 2003), available online at http://www.expert magazine.com/EMOnline/RC/part2.ht (accessed December 23, 2007).

3. Jean Piaget, *The Moral Judgment of the Child* (New York: Free Press, 1965).

4. The film can be ordered here: http://www.2mminutes.com.

AFTERWORD TO THE PAPERBACK EDITION

1. General information in this Afterword about Virginia Beach City Public Schools is quoted from the district's website: http://www.vbschools.com/ (accessed January 2, 2010).

2. As we learned at the beginning of the book, the U.S. high school dropout rate—especially among minority students—lies at the heart of the education crisis, yet very few district administrators—let alone teachers and parents—know their real cohort graduation rates. There is a specific reason for this: Despite the fact that all fifty state governors signed a pact in 2005 to use a standard formula for calculating a school district's graduation rate, there is still no common standard or significant accountability requirement for reporting graduation rates or improving them. In 2008, then–Secretary of Education Margaret Spellings announced that all states must use the same formula, a requirement that won't be phased in until 2011. In November 2009, the U.S. Department of Education announced the criteria for federal "Race to the Top" state education grants, which require states to develop plans for reducing their high school dropout rates and transforming their most underperforming high schools. It remains to be seen what impact these efforts will have.

3. An invaluable resource for more meaningful accountability, the National Student Clearinghouse tracks current and prior students' records in more than 92 percent of the colleges and universities around the country, enabling districts to know which of their students went on to college, whether they received a degree, and how long it took. More information about this service is available online at http://studentclearinghouse.org/highschools/default.htm (accessed January 6, 2010).

4. Quoted from http://www.vbschools.com/compass/LearningWalks.asp (accessed January 2, 2010).

5. Quoted from the Rhode Island Department of Education website: http://www.ride.ri.gov/instruction/diploma/FAQ.html (accessed January 2, 2010).

6. The video is available for sale at the Coalition's website: http://store.essential store.org/ces-essentialvisions-disc-2-student-achievemen.html (accessed January 2, 2010).

7. Detailed information on these portfolio and graduation requirements can be found at the Mission Hill website: http://www.missionhillschool.org/mhs/ Graduation_files/Graduation%20Requirements%20and%20Portfolio%20Review %20Revised%20Dec%202007.doc (accessed January 2, 2010).

8. Quoted from "Diploma Program Assessment, Principles and Practice," a paper downloaded from the International Baccalaureate Organization website: http://www.ibo.org/diploma/assessment/documents/d_x_dpyyy_ass_0409_1_e .pdf (accessed January 2, 2010).

9. See Evangeline Harris Stefanakis's *Multiple Intelligences and Portfolios: A Window into the Learner's Mind* (New Hampshire: Heinemann, 2002) and *Differentiated Assessment: A Window into the Learner's Abilities* (with a DVD of Portfolio tools) (San Francisco: Jossey Bass Wiley, forthcoming in 2010).

10. Samples of High Tech High student portfolios can be found on HTH's website at http://www.hightechhigh.org/digital_portfolios.php?school=hth, and the free digital software for student portfolios can be found at http://grover.concordia.ca/epearl/en/index.php. (Both sites were accessed on January 3, 2010.)

11. Clayton Christensen, Michael B. Horn, and Curtis W. Johnson, *Disrupting Class: How Disruptive Innovation Will Change the Way the World Learns* (New York: McGraw-Hill, 2008).

12. Consult the National Board's website for additional information: http://www.nbpts.org (accessed January 4, 2010).

13. More information about this work is available on the Council's dedicated website: http://edsteps.org/CCSSO/Home.aspx (accessed January 4, 2010).

14. See Linda Darling-Hammond's new book, *The Flat World and Education: How America's Commitment to Equity Will Determine Our Future* (New York: Teacher's College Press, 2010), as well as the excellent PowerPoint she presented as part of a December 2009 Edutopia webinar: http://www.edutopia.org/images/webinar/Assessment.ppt (accessed January 6, 2010).

15. The Alliance's Call to Action can be downloaded here: http://download.microsoft.com/download/6/E/9/6E9A7CA7-0DC4-4823-993E-A54D18C19F2E/Transformative%20Assessment.pdf (accessed January 6, 2010).

16. Additional information on New Tech High and the Indiana effort can be found on the CELL website: http://cell.uindy.edu/NTHS/index.php (accessed January 4, 2010).

17. A brief history and description of the Boston Pilot Schools can be found here: http://www.ccebos.org/pilotschools/history.html (accessed January 4, 2010).

Index

assessing skills, knowledge and
intellectual challenge, 52–53
borderline, 71–72
not choosing college and, 264–265
overachievers and the unengaged,
199–205
See also Learning; Student motivation;
Young people
Student-teacher relationship, 192–193
Summers, Mike, 26, 35–36, 39
Survival Skills
accessing and analyzing information,
36–38
agility and adaptability, 30–32
collaboration across networks and
leading by influence, 22–30
critical thinking and problem solving,
14–22
curiosity and imagination, 38–41
importance for citizenship, 100
initiative and entrepreneurialism,
32–34
significance of, 14
useful to all vocations, 266–267
will not become obsolete, 267

Taosaka, Sandra, 161–162
Teacher collaboration, 285–288
Teacher credential program, 223
Teacher development
at Francis W. Parker Charter Essential
School, 248–249
at High Tech High, 222–224
narrative of, 135–139
successful schools and, 259–260
transforming, 150–152
using videos of teachers, 142
Teacher evaluation
account of, 135–136
at High Tech High, 222–223
standard approach to, 52
Teacher preparation
core competencies vs. content
coverage in, 148–150
credential program, 223

criticisms of, 144–146
graduate program, 224
licensing, 150
narratives of, 133–135, 143
in pioneering schools, 223, 260–261
Teachers
academic content standards and, 63–65
assessing effectiveness of, 280–281
barriers to removing, 156
certification, 287
the culture of the education
profession, 154–157
dropout problem, 146
issues affecting the effectiveness of, 52
Japanese, 164
narrative of teaching in private
schools, 137–139
narrative of teaching in public schools,
135–137, 143–144
NBPTS-certification and, 148–150
pay-for-performance plans, 280
in pioneering schools, 260
portfolios for, 286–287
rethinking the role and authority of,
192–193
strategic objectives for, 277
tenure, 52, 151, 260
Teachers' unions, 144, 151
Teaching
adaptation to contemporary needs
and, 255–257
creating accountability for, 278
excellent, 56, 65–66
as a focus in successful schools, 258
in private schools, 137–139
in public schools, 135–137, 143–144
standards-based, 59, 63–65
Team-based leadership, 22
Teamwork, virtual teams, 22–23
Technology
cautions and concerns, 182–187
digital divide, 172
impact on young people, 170–177
new learning styles and, 178–187